NOT FOR THE
FAINT-HEARTED

NOT FOR THE FAINT-HEARTED

My Life Fighting Crime

JOHN STEVENS

Weidenfeld & Nicolson

LONDON

First published in Great Britain in 2005
by Weidenfeld & Nicolson

1 3 5 7 9 10 8 6 4 2

© Lord Stevens of Kirkwhelpington 2005

A CIP catalogue record for this book
is available from the British Library.

ISBN-13 9 780297 848424
ISBN-10 0 297 848429

Typeset, printed and bound in Great Britain by
Butler and Tanner Ltd, Frome and London

Weidenfeld & Nicolson

The Orion Publishing Group Ltd
Orion House
5 Upper Saint Martin's Lane
London WC2H 9EA

The photographs which appear on the back jacket are as follows:
(clockwise from top right) the aftermath of IRA terrorist bombing in Hyde Park,
20 July 1982 (Mauro Carraro/Rex Features); a plume of smoke over the city of London
after a lorry bomb in Bishopsgate, 15 April 1993 (Rex Features); police officers facing
the anti-capitalism riots, May Day 2000 (Jeroen Oerlemans/Rex Features); John Stevens
at the press conference announcing the 30,000th police cadet, Hendon police training
school, 15 January 2004 (Rex Features); John Stevens, Ken Livingstone and cadets at
Hendon police training school, 15 January 2004 (Rex Features).

www.orionbooks.co.uk

This book is dedicated to the outstanding bravery and commitment of police officers and support staff, past and present.

Proceeds from it will be used to found a university scholarship for serving police officers.

CONTENTS

ILLUSTRATIONS

Sections of photographs appear between pages 182 & 183

Metropolitan Police training school, 1963
JS at the time of his engagement to Cynthia
Metropolitan Police detective training school, 1966
Two pages from JS's Criminal Investigation Department diary, 1965
With Vince McFadden at the end of the Stevens One inquiry
Giving evidence in No 2 Court at the Old Bailey
May Day 2000 riot control[1]
JS wearing riot control gear[2]
In New York with the Mayor, Rudolf Giuliani, and the Commissioner of the
    NYPD, Howard Schaeffer
With the Mayor of London, Ken Livingstone[3]
With David Blunkett, Home Secretary, and Jack Wraith[4]
With Charles Clarke, Home Secretary[2]
With Ian Blair, JS's successor[5]
Celebrating the Metropolitan Police's thirty thousandth's police officer with
    Ken Livingstone and Lord Harris
JS and cadets celebrating the Metropolitan Police's thirty thousandth's police
    officer[5]
Visiting Amritsar with his wife, Cynthia[2]
At work in Paris on the inquiry into the deaths of Diana, Princess of Wales and
    Dodi al-Fayed[6]
JS's farewell photograph as Commissioner[2]
In the cockpit of JS's twin-engine Cessna

The photographs are drawn from the author's personal collection except where stated.

1 Rex Features/Jeroen Oerlemans
2 Courtesy of the Metropolitan Police Press Office
3 Rex Features/Alisdair Macdonald
4 Rex Features/Nils Jorgensen
5 Rex Features
6 Rex Features/Paul Cooper

ONE

A Night to Remember

Monday 10 January 1990: a night never to be forgotten. At about 10 p.m. I was lying on the bed in my room at the Magheramorne House Hotel, outside Belfast. I'd already had a bath and was in my pyjamas, relaxing for a few minutes in front of the television before turning in for an early night. Our team had a major operation lined up for the morning: we were due to go out at 5.30 a.m. and launch a series of arrests at 6.00.

The room next to mine was occupied by Detective Superintendent Laurie Sherwood, who was acting as my special assistant in Northern Ireland. My mind was not on the television, because I was mentally running through our preparations for the dawn raids, when there came a knock on the connecting door.

'Guv,' said Laurie quietly, 'the incident room's on fire.'

'*What?*'

For a moment I could hardly grasp what he was telling me. I had to count up to ten to collect my wits. Our incident room was in the heart of a secure compound in Sea Park, the headquarters of the Royal Ulster Constabulary's Police Authority at Carrickfergus. The seventeen-acre complex was surrounded by high chain-link fences and guarded by armed officers in fortified bunkers. How could our office be on fire?

'You're joking,' I said.

'No. Sarah Bynum's just phoned. She says the place has been burnt out. A car's on its way to pick us up.'

I pulled on some clothes and ran downstairs. I had come to Northern Ireland at the express request of Hugh Annesley, Chief Constable of the RUC, and our team of twenty-eight officers had been working for four months on my first inquiry into collusion between the security

1

forces and paramilitary groups. We had made a certain amount of progress, but we had also met a barrage of aggravation. Not only had we been told obvious lies by the British Army: there had also been a whispering campaign, and continuous attempts, through the newspapers and television, to discredit us. But, as one of my officers remarked, whenever we had needed to knock down a door, we had knocked it down, either by shoulder or foot, and carried on.

The car took a few minutes to arrive. My normal driver, Detective Sergeant Grahame Foote, was away on annual leave, and the man who came to collect us – a member of the RUC – smelt of smoke. I dived into the vehicle, and we covered the six miles to Sea Park at high speed. It was a typical Northern Ireland winter night, cold and drizzling, and the tyres swished over the wet tarmac.

As we arrived, I was expecting to see the whole building enveloped in a ball of flame, but the blaze had already been put out. All the same, it was obvious from the number of engines and police vehicles on the scene that there had been a major conflagration, and smoke was still billowing out of the windows on the second floor, where we had our offices. The smell of burning hung in the air. As we drew up, Laurie and I wondered if the whole thing was a come-on, and if we were being lured into an ambush – but I reckoned that there were already too many good targets on the scene for that to be a possibility.

The building in which we were working – square, modern and flat-roofed – had been a cigarette factory. The RUC had taken it over, and our incident room was in the part normally used by the Police Authority. The fire chief appeared and agreed that it was just about safe to go up to the second floor – but at the top of the back stairs stood a senior RUC officer, a barrel-chested fellow with a stentorian voice, renowned for his bullying tactics.

'Stop!' he cried. 'Who are you? You're not going any further.'

'Wrong,' I told him. 'I'm the deputy chief constable in charge of this inquiry, and I need to secure our documents. I'm going in. Get out of the way.'

He looked daggers at me, but moved aside, and I hurried on through the corridors along the tortuous route to our offices. The sight that greeted us was horrendous. The electricity had gone off, so that the illumination was dim: apart from the firemen's torches, some light was coming in from the corridor, through the burst glass that ran along the top of the partition wall. In spite of the gloom we could see all too well.

Our desk-top computers had melted into puddles of crumpled, twisted metal and plastic. Steel filing cabinets had buckled in the heat, setting fire to the documents inside. Piles of burnt paper were still smouldering. The green-and-white carpet had caught fire and shrivelled. Polystyrene tiles had melted and fallen from the ceiling, and there was extensive water damage. Hot metal clicked as it cooled.

I was aghast. For a minute or two we surveyed the chaos, trying to assess what we had lost. Soon several senior RUC officers appeared, looking very long-faced. Then one of my detective constables, Peter Knight, who had been responsible for keeping the office tidy, came up to me and said brightly, 'Shall I hoover through now, sir?'

His little crack broke the tension and fired everyone up. I think all of us, at that moment, became determined to carry on with the inquiry, come what may. That, however, was not the intention of the RUC officers. 'I suppose you'll have to go home now,' said one of them, 'because you've lost everything.'

For anyone surveying the wreckage, that was a reasonable assumption. In fact the man was plumb wrong. Neither he nor any of his colleagues knew that from the start we had been backing up all our information to the mainland. Right at the outset Laurie Sherwood had insisted on this as an essential precaution. Unknown to outsiders, our main incident room was not in Belfast at all, but in Cambridgeshire, and all we had in Northern Ireland was a satellite station, linked by computer to base. Every document we typed out went straight across to East Anglia electronically, as did photographs. The only original document we lost in the fire was a typed version of an original statement, obtained that day from an important agent. After being typed into the system and e-mailed to England, it had been left in a tray on the corner of a wooden table.

Quickly we pieced together the sequence of events. A small rear-guard of our team had worked late; when they left the office, at 9 p.m., they knew that there were four more officers still out, completing their day's investigations, but because those members of the team had their own keys, the rearguard locked up and went back to our hotel. Within twenty-five minutes of their departure, the remaining four came back to the incident room and found the place alight.

The nearest telephone had been put out of action, so one of them, Detective Sergeant Sarah Bynum, ran downstairs to the control point on the ground floor – but the phones there did not work either. The security guard then called for assistance over his personal radio. Meanwhile the others tried to tackle the blaze, but found there was no water in the system, and they had to drag another reel of fire-hose up the stairs to the second floor. They got some water going, but not enough – and in any case, they were too late. During their attempts at fighting the fire, two of them, Detective Sergeants Dick Harrison and Phil Coundley, had inhaled smoke and been taken to hospital. Sarah Bynum had also been affected, though less severely.

In my own office, which was separate, I found the phone was still working. My first call was to the hospital where my officers had been taken: the men were still being treated, and I learnt that all three had shown great courage in trying to fight the fire.

I stood there in my office, with wisps of smoke curling about, and wondered what the hell we were going to do. By then more of the team had arrived, and it was obvious to all of us that the incident room had been the seat of the blaze. Why should the fire have begun in *our* office, rather than in some other part of that vast rabbit-warren of a building? Tell-tale signs abounded. None of the warning systems – neither the smoke alarm nor the heat sensors – had gone off. The telephone lines had been cut.

A member of the RUC tried to tell me that the fire had been started by one of our women throwing a cigarette butt into a waste-paper bin. I did not believe this for a moment, and later exhaustive inquiries confirmed that it was pure invention. On the night, Detective Chief Superintendent Vince McFadden stood by that bin and heard the fire expert whom we had summoned declare that the blaze could not have originated there: the seat of the fire was several feet away, under a heavy wooden table next to the door, where paper sacks had been stacked.

Vince, Laurie and I were convinced that we had been victims of an arson attack; and because I didn't like the sound of what the RUC were saying, I immediately sent for the head of the Special Branch, and the Assistant Chief Constable, Crime, Wilfie Monaghan.

By then it was nearly midnight, but both men came round, and both said, 'We think we know who did this.' That was the first time I heard of a unit called the FRU, and the first time I heard the name of a certain colonel. It was whispered in my ear – I will not say by whom – that he and the Force Research Unit were directly responsible for the fire. The FRU, Wilfie told me, was a secret British unit responsible for running Army agents. So much for the Army's claim, which they had made explicitly to us, that they had no secret agents in Northern Ireland. They had told this to our whole team at a special briefing. Not only had they volunteered the information: when we put specific questions to them, they had denied absolutely that they were running agents in the Province.

What were we to do? In England I had a small group of senior advisers, which included my own boss, Ian Kane, the Chief Constable of Cambridgeshire (I was then his deputy). Every now and then over the previous four months I had gone back to report on our progress and get ideas about how to press on. Now, in the middle of the night, I rang up Kane and told him what had happened.

His response was anything but reassuring. 'You're in deep trouble,' he told me. 'This is very serious indeed. You and the team are in danger. Here, I'm issuing an immediate order for Cambridgeshire Constabulary Headquarters to be surrounded by police dogs – and they'll be here until I deem it necessary to get rid of them. *Your* decision is whether you stay or pull out and come back. You're the only person who can decide.'

'OK, sir,' I said, 'but the team have got to decide, as well.'

Leaving a guard in place, we went back to the hotel. There we found that some members of the team who had already gone to bed had come down to the bar and were having coffee, awaiting our return. When we arrived, the whole lot crowded into my room and held a meeting to take stock. The fire would make the headlines in the morning – and if I pulled the team out, the news would be even bigger. Our inquiry had obviously been tampered with; it could have been thwarted entirely, and lives could have been lost. It was this last pos-sibility that made me absolutely furious. Whoever had set the fire must have known that there was a possibility of our people coming back and being caught in the blaze.

All of us were shocked by what had happened. First, that people could come and start a fire like that; second, that they could get away with it, and third, that after numerous earlier scandals, the RUC would allow our inquiry, which was trying to do something of substance for *their* reputation, to be disrupted. Before us, no one had ever been over to Northern Ireland on an inquiry into collusion and succeeded. No one had ever got a conviction. The last person who had tried to do so, John Stalker, the former Deputy Chief Constable of Manchester, had been hastily withdrawn, his career ruined by allegations that he had associated with members of the Quality Street gang of criminals in Manchester. So for the RUC to obstruct an independent inquiry, which aimed to prove that their organisation *could* be investigated by an outside force, made no sense at all.

The fire was only the latest and most drastic of several attempts to get rid of us. Various unpleasant incidents had already forced us to shift our quarters several times, and we had moved from hotel to hotel, to present the opposition with a moving target. One of our temporary bases was a place formerly owned by a judge, whose daughter had been murdered in the garden. On one occasion, as we returned there in the evening, the hotel's deputy manager hurried out to warn me that some unsavoury characters were waiting in the bar. 'There's a load of UDA* people asking after you,' he said. 'If I were you, I wouldn't go there.'

'Rubbish!' I told him, and walked in. Sure enough, they were in there drinking – maybe eight or ten of them. Two of them were particularly notorious Loyalist murderers, already well known to us from our own intelligence, and their leader was a big, fat individual with the name of Winky Dodds. They may well have been carrying weapons – I had no means of knowing. On the other hand, *they* didn't know that I and my team were unarmed. Obviously they'd come to scare us off, but I went across to them and said, 'Look – you're not

---

* The UDA (Ulster Defence Association) was the political wing of the Protestant para-militaries, and, largely as a result of our inquiries, was proscribed. The UFF (Ulster Freedom Fighters) were the military wing – but in fact the UDA controlled both. The Ulster Defence Regiment (UDR) is a regiment of the British Army, in the main recruited locally.

going to frighten us. Bugger off.' Winky looked furtively around at his mates. He may well have thought that he was about to be arrested. A moment later they all turned tail and trooped out, leaving their drinks unfinished.

Another instance – widely reported in the newspapers – took place when somebody left sensitive-looking documents under a chair on the floor of a conference room in our hotel in Bangor. The papers, which were handed in to the RUC, were only lecture notes and leaflets from the Overseas Command Course, which officers from the Bramshill Police College in Hampshire had been taking in Northern Ireland. But because our team was staying in the hotel, someone told the press that the documents were ours. With the help of the RUC Senior Press Officer, we managed to prevent the *Newsletter* newspaper leading with damaging headlines, to the effect that we couldn't even look after our own documents, let alone conduct an inquiry. I achieved this only by personally confirming that the papers were nothing to do with us. Needless to say, when the documents proved to be harmless, further press stories did not link them with us.

Just before the fire, we had been subjected to yet another provocation. At the end of the previous week most of the team had gone to the mainland for a short break, and as we flew back to Belfast on the Sunday afternoon, prepared to carry out our raids on Monday morning, lo and behold, on the plane were two journalists saying, 'We've come for the arrests.'

'What arrests?' we said. 'What are you talking about?' And sure enough, because of their presence, there weren't any raids on Monday morning, because we cancelled them. It was obvious there had been a leak, and after a quick conference we decided to postpone our operation for twenty-four hours: if the main players were expecting us on Monday, they wouldn't be at home. We therefore planned for Tuesday morning instead – and on Monday night came the fire.

By then we were well used to threats, and the only result of the conflagration was to increase everyone's determination. I myself was hell-bent on getting to the bottom of the outrage. The enemy were *not* going to fire-bomb us out of the country. We were representing the law, and they were *not* going to defeat us.

None of us got much sleep that night – the fire had put everyone on edge. So when, in the small hours, Vince McFadden went into his bathroom and noticed that the panel on the side of the bath appeared to have been loosened, he at once suspected a booby trap. We sent for the hotel manager, who was not pleased to be routed out of bed, and because he could throw no light on the matter, we called out the local RUC. After a long interval an inspector arrived, but he was as perplexed as everyone else.

What were we to do? Evacuate the hotel? Call out the bomb-disposal squad? In the end we decided to make a very careful inspection ourselves. We found nothing untoward, and concluded that repeated opening and shutting of the bathroom door had created enough air pressure to pull the bath panel slightly out of place. But the incident, tiny in itself, showed how the tension in our team had been heightened.

Then, before dawn on Wednesday, in company with some 250 RUC detectives, uniformed officers, drivers and auxiliaries, we set out on our big swoop. As Laurie Sherwood went down the drive from our hotel in a vehicle with Graham Woodcock, a captain from the Military Police, they saw that a coach carrying some of our people had stopped, and Graham, fearing an ambush, readied his sub-machine gun – so jumpy had everyone become. At about the same time, a small party returned to Sea Park to secure what was left of our ruined office, and to start setting up a new incident room in the Antrim Road barracks, a location that I had already identified as a possible alternative.

Our most important target that morning was Brian Nelson, the double agent who, in Wilfie Monaghan's classic phrase, was at the centre of 'a can of worms'. We rounded up eight other leading suspects, including another prime target, Tucker Lyttle, head of the Ulster Defence Association, but – surprise, surprise – Nelson had flown, and members of the media were waiting outside his door. Later we heard that he had been spirited away to the mainland. Obviously someone had tipped him off, and, with that number of local people involved, it was hardly surprising. A clear audio-track that we followed up showed that a warning of the big raid had been leaked by the RUC to the FRU, and gone from the FRU to their agents.

As for the cause of the fire – we never managed to establish it with any certainty. The RUC's investigation was perfunctory: their report was not completed until months later, and their conclusion – that the

damage had been done by a carelessly thrown-away cigarette end –
was disproved by our own inquiries. Nevertheless, the woman at whom
the accusation was levelled, Woman Police Constable Patricia Tosney,
was put under severe stress. She was from the Met, and she was well
supported by Arthur Mandry, head of the CID in Hampshire, who
was with her on the night and had helped her lock up the office, so
that he knew perfectly well that what the RUC were alleging had not
taken place. Nevertheless, she came under such pressure that she fell
ill and had to be sent home. She later became phobic about being
accused of doing things that she had not done, and as a result had to
leave the service.

We ourselves never set up a full-scale investigation into the fire, but
Vince's clear memory from the night showed unequivocally that the
conflagration had *not* started in the waste-bin, as the RUC report
claimed. The only patch of carpet that had survived uncharred was
the one directly under the bin, proving that the receptacle had protected that area, rather than igniting it. Moreover, most of the paper
in the bin had remained unburnt: only the topmost sheets had been
scorched by a half-melted polystyrene tile that had fallen from the
ceiling. Under the first few sheets was a gold-coloured Benson &
Hedges cigarette packet, in among the pristine paper. In spite of this
clear evidence, word was put about that the fire had started in the bin.
A much more realistic scenario was that an intruder had crawled along
the four-foot space between the suspended ceiling and the roof, lifted
polystyrene tiles off the metal grid, dropped something into the room
and set fire to the abundant stocks of paper. No accelerant such as
petrol had been used – there was paper enough and more to start a
blaze.

Suspicious circumstances abounded. One curious fact concerned
the armed guard who was normally on duty outside the back door –
the entrance we always used. He, for some reason, had walked across
to the sangar at the main entrance of the compound, out of sight. The
duty sergeant was also away from his post, having gone to the back of
the seventeen-acre site to supervise a delivery of oil – so that when our
officers left, after locking up, there was nobody on the outside door,
and anyone could have walked in unobserved. The only person who
might have seen an intruder was the duty officer in the control room –

but to get a view of the entrance, he would have had to be peering through a small hatch in the brick wall.

Later we heard from an FRU agent that a team had been sent over from Ashford specifically to do the job, and that a member of the party had told him about the mission. Whatever the truth, the fire was a sure sign that our inquiry was making people uncomfortable. In almost thirty years as a policeman, I had never found myself caught up in such an entanglement of lies and treachery. As Vince McFadden remarked, we felt that the only friend we had in Northern Ireland was the cleaner on the Belfast ferry – and when that outfit went into liquidation, we knew we were in trouble. Nevertheless, one of my favourite maxims has always been, 'Go where the evidence takes you.' That was just what we intended to do.

TWO

Rough Start

Back to the beginning. I was born on 21 October 1942, but I have no recollection of my natural father. An aircraft engineer, he had met my mother sometime early in the Second World War, and they had got married; but he never wanted her to become pregnant, and when she did, he left her. I was less than a year old when he disappeared, to live in Holland. His surname was Vickery, so that I grew up as John Vickery. I never knew my father's Christian name: I don't even know what he looked like, and I've never bothered to follow it up. I'm not interested.

My mother, originally Sybil Raines, came from Hunstanton, in Norfolk, and the family name is still well known in the area. In her younger days she was extremely attractive, fair-haired and blue-eyed, and she had – still has – a forceful personality. I think most of my height derived from her – I am 6 foot 4, and she is at least 5 foot 10. In my earliest memories she and I lived together in a small flat in Wimbledon, sleeping in the same room.

As she was working, I was looked after for some of the time by my aunts – Maud, Ethel and Norah – who lived at 34 Mandrake Road, Tooting Bec. The trio had stayed together for the simple reason that all three had lost boyfriends in the First World War. Two had been engaged to be married, and one had been informally attached, but after losing their loved ones none of them ever took up another relationship with a man. They were superb people, working class, but proud of who they were and of the jobs they were doing.

Often as a boy I made the long train journey to Connah's Quay, on the Dee below Chester in North Wales, sometimes accompanied by an aunt or aunts, sometimes by my mother. There her parents – my grandparents – lived in a modest terrace house. They had no bathroom as such, and whenever I did have a bath, it was in a tin tub in front of the coal fire. I remember once sitting in the tub, being washed by my grandmother, and asking her where my father was. She gave some evasive answer, about him being away at the war – and that was the only reference anyone made to him.

The family played an active part in the community. One member ran the pub in the village, another the general store opposite. A great treat for me was to go down to the store, where I was given special rates on the sweets – and altogether the village was a warm and friendly place. Although we had little money, I was never hungry, and never felt deprived. Quite the opposite: I thoroughly enjoyed myself, running around happily with the other boys, fit as a fiddle. We would play football and cricket in the alleyway behind the house, and down by the river. The railway line passed close in front of the house, and I loved standing on a bridge to watch the trains pass underneath.

Beyond the railway lay some marshy ground, with the Dee running through it, and it was there, as a boy of six, that I saw my first dead body – something I will never forget. One of our gang fell into the fast-flowing water and was swept away downstream. We ran, shouting and screaming for help, and people came rushing from the village, from the factory and the docks. They got a rowing boat and managed to pull the boy out, and on the bank they tried to revive him by pumping his chest. That's what I can still see most vividly – the green water gushing out of his mouth as they worked on him. By then my grandmother had run down to the river, and as the rescue party were more or less giving up their efforts to revive the casualty, she got me and all the young children away. We heard later that the boy had died, but at that age it didn't mean a great deal to me: I was more curious than worried.

My mother never mentioned my natural father, and I never asked her about him, because the man she married later, Cyril Stevens, became a real father to me and gave me everything I've got. Strictly speaking, he was my stepfather, but I never thought of him as anything except my true parent, and I have referred to him simply as 'my father' ever since.

During the Second World War he had been a captain on Sunderland flying boats – a Warrant Officer Class 1, who never accepted a commission. When peace came, he and two friends started up a private airline, BKS (Barmby, Keegan and Stevens), and did a lot of flying round Africa in Dakotas – civilian versions of the twin-engined aircraft widely used by the Allies during the war. By today's standards they were primitive: slow, noisy, unpressurised and small, carrying only about thirty passengers, but at least they were reliable.

At first he managed BKS with his partners, but later he ran the company on his own, and in its heyday it carried a million passengers a year. The head office was in Baker Street, and the engineering base at Southend; but the hub of operations was in Newcastle. BKS was the first domestic airline to run scheduled services, and it also did inclusive tours.

During the summer and autumn of 1948 my father took part in the Berlin airlift, when the Russians attempted to seal off the former German capital from the outside world, and the Allies flew thousands of tons of food and other supplies into the blockaded city. It was about that time, just before my sixth birthday, that I became fully aware of him. My mother and I were still living in the flat in Wimbledon, and she was working as a secretary in Baker & Walls, a stationery producer in the City of London. I know that Cyril met my mother at a party, and I think he courted her for several months before proposing to her; then, late on Christmas Eve, he slipped into our bedroom to leave a present, when he thought I was asleep but in fact I was awake, thereby inadvertently destroying my belief in Father Christmas.

Probably because my mother was divorced, and second marriages were frowned on in those days, he seems to have moved cautiously – but finally the pair got married, went on honeymoon to Switzerland, and suddenly our world changed. One day we were crammed into the little flat; the next, we had been lifted – maybe 'air-lifted' is the phrase – into in a mock-Tudor detached house at Worcester Park, in New Malden, Surrey, with a bedroom for me, a garden, a wire-haired terrier that used to drive us all mad by constantly escaping, and all the space in the world. That was light years from anything I had known – and, I think, from anything my mother had experienced.

When my grandmother fell ill, she came down from Wales to live with us in our new home, and my mother nursed her there until she died of cancer. By today's standards, she was not at all old – I think about fifty-eight – and I shall never forget how, when she had gone, I slipped into her room to sneak a look at her. I was curious to know what a dead person would be like, and when I saw her, I felt reassured. Far from being afraid of the corpse, I thought she seemed very peaceful, and I just felt sad that a good friend had gone into another world.

After her death, my grandfather, Eric, moved down from Connah's Quay and went to live on the top floor of my aunts' house in Mandrake Road. A big, tall man, tough as old boots, he had spent thirty years as a constable in the police, mostly working in Brixton. When he left the force he became a security officer in Hawarden, but one day, as he stepped off a bus, he slipped and badly injured his right leg, after which he was something of a cripple. He used to walk around with a stick, and in Tooting Bec he was frequently irritated by the lack of police activity, particularly by the local officers' failure to reprimand young-sters who took the mickey out of them. 'In the old days,' he'd say, brandishing his stick, 'I'd have given them a *wallop*.' He would have, too: one of his favourite expressions was 'This is the way to deal with them!' and he'd bring his hands together with a loud smack. He was a bit of a martinet, and my aunts used to play him up, but he gave as good as he got. He enjoyed a drop of stout, and was something of a wheeler-dealer on the side. He would have liked to become a councillor in Brixton, but he couldn't, because he was a police officer.

Because I often stayed with my aunts, my grandfather and I became very close, and we had many chats about the police: he would tell me stories of derring-do, and gave me a bit of a feel for the police service. Before his accident he had been very fit and strong, and one of his favourite stories was about how he arrested a burglar after a tre-mendous chase, which he claimed lasted three miles and ended in fisticuffs. Some of his yarns concerned the General Strike of 1926, in which he was caught up. When I was older and away at school, I used to go and see him, and he always gave me a £10 note – a lot of money in those days. I still have his gold watch, which he left me.

My father Cyril was a distinguished-looking man, wonderfully modest, of enormous integrity. He never talked about his war, and he was not particularly sociable, but he was extremely proud of his house, and he loved his garden, in which – like Winston Churchill – he built brick walls as a hobby. I never saw him lose his temper. He was fond of fast cars, and among the ones he owned was a Jaguar, which he used to let me drive in and out of the garage. One day, as my aunts were waiting outside, I went to bring it out; but I'd left the front wheels turned to one side, and as I put my foot down on the accelerator I hit the garage door: I took half the garage away and did massive damage to the car – but he never said a word.

In due course my mother had three children with him – two boys and a girl – but the first of the new brood did not arrive until I was twelve. As the family expanded, we moved to a still larger house in New Malden, near Kingston, where we had a tennis court and swimming pool.

Long before that – soon after his arrival in our lives – Cyril had taken up responsibility for me, and in the autumn of 1949, when my mother was finding things too much for her, he arranged for me to be educated privately. Because he was often away flying, and my mother was going out to work, I was sent off to boarding school at the age of six and three-quarters.

I had quite enjoyed primary school, but it was a severe shock for me to be dragged out of my familiar environment, and for my first year at prep school I was acutely miserable. That establishment, in a country house, was in Sussex: the regime was Spartan, and there was a lot of bullying and unpleasantness, not least from the teachers, one of whom was aggressively disciplinarian, and after a year my parents took me away.

Heathfield House, to which I went next, was a great deal better. Another private school based in an old house on the outskirts of a village, it had extra classrooms built on, and first-rate playing fields. It was a good school, well run and well supported: the headmaster was a talented teacher, and sport was strongly encouraged. My own experience of it was so good that my mother's sisters in Canada also sent their children there.

I enjoyed myself and prospered at Heathfield, became captain of cricket, captain of football, and Head Boy. At cricket I was both bowler and batsman. Later, at public school and playing for the police, I became a fast bowler, but in those days I used to bowl slowly. The ground was set on a slope, and I always bowled from the same end, getting the pitch to help my natural movement away from the bat. I also used to open the batting. One of my failings is that I am incredibly impatient: I always want things done yesterday, which I guess is a weakness and also a strength. You might therefore think that at the crease I would have been a whirlwind hitter – but no. The curious thing was that when I went in to open the innings, I had all the patience in the world. I'd take my time, get my eye in, and wait for the bad ball to come along.

My father's love affair with aircraft persisted all his life. He introduced me to flying, and when I was no more than eight started letting me have a go in the cockpit, which of course I found tremendously exciting. At one stage he acquired an Airspeed Anson, a small, twin-engined plane, seating six or seven people, of the kind used by RAF Coastal Command for spotting submarines and general surveillance. We used to take it to Le Touquet for holidays, and one of my greatest delights was to sit up front with him or another pilot and take over the controls. Not surprisingly, I inherited his passion for the air.

One day, when I was about ten, my father asked if I wanted to change my surname. I was surprised, but really there was no alternative. So I became John Stevens, instead of John Vickery, and it proved quite traumatic, because I took a lot of ribbing at school, where an Irish Catholic master maintained that to change one's name was as bad as getting divorced and remarried.

For years I didn't realise that I am one of those people who, in order to pass exams, has to concentrate intently on their work. Early on, I had trouble learning to read, and I was very slow – not because I was dyslexic, but simply because I tended to take things too casually. By no means a natural scholar, I failed my 11-plus exam, later botched a science exam three times, got only three O levels at my first attempt, and failed my first two exams at police training school. Only when I went into the police service did I grasp the fact that I was not clever enough to sail through life without making a real effort. But then, belatedly, I saw that unless I worked absolutely flat-out before exams came up, I was not going to do well.

At prep school I did manage to pass the Common Entrance exam, and when I was twelve my father took me to Lancing College for an interview with the headmaster. We turned up in my father's spanking new Jag, and after a bit of chat with me about Latin and other subjects, the headmaster turned to him and said, 'And what do *you* do, Mr Stevens?' My father, not wanting to let on that he owned an airline, replied casually, 'Oh, I work at Heathrow Airport.'

I could see the headmaster thinking, This is some crafty loader, who works at the airport, and somehow he's acquired a Jaguar . . .

I never got into Lancing! But for my next attempt, at St Lawrence College, Ramsgate, when I was thirteen, I was taken for interview by my headmaster instead of my father, and was accepted. St Lawrence, a minor public school, was then one of the best hockey schools in the country. I had a highly enjoyable time there, and made many friends whom I still see.

I now realise that I could have worked harder, but I greatly enjoyed all the sport: I was in the first XV for rugby, and won colours in the cricket second XI, bowling fast (but none too accurately) off a long run. My main passion was the Combined Cadet Force, in which I became Senior Under-Officer. The Head Boy of the school, Michael Beggs, used to boss me around for most of the time; but on Wednesdays I would get my own back, because he was on parade as one of my sergeants and I could legitimately bawl orders at him (I'm glad to say he has remained a good friend). Every summer we went out to a camp and lived under canvas, doing field exercises and firing live ammunition from Lee Enfield .303s and Bren guns. My last camp was at Otterburn, in far-off Northumberland, and on the way back we managed to cadge a lift in one of my father's aircraft, which impressed my friends enormously.

On top of all my other activities, I started up a band, which became semi-American in character, and proved a great success. At first I was a bugler, but then I became the individual at the front, twiddling my stick and throwing it up in the air. We were one of the first cadet-force bands to play numbers like 'Dixie'.

When I left school, just before my nineteenth birthday, my ambition was to become a pilot. Through my cadet force I had already done some flying training with the Fleet Air Arm at Gosforth, and although I had not passed all the tests necessary for a private pilot's licence, I had gone solo in a Chipmunk. Now I had to decide whether or not to make flying my career. I had one great advantage, denied to most beginners, in that I could get some practice floating around with

Father's airline, which then had Elizabethans and Dakotas, and I was often up on the flight-deck.

Yet after only a few months my hopes were dashed, because my eyesight let me down. When I was only six or seven, I'd had an operation at Moorfields Eye Hospital to correct a squint in my left eye; and in my late teens I found that when my eyes got tired, the left one began to lose focus. Later in my life the problem disappeared, and to this day I have a pilot's licence to fly multi-engined and jet aircraft; but at the time there were worries that the defect, slight as it was, might be dangerous for a commercial pilot. The deciding factor was the opinion of two Harley Street surgeons that the disability was likely to grow worse: that my left eye would grow weaker as I got older, and that by the time I was twenty-five or twenty-six, I would no longer be fit to fly. As one of the specialists was Dr Wambeck, who did all the tests for the British Overseas Airways Corporation, we felt bound to accept his advice, and with immense reluctance I abandoned my hopes of a flying career.

My father naturally shared my disappointment; but my mother, whose own father had been a policeman for thirty years, was delighted when I opted for my second choice and applied to join the force.

THREE

Raw Recruit

I joined the police on 8 October 1962, just short of my twentieth birthday. My call-up papers directed me to report to the Met's training school at Peel House, a tall, nineteenth-century former town house, near Victoria, in the centre of London. I spotted the intimidating façade of dark-red brick easily enough, but I had a few minutes in hand, and before I committed myself I went into a café on the corner for a cup of coffee. As I sat there, other young men – obviously fellow recruits – appeared.

One came up and asked, 'Are you joining the police?'

'Yes,' I said, so he sat down with me, and we had a chat.

His name turned out to be Ian Coates, and he came from Kent. Another of our number, Brian Sinclair, had been a milkman, and I was immediately struck by the variety of backgrounds from which we derived.

I was nervous as I went up the front steps into the hall of Peel House, and I had a peculiar feeling about the whole enterprise. I kept thinking, This is the beginning of a long, long journey.

It wasn't as if I was going into a tunnel: just that I sensed the road ahead stretched far out of sight. And yet, at the same time, I had not the slightest doubt that I was going to devote my whole working life to the police.

Inside, I was met by Sergeant Checkley, an impressive figure in uniform, with a magnificent moustache, who was going to be our instructor. Seeing a large policeman in full regalia, close up, gave me another strange feeling: soon *I* would be dressed like that.

There were twenty-odd in our intake, and I quickly became aware that most of them, although aiming to join the Met, were not from

London at all. On the contrary, they came from far and wide – Scotland, Wales, the north of England, even Northern Ireland – and spoke with a variety of accents. Some of them were not that easy to understand, and they in turn had difficulty making out what Londoners were saying. Another disadvantage that the outsiders suffered was that they were on strange ground: they didn't have a clue about the geography of the city, and when they went out on the streets, and someone asked them for directions, they had to refer to their little red books to give even the simplest instructions.

Our first task was to draw our kit – uniform, helmet, truncheon and so on. Then we settled in, and training began. Peel House itself was depressing – dingy rooms, battered old desks and chairs, and food so tasteless that some people had parcels of extra supplies sent from home, as if we were in a prison camp. There were no bedrooms as such: the dormitories on the top two floors were divided up by low partitions, like horse-boxes, so that we had no privacy. They were equipped with wooden lockers, metal beds and a couple of green blankets. But what worried me more than the physical surroundings was the fact that everything depended on learning by rote. We were required to memorise an entire instruction book word for word, as if we were actors, and if anyone got a single syllable wrong in a test, he was marked down. I found this very difficult, because at school we had been taught to use a bit of creativity – and in police training no creativity was allowed. Word for word meant literally that.

Our existence was claustrophobic in the extreme. The days consisted of one lesson after another, broken up only by periods of Army-style drill in the back yard, which was so small that our squad had to execute continuous about-turns as we marched up and down. Our parades were farcical, but the instructors took them very seriously. We tended to spend the evenings revising what we had learnt earlier, but every now and then we would repair to the White Swan – the pub known as the Mucky Duck – round the corner.

After two weeks at Peel House we went off to the Police Training College at Hendon, which had better facilities, far more space and a much wider curriculum. The buildings were grouped round an old country house, and surrounded by playing fields. The complex also included the driving school, and the old detective training school, and altogether I felt part and parcel of something worthwhile.

The accommodation was far more comfortable than in London, and I shared a room with Sinclair, the former milkman, who regaled me with stories about all the interesting encounters he had had on his rounds, especially with housewives. In those days I was pretty naïve, and my own experience of women was limited, to say the least. But Sinclair's narratives rapidly advanced my knowledge of female habits and behaviour, and on the whole I believed his stories, for they had the ring of truth. (In fact, so much of his energy went into the activities he described that he survived only two years in the police.)

Again the atmosphere was military: reveille at 6.30 a.m., followed by a drill parade. There was any amount of drill, and we were chased about the parade ground by a big bull of a police sergeant – but I didn't mind that: at school I had been leader of the drill team that won several CCF competitions. We also had no end of PT and self-defence lessons. Luckily the food was good, and there was plenty of it: we needed it, to replace all the energy we were putting out.

Our instructors were, naturally, of an older generation, and because of the war, their experience was entirely different from ours. Most of them were former servicemen, and many wore the ribbons of campaign medals on their tunics. They made no secret of the fact that they thought we were pig-ignorant – and they were absolutely right – but we ignored their contempt and looked up to them, because they had fought for our country.

We learnt much about police procedure: how to arrest people, how to give evidence in the witness box, how to fill out reports. Later, of course, the job itself turned out to be totally different from what we'd been led to expect: if work had been anything like what I experienced at the training school, I'd have left the service within the first three or four weeks. Not only was the instruction incredibly unimaginative: we were practically taught *not* to use our discretion, or even our intelligence.

There were two kinds of reports that we had to master: 'A' and 'B'. The A reports – the most important – including all legal definitions, for instance of larceny, had to be learnt word-perfect, and whole sentences remain lodged in my head to this day: 'The primary object of an efficient police force is the preservation of public tranquillity,' and so on. B reports could be paraphrased, but not much. In exams, if we deviated by so much as a single word from the set definitions of the A report, again we lost marks. There was no leeway. In general, the language used was ridiculously restricted, and evidence in court had to be given in similarly stilted jargon: 'On such and such a date I was proceeding in an easterly direction down so-and-so street at whatever time it was when I saw someone whom I now know to be . . .'

The formula did give you a certain discipline, but one of the weaknesses of the training was that it did not allow you to describe grey areas: everything had to be black and white. Of course, in real life things are not like that. The result was that sometimes in court police officers were tripped up by barristers if they refused to admit that they were wrong, or could not fully describe what they had seen. The saving grace was that, in those days, the courts tended to believe what police officers said: the general presumption was that they told the truth, and magistrates backed them up. Today officers have to give their evidence in more natural language, and in words less open to parody.

Often at Hendon my mind went back to my housemaster at school, Mr Drew, who, during our last six months, talked to us about possible careers. He thought the police might be good for me, but he warned me by saying, 'The day we can't laugh at our police officers will be the day we're in trouble.' He meant that if people were frightened of the police, because they reacted like humourless automatons, we would be in danger of living in an overbearing police state. The truth of his remark came home to me at Hendon, and has stayed with me throughout my career.

The best feature of Hendon was that we were confronted with realistic scenarios and incidents, such as traffic accidents, and had to work out how we would deal with them. The roads inside the college grounds were equipped with pedestrian crossings and police boxes, and cars were deployed as they might be out on the street. Some of the staff would act as complainants or injured persons, and we, as PCs, had to go up and ask, 'What's happening here, sir?' Then we had to follow through, deal with the incident or accident, and note down details in our pocket-books. Later, the books were marked, to make sure we had got everything right. We were also taught unarmed combat, and jumped off high diving boards to learn life-saving – in those days every officer had to be a proficient swimmer, able to save anyone who fell into the Thames.

Once again, the physical part of the twelve-week course presented me with no problems. During the winter of 1962–3, whenever the freezing weather allowed, I played rugby for the college, being large enough – at 6 foot 4 and thirteen stone – for a second-row forward (today I would need to be four inches taller, and three or four stone heavier, to compete with the second-row giants who power the pack and dominate the line-outs). As always, it was the exams that nearly proved my downfall. We had one every couple of weeks, and, having failed the first two, I was given a warning by the chief instructor, after which I took to getting up at six or even five in the morning for sessions of intensive revision. I found the work very difficult – and had I failed yet again, my police career would have come to an abrupt halt; but in fact my extra effort paid off, and in the final exams I passed out in the upper third.

Strangely enough, I got little encouragement from the family. Most weekends I went home on the tube, and my mother always asked eagerly how I was getting on: because her father had made his career in the police, she loved to compare notes. But my father was curiously ambivalent. Considering how positive he was about most things, I was surprised and a bit disappointed by his attitude. When I told him I was having a hard time learning everything, he'd say, 'Yes, well – you may find that being in the police isn't quite what you expected.' He never came out with heavy advice: that wasn't his style. Rather, he would make suggestions, and gently manoeuvre people in the direction he thought it best for them to go. His doubts persisted for my first two years in the force: I never really knew what he was thinking, but I believe he instinctively felt that there were better things I could do.

Some of his doubt percolated through to me, and I did not enjoy Hendon. The regime was so dour as to deaden the mind and soul: instruction was unimaginative, male-chauvinistic and utterly lacking in humour. Nothing was injected with a bit of fun: I found the whole course depressing. We had no such sophisticated training aids as videos: it was all chalk and talk. The instructors – police to a man – knew their business, but there was a bullying atmosphere, and whenever the chief superintendent who ran the school came into a mixed class, he would make obscene remarks about any women present.

There was certainly a great deal to learn, especially about the law, but the approach was far too narrow. Maybe this was inevitable – because if you're a police officer chasing someone over a roof, you must be confident you're doing the right thing: there's no time for doubts about the propriety of your actions.

Through the perimeter fence, across the road, lay RAF Hendon – still an active airfield – and of course, given my father's background, a place of some fascination to me. Often I looked across, watching planes potter in and out, and thought wistfully, Gosh, I'd rather be there than here.

In my time at Hendon I boxed for the college, as a light heavyweight, and did all right until my last fight, in which I met someone from whom I couldn't run away fast enough. The result was that I took a good hiding. When I came home with my eyes all puffed up, black and blue, my mother was horrified, and my father was in a better position than ever to keep up his gentle pressure: 'Are you *sure* you're doing the right thing . . .?'

I expected that at the end of the twelve-week course there would be some sort of ceremony and a passing-out parade, with a band playing and parents in attendance – but no. I was just given my warrant card and told to report to West End Central police station on a certain day. With that, I was on my way.

FOUR

On the Beat

We were given no choice as to where we were posted. One of the units I did *not* want to join was A Division, which operated out of Cannon Row: everyone I knew urged me not to go there, claiming that if I did I would be on static points, guarding places such as Buckingham Palace, and have no chance to do the kind of police work I wanted to do. I greatly feared that might be my fate – so when I heard that I was bound for C Division, which comprised West End Central and Tottenham Court Road, I was overjoyed.

One formality that we all had to go through at Old Scotland Yard – between Whitehall and the Thames – was the ceremony of taking the oath of allegiance to the Queen in front of an Assistant Commissioner, who in those days was a Justice of the Peace. Some forty of us swore, in unison, to serve the Queen, to act on her behalf, and so on. The JP's address concentrated on a sense of duty – something that was still ingrained in the police service. Ever since, I have kept in my mind – and often used in speeches at long-service ceremonies and passing-out parades – the famous quotation by the American Civil War General Robert E. Lee: 'Duty is the most sublime word in our language. Do your duty in all things. You cannot do more. You should never wish to do less.'

My first day as a constable is still vivid in my mind. Three of us new boys went upstairs together at West End Central, and we received no formal greeting. An inspector merely said to my companions, 'Well, you two are staying here, but Stevens, you're off to Tottenham Court Road today.' For a few minutes I was disappointed. Yet, as it turned out, it was the best thing that ever happened to me, because that area was a fine learning ground, well away from other stations. It encompassed a self-contained community, and covered the north side of Oxford Street, as well as London University, and two major hospitals, the Middlesex and University College – both great places for meeting nurses, which is one of those arduous pursuits that policemen feel obliged to follow.

I was driven to Tottenham Court Road, and as I was about to go into the station through the back door, there in the yard I saw a man cleaning a beautiful white Austin Healey 3000 sports car.

'Who's that?' I asked the PC escorting me.

'Oh,' he replied, 'that's Detective Constable Charlie Heaver.'

I didn't know at the time that Charlie was an outstanding rugby player, and had had a trial for the England XV; but I did immediately think that the CID would be a good place to work, if you could drive a car like that, and I fancied the idea of becoming a detective.

Inside the station I was met by the duty sergeant, who seemed to run the place, and by an inspector. The sergeant was an impressive figure – three stripes and a crown on his uniform – and boy, was he powerful, able to put you on early turn, late turn or whatever. As I soon learnt, the building was entirely functional. On the right was the duties office, where rotas were worked out; behind that was the charge room, and the cells were to the left. Down below were the lockers and parade room, reached via a sloping ramp. Upstairs to the left, beyond some offices, was the canteen – one of the most important rooms in the building. Out at the back, down some steps, was the yard, on the left of which lay the drivers' room, used by the officers who drove the fast-response cars (area cars) and were known as the 'Knights of the Road'.

On my first morning, after a brief introductory talk, I was put straight on to learning beats with two other constables, Tony Coppellotti and Johnny Batten, who had joined the force a few months ahead of me. Johnny was relatively short and stocky, but Tony was a huge lad – about 6 foot 3, and an amateur boxing champion. If you were lucky, as I was in finding these two, you went out on the streets with an energetic leader who taught you a good deal. I remember Johnny telling me, 'Never just walk along. Always look up. Always take in whatever's going on. There's a lot happening up above, in buildings, on roofs.'

By no means all Johnny's colleagues were so informative. There was one crotchety old PC, who had been an area car-driver, used to cruising about in nice Wolseley saloons. He'd been taken off that duty, and was none too pleased. During our eight hours on the beat, he did not utter a single word: he just walked and walked in gloomy silence.

Apart from that, my new life was a revelation. I was working in an environment entirely different from that of Hendon, with different disciplines and a different way of talking. This was life for real. I felt reinvigorated, and knew I had started on a career that I would not want to change for any other.

At first I was allocated accommodation in a section house in Beak Street, a dreadful place in darkest Soho, where the bedrooms – if you could call them that – were strung out along a corridor, separated only by low partitions. As people were on shift work, comings and goings continued all night long, and the constant disturbances, combined with the normal noises and smells of a dormitory, made sleep difficult. Fortunately, after only about four months, I moved on to Trenchard House, another section house, in Broadwick Street, in the centre of Soho, where I had a room of my own and was much more comfortable. But whenever I went on duty I had to walk, in full uniform, from there to the station in Tottenham Court Road, and vice versa – a distance of maybe a mile each way, which added a good deal to my working day.

Learning beats was absolutely fascinating, but exhausting, too. I was on my feet for eight hours a day, and before my feet hardened up, a new pair of boots gave me a blister. The result was a poisoned heel, which put me off duty for one of only three times in my entire career. In spite of that, I *loved* being on the beat. We would set out from the station in pairs, but then we would separate, and each go his own way. I shall never forget walking out on my own for the first time. There I was, with my whistle and truncheon, thinking, Wow! If anything happens, I'm going to have to deal with it. When people came up to me and asked for help, I realised how much they were relying on my presence and support. I felt that simply by being there I was doing something for the community. Also, it seemed to be easy to make friends with people in shops, at the pubs, in the hospital casualty departments: they all had good relationships with the local coppers and were glad to see me.

I soon discovered that a few constables were rather too fond of pubs. Drinking on duty was a sacking offence, but occasionally a colleague was willing to take the risk, and one night, while still learning, I went out with a fellow who was determined to slake his thirst. He knew just where to go. At the back of a pub in Titchfield Street builders had put up some scaffolding, so we climbed a ladder, went in through a window, and there was the publican. I wasn't brave enough to drink anything, but my friend sank a couple of pints in quick time, and then exclaimed, 'I think I'm all right for the night now. We're off!' And away we went.

Constables on the beat were not supposed to smoke either – and in fact I myself never smoked cigarettes at all – but at night it was easy enough for my colleagues to nip into a doorway for a quick drag, and in those days almost everyone did smoke. The air in police offices was thick as fog. Johnny Batten reckoned he got through more than forty cigarettes a day: a packet was then so cheap that if you took it out in the canteen, you'd just hand it round, not noticing if you gave half a dozen away.

There was far less traffic then than now. Parking meters were only just coming in, and in any case they were not our concern, being operated by a special unit of the police. Tottenham Court Road itself was still two-way (it is now one-way north), and the whole area had an easy-going feel.

My salary was the princely sum of £8 a week, and every pay day brought an antiquated ceremony – much the same as in the Army – when we paraded in the station, went up to the desk one at a time, saluted, and collected our money in cash, in a packet. Although pay was low by today's standards, we were not badly off: we had free accommodation, and it was perfectly possible to live on the money we got. We knew that our predecessors in the 1950s really *had* been hard up: before the pay rises introduced by the Royal Commission of 1960, officers had been going to work at the end of the week with sandwiches that had no fillings. We were never reduced to surviving on bread alone; but all the same, I could barely afford to run a car – even an old banger – and when I wanted to get married I had to sell my ancient, six-cylinder Vauxhall Velox (which I had bought at umpteenth-hand from a friend of my father's) in order to buy an engagement ring.

*

The first arrest I made was with Johnny Batten. We were walking down Tottenham Court Road towards St Giles' Circus when Johnny, whose powers of observation were superb, suddenly said, 'Look at those guys – they're molesting the women over there.' I hadn't even noticed, but he was right: in the entrance to Kirkman Place two men were obviously harassing a pair of women.

'Quick!' snapped Johnny. 'Come on!'

We ran across and grabbed the villains. Sure enough, they had insulted the women and tried to take hold of them. In those days we had no handcuffs, so we frog-marched the men back up the street to the station, put them in the cells and charged them with insulting words and behaviour. One quick entry in the book, and within quarter of an hour we were back out on the street, patrolling again. That first time, I was so frightened of giving evidence in the morning that I didn't sleep a wink – but in the event I need not have worried, for the men pleaded guilty, and no evidence was required.

A more traumatic occasion came on the day I arrested a violent drunk in St Giles' Circus. He was a hulking great fellow, and when I accosted him, he pushed me away, muttering, 'Piss off! You're not big enough for me.' I had doubts about whether I could handle him, but I managed to get him in a wrist-lock, and marched him up the street. By the time we reached the charge room, I was exhausted and soaked in sweat.

At first, I know, some of my colleagues were nervous about making arrests: obviously, if they saw some incident occurring, the easiest thing was to take no action. I never had any such inhibitions. Already my ambition was to become a detective, and the next step up the ladder was to be promoted to the category known as aide to CID; but I knew that uniformed constables were normally on probation for their first two years, and it was most unusual for anyone to become an aide in a shorter time than that.

Every six months, as probationers, we were required to submit returns of the arrests we had made, and if we hadn't scored high enough, we were criticised. Luckily, I found that I was a good observer of people, that I had a knack of chatting them up, and that these assets gave me an unusual ability to detect criminals. Some sort of telepathy may have been involved, or it may be just that I was lucky. I used to stop and talk to a great many passers-by, and I could usually tell from their manner what sort of people they were. Sometimes I could sense, simply by looking at a person walking along a street, if he or she had a guilty secret; and of the people I stopped, about one in three, or sometimes even one in two, would turn out to be wanted, or to have something in their possession that allowed me to arrest them. Occasionally I used to take a look at a person, get a hunch, and follow him to see what he was up to – and I soon had an incredibly high hit-rate.

Stopping and searching was much easier then than now, because the rules were far more relaxed. Especially at night, you could walk up to anybody and say, 'Excuse me, what are you doing? Where are you going?' Even if he was on perfectly legitimate business, he wouldn't take exception.

Success came in part from having a thorough knowledge of the patch. A strange face in a strange place immediately aroused suspicion. If I saw somebody walking about at one o'clock in the morning, I would want to know what he was doing, especially if he was carrying a bag: if it was someone I recognised – maybe a waiter going home from one of the restaurants, or a cab-driver having a break – all well and good. But if his answers weren't plausible, I would ask him what he had in his pockets – and under Section 66 of the Metropolitan Police Act, 1829, I had the power to search anyone I stopped, providing I had 'reasonable grounds for suspicion', and those grounds could be entirely subjective.

The question of what did or did not constitute a criminal offence was somewhat arbitrary. Strictly speaking, drunkenness was a criminal offence; speeding was a criminal offence, but parking was only a traffic offence. Theft, robbery, criminal damage and serious assault were always criminal offences. But in practice we classed lesser mis-demeanours as 'vagrancy offences', among which were drunkenness, threatening behaviour and moderate fighting.

Now and then our patrols clashed with the work of the CID. Some-times, as I reported from a police box, I'd be called back to base, and the detective on duty in the CID office would tell me to keep out of a certain area, because the chaps from the Yard had an operation going on there. Once Johnny Batten and I got some rather vague information from a resident in Rathbone Street, who reported people behaving suspiciously. When we went down, we found three Greek Cypriots, stopped them, and took them into a doorway to search them. While we were at it, who should come along but Detective Sergeant Jack Slipper (later famous as Slipper of the Yard), with Detective Sergeant John Vaughan, both Flying Squad officers. 'We've been watching these guys,' they said. 'Leave them to us.' So we pulled off – and back at the station one of the Cypriots was found to be carrying a loaded handgun.

With 99 per cent of my stops, there was never the slightest aggravation; provided I talked in a reasonable way, nobody cut up rough. Once, though, I stopped a man who said he worked in a West End hospital, and for no apparent reason he became abusive and violent. Because he seemed so volatile, I couldn't search him on the street, so I took him to the police station, where we found he was carrying a knife. Later, he tried to murder the South African High Commissioner.

What we did *not* have were radios on which we could summon help or check with the station to see if a person we had stopped was wanted. Our only means of attracting attention or calling for assistance were our whistles. Luckily different beats were usually quite close to each other, so that a colleague might be within earshot – and in any case, it could be said that our very lack of equipment was an advantage, in that it encouraged us to make friends in the community, so that there were plenty of people who would come to our aid in an emergency. The newspaper-seller, the ladies in the bakeries, the milkman – you knew that if any of these saw you rolling around on the floor, they would quickly make a phone call.

Beats were precisely delineated, and often quite small. One was no more than 500 yards up and down Tottenham Court Road, and each of us was limited to one side of the street: we didn't cross over. One of the most interesting areas was round Eastcastle Street, which was then the home of the rag trade, and full of dress-making shops.

In retrospect, my colleagues and I seem to have been incredibly naïve. I have no doubt that corruption existed in higher reaches of the police, but down on our level we were totally innocent. Even accepting a free cup of tea gave me a twinge of guilt – what would the sergeant say if he got to know about it? – and an incident in which Johnny Batten became involved showed how guileless we were.

One evening he was walking his beat in Russell Square when a big Rover came limping past, with a flat tyre flapping on the road. The driver was got up in a dinner jacket and black tie, obviously on his way to a smart party. When Johnny commiserated with him through the open window, he confessed that he didn't even know how to use his jack – so Johnny changed the wheel for him, whereupon the man thanked him effusively and handed him two £1 notes. Two pounds! Johnny couldn't believe it. He tried to wave the money away, but the driver insisted on handing it over. For the rest of the night Johnny was in a sweat, tormented by guilt.

Other contemporaries would have positively refused the tip. One morning Tony Coppellotti found a shop in Tottenham Court Road standing open and unoccupied, so he put in a call to the station, to report that the premises were insecure. When the key-holder came back, he tried to give Tony ten shillings – and was offended when his offer was declined. There were two thoughts in Tony's mind: one, that the rules strictly forbade him to accept money, and two, that he was being paid to do a job, and did not want to be tipped like a porter on a railway station.

Looking back, I can see that I was very ambitious, and eager to get on. But I hope I never became pleased with myself or boasted about what I was achieving. After twelve months, I had a record number of crime arrests, but the chief superintendent criticised me because I had no motoring prosecutions. Stung into action, I responded by going down to Oxford Street and giving eighty motorists cautions, either for not leaving their lights on or for parking their cars pointing in the wrong direction, both of which were offences in those days. As I was doing it, some people came out of a cinema, and a man said, 'What the *hell* are you doing?'

In a jokey way I replied, 'Don't worry. This is just to remind you' – and everyone ended up laughing. But by that single strike I boosted my traffic offences to a satisfactory level, thereby demonstrating the ludicrousness of having to meet targets.

My favourite stint was night duty, when I went on at 10 p.m. and did not come off until 6 a.m. After midnight, I felt that the streets were mine. The traffic had died away: there were few people about, and I got an extraordinary sense of ownership, which I never had during the day. I think I was driven partly by the natural curiosity that is the prerequisite of any successful detective. Why's the milkman out at 3 a.m.? He's not usually here till four. It must be someone new on the round – and so I would have an excuse to introduce myself and chat the fellow up.

Because I was making so many arrests, I was having to work very long hours. Sometimes I would finish night duty at 6 or 7 a.m., go into court at 10 a.m., and maybe spend all morning and afternoon there, so that I would be dog-tired when I went back on duty in the evening. The compensation was that we were paid overtime for our court appearances – and for young men on a weekly wage of £8, that was very important. Besides, I found a remedy for exhaustion. Once or twice I and a colleague from a neighbouring beat, PC Jimmy James, climbed over the railings in Bedford Square and took refuge in a little pavilion screened from view by bushes. There we gratefully lay down on the slatted wooden benches and had a nap. But one morning we dropped off so soundly that when we awoke with a start, we found to our horror that the time was already 5.50, and we were supposed to be back at the station, booking off, by 5.40. There was frost on our eyebrows and all over our uniforms, but we brushed it off and ran like hell for base, arriving just in time to keep out of trouble.

In those days Tottenham Court Road was the centre of the beatniks, and off Gower Street, round the back in Fitzroy Place, the fraternity used to congregate in large numbers, squatting in derelict buildings and using the Fitzroy Arms as a meeting place. On a Friday there could be two or three hundred people milling around inside and outside the pub. Often some of them were high on Purple Hearts or other drugs, and we used to have the odd lively battle – nothing so uncivilised as knives, but sometimes a bit of a punch-up when we went in to make arrests for drugs. Naturally, the restaurants in the area objected to the beatniks' presence, and, without being too aggressive, we tried to balance up the wishes of the locals. Drugs like Purple Hearts were just coming in: the big buzz, on a Saturday night, was to go and buy a few tablets in the Charlotte Street area. We knew who was selling the stuff, so we used to keep an eye on the clubs: we would watch a steady stream of customers come strolling up from the West End and disappear down steps into a basement. Then, as they re-emerged and were walking away – *wham!* We'd grab them.

In those days the blue uniform commanded far more respect than it does now, and members of the public did what you told them. For instance, there was a law against drinking in the street: if people had spilled out of a pub on a hot summer evening, and you told them to get back inside, they'd go. You couldn't do that now. Today, people freely insult the police, using filthy language; we wouldn't put up with that. If anyone started swearing at us or threatening us, we would arrest him for insulting words and behaviour, or for being drunk and disorderly. We had a saying, 'No one insults the cloth': it sounds a bit pompous now, but it was true enough at the time. There was general acknowledgement that to take on a police officer was unwise, because if someone beat up one of our colleagues, we became pretty robust and might well retaliate in kind.

In fact, it was exceedingly unusual for anyone to hit a policeman. Even if an individual was drunk, he wouldn't put his hands on you. There was a certain respect, in both directions, and members of the public sometimes volunteered assistance: once when Tony Coppellotti was struggling with a drunk, a car-driver pulled up and offered to help him.

Even criminals were much less likely to assault a policeman than they are now. Once in Old Compton Street Tony came on two men attacking another, kicking him as he lay on the pavement. The thugs ran away, but Tony, having shouted at a passer-by to ring for an ambulance, chased them until they ran into a restaurant. There they stood at the back, with knives at the ready, and he remained in the doorway, blocking their escape. As they began advancing towards him, he stood his ground, not moving or saying anything – and his immobility made them hesitate until it was too late: reinforcements arrived, summoned by a call from the restaurateur, and the pair were arrested. Their victim had been badly injured, losing an eye, and they both went to prison. Today, in similar circumstances, the criminals would never have hesitated to attack the policeman, and he might well have been killed.

Six months after I started on the beat, I was swept up into the incident that led to my first commendation for bravery. I was on early turn, which started at six in the morning, so I paraded at 5.30 at Tottenham Court Road, and by 6.00 I was out on the beat. The weather was freezing, and I was paired with PC Clive Young, a strapping great lad from East Anglia. We set off northwards, then turned right and left into Goodge Street, where there was a strip and drinking club, then run by a Greek Cypriot called Paphos.

At about 6.10 Clive and I stopped in a recessed doorway (which is still there), with a glass partition at one side of it. We hung about for a few minutes, partly to keep out of the cold, partly to keep an eye on what was happening over at the club, which was open for twenty-four hours a day, and where, we knew, drugs were sold. A few people were still going in and out. From our little hide-out we could see through the glass partition, but because it reflected light, no one could see us.

At 6.25 up drove a car. Out got four large men, who nipped round to the boot, opened it, and took out a machete, an axe, knives and other implements. Thus armed, they hurried into the club without spotting us, even though we were in uniform. It was apparent that they had seriously unpleasant intentions, and were, in our terms, top-rate villains.

'Come on,' I said. 'We'd better do something about this.'

We ran across to the entrance. One of the four tried to slam the door in our faces, but we put our shoulders to it and smacked our way in – to find blood all over the place. The raiders had lost no time in literally carving up the owner of the club.

Clive stood in the doorway to prevent anyone escaping, and blew his whistle furiously. Inside, the scene was nightmarish: the walls were dripping with blood, wounded people were hollering and screaming. The manager of the club was clutching one arm, which had been half-severed. In front of me, the villains ran away though the building into the back yard. I chased after them and saw them going up a fire-escape ladder on to the roof of the three-storey block. I climbed after them, hand over hand, and just as I reached the top, one of them rushed back, trying to kick me off the ladder.

I held back till he moved away, then, as he ran off, I pulled myself up to see where he had gone. A few seconds later, from away to my right, came a crash of breaking glass. I realised the fugitives had dropped through a skylight, so I slithered down the ladder and ran back through the blood-soaked club, out into the street, to find that they had landed in a depot where milk floats were loaded, and had used one of the floats to smash their way out through the doors. By then the cavalry were on their way – more police officers had deployed rapidly from Tottenham Court Road – but I started chasing a man who ran off, a big, strong fellow with red hair, carrying an axe in one hand.

'Stop! Stop!' I yelled, but he had no intention of stopping, so when I caught up with him I began to belabour him over the back of his head with my truncheon. Blood spurted out of his hair. The truncheon broke. Luckily for me he didn't turn round. The next I knew, he dropped the axe, and we were both down on the pavement, struggling and trading punches. Soon I started to get the worst of it: he was hell-bent on scratching my face or gouging out my eyes. Just in time, some of my colleagues caught up with us, dived on him, suppressed him and saved me from taking more of a hiding.

It turned out that he was Irish, leader of the gang. The other three were arrested as well, and inquiries revealed that the club owners had not paid their protection money – or else they had paid it, but to other people. The criminals we captured were very powerful in the West End at that time, and they had decided to exact revenge. When they came up at the Old Bailey, they all got long terms of imprisonment, while I received a commendation from the High Court judge and also from the Commissioner. That was the first of the awards I won, but it has always remained the one of which I am most proud. In court the judge praised my courage – but I would hardly call it that: rather, I acted instinctively in a crisis. Everything happened so fast that there was no time for doubt: once the chase was on, adrenaline took over.

When I was commended, my father at last realised how much I was enjoying myself. Seeing that I revelled in the camaraderie of the force, and in helping the community, he abandoned his latent opposition and backed me from then on.

More than ever, I wanted to get into the CID, and I knew that the more crime arrests I made, the better my chances would be – for in those days the only way to become a detective was to succeed as a crime-arrester. There was a league table in the West End Central station and if your name was at or near the top of it, your chances were good.

Among our favourite targets were the rogues who played 'Spot the Lady', also known as 'the three-card trick' – a typical sixties craze. They operated all over London, especially outside football matches and greyhound tracks. Little groups of five worked in Oxford Street and around the bottom of Tottenham Court Road: one man to deal the cards, two spotters to keep look-out (one in either direction) and two to play the game and win tempting sums of money, thus encouraging genuine punters to have a go.

It all looked terribly simple. The croupier flicked out three playing cards, face down, on top of a box, and invited gamblers to put money on the one they reckoned was the Queen of Spades. After a couple of wins by the home team, strangers would start to have a go, and inevitably lose their stakes – but at the first sign of trouble, the ring-leader would sweep up his cards, kick the box over, and vanish into the crowd, along with his mates.

Because there were so many people passing in and out of Woolworths, they liked to work in front of the shop's doors – but that was good for us, too, because we could slip through the store from the back, come out behind them and grab at least one of them before the rest scarpered. One PC used to take a ride on a bus and hop off right opposite their pitch, to take them by surprise. Whenever we did catch them, we'd take them into the police station and charge them, not with any gambling offence, but with obstruction of the footway.

By no means every incident ended so well. Once, in pursuit of nurses, I went into the Middlesex Hospital for a cup of tea at three o'clock in the morning, and in particular to chat up one of the staff nurses, a girl called Macdonald, whose father was an Air Commodore and used to write for *The Times* on air defence matters. In the Casualty department on the ground floor everything was quiet – until I was challenged to a sack race along one of the corridors.

Three or four nurses entered, and I was lying second, with one ahead of me, when suddenly, outside the window at the end of the passage, up loomed the face of Sergeant Eddie Stone, the station officer at Tottenham Court Road – who was liable to blow you up if he saw you so much as stray on to the wrong side of the street during your beat. This time, as I tried to disappear, he growled, 'I'll see you in the station, lad,' and I feared I was going to be disciplined. Fortunately, he showed his other side: possibly influenced by the fact that the nurses in the race had been extremely good-looking, he saw the fun of it, and just gave me a gentle ticking-off.

Stone was an unusual character – a brilliant mathematician, with strange, staring eyes. He was one of the first policemen to wear glasses – normally no one who needed them was accepted by the force – and to us he seemed terrifically old. He was probably all of thirty-five, and he was in the wrong job: he was harmless enough, but he should have been an academic. His tendency to pick on people was probably a manifestation of his frustration.

He had one memorable confrontation with Chief Superintendent Starrett, known as 'Big Jim', who was in charge of C District in the mid-1960s. Starrett was from Northern Ireland – he looked and sounded a bit like Ian Paisley – a feared character, tall, with a big face. If ever you heard he was coming, you cleared off out of the way, and when he walked into a police station, everybody froze. He was always immaculately turned out, and a stickler for tidiness. A story was told of how once, as a chief superintendent, he walked along Oxford Street in plain clothes, and when he came on some street traders, he told them to move off. They refused, so he said, 'All right, you stay there, then' – whereupon he went back to the station, put his uniform on and returned to the spot: 'Right you're nicked!'

Another time at Tottenham Court Road he tried to blow Eddie Stone up for some misdemeanour – and anyone with a normal sense of survival would have just kept quiet and let the storm die down. Yet as Starrett ranted, Eddie kept answering back: 'Well, no, sir, that's not true, actually. That's not the case, sir.'

When, in exasperation, Starrett roared, 'THAT'S TYPICAL, SERGEANT STONE, ISN'T IT?', Eddie remained unmoved. 'No, sir,' he replied evenly. 'That's not at all typical. As a matter of fact ...' Starrett ended up as Sir James, the Deputy Commissioner.

One feature of police work that fascinated me when I first went out on the beat was the rapport between coppers and criminals. At school, as part of our social studies training, we had once been taken to a magistrates' court at Broadstairs, Kent, and I had been puzzled by what seemed to be the remarkably good relationship between the villain, who had been charged with larceny, and a local detective constable. When the accused man came out of the dock, he chatted away with the detective most amicably. At the time I couldn't understand it – but when I went on the streets, it suddenly made sense. Relationships between criminals and police generally *were* quite easygoing: the only times they broke down were when villains committed offences of outright brutality or cruelty, especially against children or one of our own people. Very few police officers can stomach crimes that they perceive to be totally against human nature and decency.

In general, there was a sense in which we, the cops, were the top gang. We had more resources than the criminals, and they knew it: they knew that the courts would back us, and that punishments would be severe. The result was that even men as vicious as the Kray twins could make themselves very charming to the police, and go to their aid, if they thought it would gain them temporary advantage.

After a few months on the streets. I knew every inch of the Tottenham Court Road area. There was no science in my perambulations, but during the course of a single night, from ten to six, I might potter along the same street five or six times – varying my route, of course. I knew every thoroughfare, every mews, every alleyway, every building. I also knew where some of the hot spots were, and where the aggravation was likely to be. I noticed at once if any detail of the urban landscape had changed, due to a break-in or some other cause like fire or storm. I also knew a great many of the local people – shopkeepers, night-watchmen, porters, bakers, and (most important) the personnel of the casualty departments in the hospitals.

The casualty departments were regular ports of call, especially when we were on nights or early turn. Depending on which side of Tottenham Court Road we had been allocated, one of us would drop into University College Hospital (to the east) or the Middlesex (to the west): we were in and out almost every day and night, checking on the results of accidents and cases of assault, and we had a tremendous relationship with the staff on the counter: at six in the morning, with nothing much happening, they always had time to find us a cup of tea or a piece of toast. In those days hospitals had no security guards: we, the police, were their security, and the synergy between us, the medical staff, the doctors, the nurses, the porters and the receptionists was outstanding. If any of those people had information that might help us, they passed it on: the only people who would never communicate were the hospital authorities.

It was in UCH that I met my wife-to-be. Tony Coppellotti and I used to go in there for cups of coffee, and one night he pretended to have a headache – so we looked in, drawn by a rumour that two exceptionally attractive nurses would be on duty. They had a little alcove just off the Casualty department, to which they would repair for a cup of tea and a chat. The one I particularly fancied, the tall and slender Cynthia Huggins, didn't show much interest in us policemen at that first meeting, because she was going out with a medical student, and in any case she had plans to go and work in Africa; but I discovered where she kept her bicycle, chained to the railings on the street outside her nurses' home, and I put a ticket on it saying that it had been parked without lights, and she should see me to make sure I didn't report it. That, and a few exclamation marks, did the trick.

I found out that she came from Lancashire, where her father was the vicar of Stalmine, a village between Fleetwood and Blackpool. She'd been to Casterton, a major girls' public school in Westmorland, and afterwards had spent a year in France, working for a family in Paris and at their various grand country houses. Back in England, she went to train at the Great Ormond Street Children's Hospital, and then did her general nurse's training at University College Hospital, where I met her. She was the same age as me – twenty-two – and strikingly attractive. One or two other officers had their eyes on her, but somehow I got ahead of the field. At first her father naturally wondered who I was, but luckily for me *his* father had been an inspector in the police, and I think that prejudiced him in my favour. It was not long before we knew that we wanted to get married; but, unlike today, when people get engaged one day and married the next, we had to be patient and wait nearly two years.

On the beat, if anything untoward was happening, the locals would tell me; and although none of us had radios, I had a very good idea of what was going on. Our only mobile means of communication were the area cars – old Wolseleys – one of which covered our whole area and was manned by senior police officers, the Knights of the Road. The only way of getting in touch with them was by telephoning from a public box, or from one of the police boxes, to which we had to report at certain times.

Our lives as uniformed constables were tightly controlled. The visits to boxes were mandatory, and before we went out on the beat, we were given specified times at which we had to report by telephone, letting the station know everything was in order. If a light was flashing in the box, it meant there was a message, and there was a flap, which we had to pull down, with a book behind it that we had to fill in whenever we called base. The process was called 'Showing a ring', because it recorded when we had rung in. Whenever I went into the station, with a prisoner, or just for a cup of tea or a meal, there was another book in which I had to sign in and out. If I stayed longer than the forty-five minutes allowed for a meal, I was in dire trouble. My job was to be out there on the streets, all the time.

The value of a constable on the beat was never demonstrated better than by the case known as that of the antiques murderer. A Welsh PC called Davies, who had transferred from Cardiff City Police to the Met, was walking along the road in Soho when he saw a man coming the other way: recognising him from a photo-fit portrait that he had been shown on parade that morning, he had the courage to accost the fellow and immediately arrest him. The sole basis for Davies's action was the built-up picture, but he was spot on: the villain was tried and convicted of savagely murdering an antiques dealer – the first time that a photo-fit identification had succeeded.

My aim was always to detain criminals, but to harass law-abiding citizens as little as possible. Tramps, for instance, caused minimal trouble, and I generally left them alone; but I did arrest one, who used to sleep in the doorway of Great Portland Street tube station, for stealing a wallet. When I searched him, he had the wallet on him – a case of what in those days we called larceny finding. Prostitutes were also treated amicably: it was rare for us to arrest one, and then only if there had been a complaint. In any case there were relatively few prostitutes in our area: most of them had been cleared from view by the Street Offences Act of 1959. Before that the streets in Soho had been lined with girls soliciting. What sprang up instead were clip joints known as 'Near-Beer' clubs, where the girls would patrol outside, to entice customers in. Inside, the punters would be sold drinks for exorbitant amounts, thinking they were going to be offered sex.

These clip joints provided some constables with unexpected bonuses. Because there had been a series of attacks on prostitutes, volunteers were paid overtime to spend four hours at a time sitting behind a curtain inside a club, in the hope that they would catch bad characters red-handed.

Occasionally we clamped down on people causing a nuisance – as when we arrested a group of meths drinkers who had settled in Euston Square and were irritating the locals by being noisy and aggressive. We were not very popular with the station sergeant, because when we brought them in they were in need of a good wash, alive with lice and (in some cases) maggots. One tramp was so badly infested that I had to take him to the St Pancras de-lousing centre: there he was stripped naked, fumigated and washed from head to foot, and because I had handled him, I was obliged to submit to the same unpleasant process. The police van had to be de-loused as well.

FIVE
Aide to CID

On the beat I made so many crime arrests that I earnt the nickname 'Swifty' Stevens. I hope it doesn't sound as though I was aggressive or vindictive: I got on perfectly well with all law-abiding citizens, and my ambition was to make society safer by catching as many criminals as I could. Under the system that prevailed at the time, my success qualified me for rapid advancement, and after only eighteen months I applied to become an aide to CID – the next step on the road to detective constable.

I think the idea of working as a detective appealed to a limited number of people – but somehow it was attractive to me. I knew that the job would mean incredibly long hours, and that there would be no payment for overtime. All I would get extra was a detective duty allowance. If I went to work at eight in the morning and finished at eleven that night, it would be just too bad. Even so, I felt a kind of commitment, and was determined to press ahead.

I did not expect to get promotion till I finished my two-year probation, so I was delighted when, in the summer of 1964, I was asked to go to West End Central for an interview. The officer who grilled me was Detective Chief Inspector Wally Virgo, who was in charge of the aides. Later, as a CID commander, he was arrested for corruption and got five years for accepting gratuities from criminals. But at the time our paths crossed he was still in a powerful position; if he didn't approve of somebody's work, that person wasn't going to go far. 'When are you going to arrest someone, son?' was one of his favourite challenges.

Fortunately he accepted me for selection, and so, on Monday, 20 July 1964, after the unusually short time of a year and six months, I became an aide to CID. I got rid of my uniform, wore plain clothes and for some of the time worked in the CID office under senior officers, learning the skills of a detective; but once again my primary role was to be out on the streets as much as possible. I literally lived on the streets, and on many days I went indoors only for meals, or when I arrested people and charged them. The delight of staying on at Tottenham Court Road was that, although in a new guise, I could continue to see all the people I knew – and knowledge of the ground is as great a help to a detective as it is to a uniformed policeman.

In those days the only way an aide could become a fully fledged detective constable was to show prowess at becoming what they called a 'thief-taker', by arresting as many people as possible. If anyone failed to make an arrest in his first two or three months, he would be sent back to the uniformed branch. In the station there was a league table, showing how many arrests each aide or detective had made. The system was quite ruthless – and of course it was open to misuse, for there was always a temptation to arrest people for the wrong reasons.

In 1964 the process was revised, as a result of the Challenor affair, in which Detective Sergeant Harry Challenor, a tough, brave former SAS man who had escaped from a German prisoner-of-war camp, and was feared by London criminals, was arrested for ordering his aides to plant bricks in the pockets of three youths who had staged a demonstration against a state visit by King Paul and Queen Frederika of Greece. The publicity that the scandal attracted led senior police officers to recognise that the system was unhealthy, and the element of competition was scaled down.

Challenor was said to carry what he called his 'gifts' – the stuff he might want to plant on people – in his umbrella. He certainly did a great deal to clear the West End of vicious gangsters: when he told them to leave the country, they would go. But whether his methods could or could not be justified remains a matter of debate. I think they could not, because if you actually break the law in trying to impose the law, you become as much a criminal as any of your villains, and lose your true perception of right and wrong. Challenor lost his own judgement, corrupted the young men working under him, and ended up needing psychiatric treatment. His case illustrated the dangers of a system in which a detective sergeant had such power.

These days, the job demands an understanding of forensic science, of fingerprinting, of DNA comparisons, and so on; but I believe a detective still needs that intuitive ability to recognise criminals and pick them out on the street. When I became an aide, my sixth sense for picking up small signals of unease and stress in the people I stopped seemed to be functioning better than ever, and I had an 'assist' on my first day – helping Detective Constable Charlie Heaver apprehend a lady in Oxford Street on suspicion of falsifying cheques.

My first arrest proper, a stop in the street, came two days later in Charlotte Street, at 10.30 a.m. on 22 July, when I was out with PC Nelson, another aide, and we pulled up a man called Barry Cunnington. Something about him jarred, so I stopped him, and it turned out that he had broken into a store in New Oxford Street and stolen some goods. He was sent down for three years. On 25 July I got another stop in the street, this time for possession of an offensive weapon: a nasty piece of work called Derek Carpenter had a knife in his pocket, which he had used on previous occasions. But he, in contrast, was only fined £5.

I can recall these details because every one is recorded in a logbook with a battered, marbled blue cover and a red spine, which has somehow survived for forty years. 'DIARY – Criminal Investigation Department' proclaims a notice on the front, and it was my bounden duty to fill it in precisely. Every minute of every day had to be accounted for, and rules for diary-keeping were strict. 'The entries will be made daily in ink,' said a notice posted inside the front cover:

> No spaces will be left in the manuscript and the entry
> for each day will start with the full date being written
> across the page. Erasures are forbidden; and
> corrections should be avoided, and if made they
> should be initialled and dated by the officer making
> the entry and by the supervising officer. Entries
> should not be lengthy or argumentative . . .

I used blue ink, and my record brings back that eventful period of my life with amazing clarity. The diary shows that nights were often long and busy:

Sunday 16 August 1964

On duty at CT [Tottenham Court Road] at 6 p.m. Engaged in office until 7.25 p.m. when to QD for refreshment until 8.05 p.m. when resumed patrol with PC Harwood of CT sub-division generally, until 9.00 p.m. when we entered the DUKE OF YORK public house and I purchased refreshment for an informant re local crime. Resumed patrol at 9.25 p.m. Visited CT 10 p.m. then resumed patrol of CT sub-division until visit to CT at 12.00 midnight. Then to 38, RATHBONE STREET at 12.35 re observation until 1.45 a.m. when I arrested DENNIS IVOR IANSON for receiving at 38, RATHBONE ST and JACQUELINE MARY TAYLOR for unlawful possession in RATHBONE STREET, W.1. To CT with prisoners then at 1.50 a.m. to GOODGE STREET with PCs HARWOOD, BATTEN AND MANSBRIDGE where we arrested ANDREW MARKOULIS for unlawful possession and MIKIS GEORGIU CHRISTOPHI for receiving at 38, GOODGE STREET, W.1. To CT with prisoners and engaged re charge until 4.10 a.m. when I purchased an extra meal. Then engaged re prisoners until off duty at 6.30 a.m.

Every right-hand page was reserved for lists of expenses, which now look modest in the extreme. An extra meal generally cost four shillings (20p), and a round of drinks for informers (known as an 'incidental') eight shillings (40p). For the week ending 18 August 1964 I entered travelling expenses of two shillings (10p), and a grand total of £1.60. In my summary for the week I recorded 'ARRESTS – 4. ASSISTS – 4. STOPS – 9. HOURS – $72\frac{1}{2}$.'

At the end of the logbook were two pages headed 'Summary of Apprehensions', with columns for 'Offence for which convicted' and 'Result'. My hit rate was so fast and furious that I soon filled the space available and was obliged to start working backwards into earlier pages. At the end of 1964 I had made forty-four arrests, and by the end of the next year I had taken my total to 106, not to mention eighty-one assists. Crimes varied widely: receiving, robbery with violence, unlawful possession of drugs, breach of probation, desertion, possession of offensive weapons, breaking and entering, threatening behaviour, taking and driving away – but the most common of all was larceny. Punishments ranged from fines to (in one case) four years' imprisonment for embezzlement and larceny.

Occasionally my supervising officer would scribble 'Good work' or even 'Excellent work' in thick blue pencil over a particular entry in my log. Most people pleaded guilty, partly because in those days there was no legal aid. If someone wanted to bring in a solicitor, he could, but it would cost him a lot of money: it was easier to go before the court, apologise, and pay a derisory fine. Today things are entirely different: with legal aid available, it costs an individual nothing to hire a solicitor, and he or she will go on defending you to the end of the world, no matter how guilty you are, because the fees are coming from the taxpayer.

Our aim on the streets was to make ourselves as inconspicuous as possible; so we dressed in nondescript clothes. It was the time of long hair, and some aides grew theirs as a form of camouflage. I never did. But, as my record shows, my relatively trim appearance did not make me any less effective at apprehending criminals.

One day, about three o'clock in the afternoon, I and a colleague, Brian Harwood, were down near High Holborn when we saw three youths behaving in a way that seemed to us suspicious. We tracked them all the way up to Euston Road, where they went round the back of a pub, broke into the owner's car and stole binoculars, a camera, cigarettes and other items. As they came back out on to the street, we were waiting for them. Brian and I were both pretty fit, and we had a vicious fight with the thieves. One got away, but we arrested the other two – all because I had noticed something odd about their demeanour.

Brian was a keep-fit fanatic, always in training: it was a standing joke that whenever he went into a pub, the barman would hand him a glass of milk, because he never drank beer. The result was that he could out-run any villain. Once, after another attempted theft from a car, he pursued a man for several hundred yards up Tottenham Court Road, jogging easily just behind him, until they came level with the police station, whereupon he accelerated and bounced him in. Johnny Batten, meanwhile, had been chasing a man who ran off in the other direction, down Great Russell Street towards the British Museum. The pursuit ended when the fugitive – a big, fat fellow – tripped over a pavement and fell down. Johnny dropped on top of him and held on, but both were so exhausted that they couldn't get up, and they lay there for several minutes like a pair of stranded dolphins, with Johnny unable to summon assistance, until a van full of colleagues came in search of him.

Most days and nights we went out in pairs, two aides together, but sometimes we accompanied experienced detectives so that we could learn from them. As the time approached when we might go before a board, to see whether or not we were fit to become detective constables, senior operators would link in with us and teach us some of their special skills, for instance interrogation. After a serious crime such as a murder, detectives would bring in us aides as members of the murder squad, and include us in the inquiry. The result was that I picked up a lot purely by observation – sometimes of good habits, sometimes of bad.

For one week in every six, I became the assistant to the detective who covered the West End of London as the night duty CID officer. If someone was arrested and put in the cells for crime, the only person who handled the interrogation and documentation was the CID officer – so that I helped deal with every crime arrest that took place at night in the West End. That involved a great deal of low-grade drudgery, mostly paperwork. But at least, in those days, the filling-in of forms was far less demanding than it is now: I could usually get in and out of the charge room within three-quarters of an hour. Now the requirements of health and safety, political correctness and human rights mean that the process takes six or seven hours – a crazy length of time.

In those days the CID was powerful indeed. It was a firm within a firm, with its own chain of command and its own rules and practices. Much imbibing went on, not only in pubs and bars, but also in CID offices, because drinking was part of the culture. Often it was done to obtain information, but drinking of any kind was not frowned upon. In fact, rather the opposite: being able to hold your drink was seen as a useful attribute for a detective. The trouble was that the most favoured beverage of the day was whisky, which is not renowned for keeping people calm.

Detective sergeants and inspectors rarely paid for anything as they made their rounds of bars: the publican would give them back in change whatever sum they had pushed over the counter. But if an aide was found in a bar by a detective sergeant or detective inspector, he was expected to put his hand in his pocket, because they'd caught him, and it was part of the tradition that he paid for their drinks. So he bought them one and got out.

There was also a fair amount of corruption – which I am sure was increased by the low level of our wages. Once, as a uniformed officer, I arrested a man for stealing bottles of milk early in the morning, and when the case came to court, I knew something had gone wrong, because he pleaded not guilty and got off. I had caught him red-handed, carrying the bottles away. In court he claimed he was suffering from a duodenal ulcer, and the magistrate, who *did* have a duodenal ulcer, let him off, on medical grounds. That was absolute nonsense – and my annoyance was doubled when, as I came out of the court, I saw the man slide off with a detective sergeant and hand him some money. Later I heard that the sergeant had known about the magistrate's medical condition, and had suggested that if the accused pleaded that he was similarly afflicted, he would get a sympathetic hearing. In spite of my indignation, I didn't put in any report, because in those days one didn't do such things – and in any case, a complaint would have got nowhere.

As an aide I sometimes went out with Detective Sergeant (First Class) Kennedy, an ex-Canadian lumberjack, a superb detective, incredibly powerful and tough as teak, who always wore his hat on the back of his head. One night, not long before he was due to go on a board for promotion to detective inspector, I came in from night duty and found the charge room in chaos: two or three of my colleagues were struggling all over the place as they tried to control a man who was fighting drunk. A couple of other PCs seemed to be just hanging around, so I said, 'Why don't you get stuck in? Grab him! Sort him out!'

One of them turned round and said, 'That's your first-class sergeant.'

I was amazed to see that the drunk was Kennedy. I went across and tried to calm him down, but he was so far gone that the only thing to do was for three or four of us to push him into the detention room and lock him in until he sobered up. It emerged that he had been working ridiculous hours. He'd also been drinking, and had then swallowed a dose of Purple Hearts, which were everywhere at the time.

The combination had put him completely out of control. He never appeared before the promotion board – and eighteen months later he went on another bender, which finished his career in the police. That was a tragedy, brought on by the stress of trying to achieve promotion, and working extremely long hours.

Interrogations were tougher then than now. Things were done more forcefully, but I never saw anyone being beaten up, and I always thought that hitting people was counter-productive. I saw people being dealt with quite firmly: if someone started screaming and hollering, he was grabbed and thrown into a cell, and the door was shut – but that was fair enough. Interrogations were carried out under Judges' Rules, and statements were taken under caution – that is, a warning that anything a person said would be taken down and used in evidence. I am glad to say I cannot remember anybody ever being convicted for the wrong reasons. My view was always that there were plenty of villains out on the streets, and it was my job to catch them without breaking the law.

Every time I made an arrest, I had to go to court the next morning to present my own case. Later, when I became more experienced as an aide, I was given other cases to present at Marlborough Street Magistrates' Court or the Crown Court, and sometimes I was in and out of court nearly every day. My expertise at giving evidence gradually increased. One case, for which I was commended, involved a man who had been arrested for possession of house-breaking implements, and who was thought by the CID to have broken into numerous premises in my area. One night I stopped the fellow as he was walking up Tottenham Court Road, and found he was carrying a jemmy, hammer, screwdriver and so on. When I gave my evidence in court, I was cross-examined by a QC, but my answers were not what he was expecting, and he gave me a very hard time. When I came out, after nearly four hours in the witness box, a sergeant threatened to report me. 'You should never have answered him back like that,' he said. 'You should have followed normal procedure.'

Next day I was in court again, for the result of the appeal. Not only did the judge and the two magistrates throw it out: the judge called me into the box, to commend me on my arrest, and on the way I had given evidence. When I looked round at the sergeant, I saw he had gone bright red in the face. I learnt there and then that evidence need not always be given in a regimented fashion. Of course you have to give it succinctly, but not like a parrot.

In the summer of 1963 at Marlborough Street I saw Christine Keeler and Mandy Rice-Davies, the girls at the centre of the scandal that caused the resignation of John Profumo, the Secretary of State for War, and nearly brought down the Government. I couldn't help taking a good look at two of the most notorious women in Britain, who had caused a furore by cavorting naked round the swimming pool at a cottage on Lord Astor's estate at Cliveden, and becoming involved with the Soviet naval attaché, Eugene Ivanov. Christine, who was twenty-one and dark haired, was extremely photogenic, but Mandy, blonde and only eighteen, was extremely pretty – and I was impressed that anyone could look as good as she did in such circumstances.

Another lasting memory, from July 1964, was that of seeing the car in which the world champion light-heavyweight boxer Freddie Mills was alleged to have shot himself in Soho (there was some doubt about what happened, but the coroner ruled that he had committed suicide). He died at the age of only forty-three, and the car was brought into the yard at the back of the Tottenham Court Road police station: the sight of it was particularly poignant for me, because my aunt and uncle lived on Denmark Hill, next to Mills and his wife, and sometimes, when I went to see them, they would ask us in to tea. They always seemed to me a delightful couple, and he in particular, with his crumpled face and thick, curly dark hair, struck me as an exceptionally nice man – not at all the thuggish, aggressive individual one might have expected. (In retirement he ran a nightclub at the top of Charing Cross Road, next to the Astoria Theatre.)

Occasionally our investigations took a farcical turn. Once Johnny Batten and I found a man slumped in a doorway behind the Lyons tea house: we asked him what he was doing, and when we searched him, we found that he had stolen more chocolate than he could ever eat. Every pocket, every bag, was absolutely stuffed with chocolate. He was loaded with such a weight of it that he could hardly stand up. Trivial as his offence seemed, we arrested him all the same – in those days we had a policy of zero tolerance: if someone had committed an offence, he was taken in. Even a peccadillo as minor as fly-posting attracted our wrath: if we saw somebody at it, we'd drag him off and charge him with malicious damage.

Another time Brian Harwood and I got an allegation of indecent exposure, so we went to see a woman who lived on the top floor of a house in Great Titchfield Street. She must have been in her late fifties, and when we met her, we asked what the problem was. 'Well,' she said, 'there's a man in the flats over there who keeps indecently exposing himself to us.'

'Right,' I said. 'Can you show us which flat he's in?' Believe it or not, she had to climb up on to a chair to get a view of the alleged culprit's window.

Working as an aide to CID was a tremendous apprenticeship for me – busy, varied and endlessly interesting. The most important element in it was the fact that I was continually being thrown into contact with people of every kind. In no other job could I have met so many diverse characters, and I don't think I could have gone through those eighteen months without the experience having a beneficial effect on my own development.

In 1965, after less than a year, I went on a selection board at Old Scotland Yard. I was twenty-three, and fervently hoping that I was on the verge of a major breakthrough in my career. As an aide to CID I'd been successful, and I knew I had got an outstanding report; but I realised that the board would be looking for experience, and might well think I was too young to become a detective.

The interview was thoroughly alarming. On the appointed day, wearing my best suit, I went to the Yard and up to the waiting-room, off a long corridor on the first floor. Four other aides were also there, poised on the edges of their chairs, all looking highly nervous.

To pass the time, I kept looking at the framed photographs hung in a row round the walls: there were twenty-two in all, portraits of former heads of the CID. I had plenty of time to study them, because I was kept waiting for more than an hour and a half.

At last I was called in. The panel, sitting behind a table, was headed by Commander Millan, one of the top men at the Yard, known as 'Hooter' Millan because of his splendid nose. The other two were detective chief superintendents, also powerful figures, intimidating to a youngster. To me they looked immensely old – they were probably in their early fifties – and they were all gods.

They asked me one preliminary question, and then Hooter Millan said quietly, 'How long have you been outside, lad?'

'An hour and three-quarters, sir.'

'You want to be a detective. You're meant to be observant. I want you to take me through all those photos of the heads of the CID.'

Fortunately I had been so bored that I really *had* looked at them. When I reached number eleven, he smiled and said, 'That's good enough.' They then launched into tough questions, and the interview became pretty grinding. All three of the panel were fierce people, and they gave me a proper grilling: Who are you? What have you been doing? Why do you want to join the department? Towards the end their manner softened a bit, and they asked an easy one: Which well-known person went to school in Ramsgate? The answer was Edward Heath, who had been at the grammar school there. But it was the final question that I shall remember most clearly till the day I die.

'Well, lad,' said Millan, 'you've done very well so far. You've had a lot of crime arrests. But you're exceptionally young to become a detective. You may get through, and you may not. What if you do? Where would you like to go to?'

From the tenor of his remarks, I sensed that I was going to make it. What I *should* have said (I realised afterwards) was, 'Anywhere you want to post me, sir,' or something on those lines. Instead, like an idiot I replied, 'Well, sir, I'm living at Trenchard House. I'm a single man. I'd like either to stay at West End Central or to go to Notting Hill, or somewhere else in the centre of London.'

'All right, lad,' he replied, in a faintly menacing voice. 'I'll make a note of that.' He wrote something down and said, 'Bye bye.'

I came out of the interview feeling shattered. What if I hadn't looked at the photographs? I'd have failed, without any doubt. Maybe I had failed anyway. A week or two later I found I had been selected detective constable – and boy, did we have a celebration! Two others had also got through – Brian Harwood and Johnny Batten – and we had a tremendous drink-up in a pub next to the nurses' home at the Middlesex Hospital. But where did I find I had been posted? To Hounslow, the furthest place possible from the centre of London!

Every day or night I would have to travel fifty minutes each way on the tube, before and after work. That episode taught me a lesson: if you want to be sent somewhere, ask for the opposite. For ever afterwards, if asked a similar question, I replied, 'Wherever you think my abilities would best suit the service.'

SIX

Detective Constable

As a newly selected detective constable, I went first to Scotland Yard, to work for a few weeks in the Criminal Record Office, to get an idea of method index and how it worked, and to learn how the office was run in general. I was put to menial tasks like answering the telephone. Then, on Monday, 4 October 1964, I started at Hounslow.

When I walked in on my first day, a nice sunny morning, there was nobody in the office but a youngish-looking man who introduced himself as Chris Draycott. He was a first-class sergeant – a powerful rank in those days – and absolutely charming: a debonair individual with a moustache, and the palest blue eyes, a lover of real ale. That evening he took me round the pubs and introduced me to Hounslow in general, where the way of life seemed a bit more genteel than that of Central London, but still quite demanding. There were some amusing characters around, among them a young detective constable called Terry Babbage, with whom I worked a lot: square-jawed and powerfully built, he was a lively raconteur, full of jokes. He threw himself into detective work with terrific energy, and since he was as keen on arresting people as I was, we made a pretty good team.

In contrast with my life on the streets as an aide, I spent a good deal of time in the office, but also went out to deal with burglaries that members of the public had reported. I used to take along a little bag full of things like fingerprint powder, but I rarely picked up clues that were any use: the bag was just for display, to show that I was doing the job. As for the business of reporting crime: my job was really to make sure that crime *wasn't* reported. Things were totally different from today: if there was any way we could 'no-crime' an incident, we'd do just that, by somehow making out that nothing illegal had occurred.

In that way we kept crime figures low. Of course, the policy was counter-productive, because if you're looking for extra resources (as we always were), it is pointless to no-crime genuine cases, thus minimising your achievement.

After nine months the head of station, DI Clark, moved on, and his place was taken by Barry Price, a tall, good-looking man, outstandingly polite, but also energetic and capable, who rose to a high level in the police service, becoming Chief Constable of Cumbria and heading the Drugs Interception Unit at the Home Office. I learnt a lot from him – as I did from Detective Inspector Jimmy Sewell, another live wire – small, with crew-cut brown hair, continually on the move – who also went far and reached the rank of deputy assistant commissioner at the Yard.

One person with whom I made particularly good friends was John Wheeler, who took over from Chris Draycott. He was quite a tough individual, and taught me a few things I have never forgotten. We were working long hours – supposedly thirteen one day, eight the next, then thirteen again, although in fact we always did more than that, often putting in twelve hours on the shorter day. We were expected to be around the whole time. One evening we repaired to the Red Lion, the pub next to the police station, together with a number of other CID officers. We were all having a relaxing drink, when some members of the group started criticising one of John's friends, a detective inspector.

John wasn't having that. 'If you go on talking like that about him,' he said, 'I'm going to have to leave the bar.'

When they persisted with their carping remarks, he did just that. He put his glass down on the bar and walked out. He could have taken a more conciliatory line – but that's how he was, and I was much impressed. Ever since, I have thought that one friend of such a calibre is a match for fifty enemies.

Working at Hounslow did nothing for my love-life. I was commuting between there and Trenchard House – fifty minutes each way on the tube – and Cynthia was sharing a flat with some other girls in Abbey Road (of Beatles fame) in North London. In those days there was no question of living together before we were married. I couldn't even take her up to my room in Trenchard, because Sergeant Perryman, in charge there, was an absolute stickler for the rules: if any woman came into the section house, she got not an inch further than the visitors' room. If you were caught with a woman in your bedroom, you were in real trouble. Our scattered lives put us under quite some strain, but our relationship survived, and whenever we could, we went north to stay with Cynthia's parents.

In 1966 the Government published a White Paper entitled 'Police Manpower, Equipment and Efficiency'. The burden of it was that the police service would never get enough recruits, given the challenges of the job and the low salaries paid. The Government therefore proposed to provide new equipment and the latest technology: cars for patrolling in, and personal radios. The theory was that each officer would have a panda car, which he could drive out around his beat, but that he would frequently stop, get out and walk around.

The police reaction was that we would become a fire-brigade, re-active service, as opposed to an actively patrolling and preventative service, that we would lose contact with the public, and that our skills would wither. The service's arguments went unheeded: this was the era in which every problem could be solved by what Harold Wilson, the Prime Minister, called 'the white heat of technology' – so the reforms went ahead; The nature of beat work *was* changed, and we *did* lose our skills. All too often constables no longer took decisions themselves, but evaded the responsibility by calling up their senior officers to ask whether or not they should make an arrest.

This was a radical departure from precedent, and, in the eyes of many officers, a lamentable abandonment of one of the police's great strengths. This had been pin-pointed by the Royal Commission of 1960, which recognised the importance of the British constable, and discussed his unique nature as a subordinate: a junior officer who had powers directly granted by Act of Parliament, with the authority to make arrests on his own initiative. He could not be ordered to arrest somebody by any superior officer, because he was personally accountable for the way he interpreted the law, and himself had to justify what he had done. The effect of the 1966 White Paper was to undermine the old idea that the constable on the beat was the heart of the service.

*

The most stirring event of my time at Hounslow was the escape of George Blake, the convicted spy, from Wormwood Scrubs. A former MI6 officer, Blake had spent nine years working for the Russians as a double agent, and had betrayed numerous colleagues. At his trial in 1961 he had been sentenced to forty-two years' imprisonment – the longest jail sentence in British history – said to have been based on the number of people whose deaths his treachery had caused. But on 22 October 1966, with the help of a young Irish inmate, Sean Bourke, and the Campaign for Nuclear Disarmament activist Michael Randle, he went out over the Scrubs' wall and disappeared. His accomplices, who collected him in a van, left a pot of pink chrysanthemums at the foot of the wall in Artillery Road, possibly as a marker, or as a derisive gesture, or as a memorial to his time inside.

At the end of October I was seconded from Hounslow to Shepherd's Bush, to work on the Blake inquiry under the Head of F Division, CID, Detective Chief Superintendent Bill Marchant, an experienced, tough and straight-talking officer, powerfully built and tending to corpulence, who would let off volleys of expletives whenever he became irritated. His worst *bêtes noires* were bureaucrats, who, in his view, were infesting the world, especially the Home Office and other Government departments. Like many of his colleagues, Bill chain-smoked and had an immense capacity for drink, without it affecting his behaviour.

With us were a number of Special Branch officers under the command of Detective Chief Inspector Harry Nichols. A mixed squad of that kind was most unusual: ours was at first eighteen or twenty strong, and we were based in a special incident room that had been set up in Shepherd's Bush police station after the murder of my friend Sergeant Chris Head and two other officers, who were gunned down in front of children playing in the street when they pulled over a van after an armed robbery. (At one stage the triple shooting was thought to be linked in some way with plans for Blake's escape, but this theory was later dropped.)

The hunt for George Blake was incredibly high profile: newspapers and television bulletins were constantly full of it. For several weeks none of us knew that he had been quickly spirited away through the Iron Curtain, and my job – believe it or not – was to trace the knitting needles used to stiffen the rungs of the home-made rope-ladder, which had been thrown over the wall for him to climb. I was given that specific task – and I learnt more about knitting needles than I ever want to know again. There were ten pairs of No. 12 needles, and I spent weeks trying to establish where they might have been bought. I went to the factory that produced them, and all the outlets through which they were sold – but it was an impossible task, and I don't think my efforts contributed much to our stock of knowledge.

Thereafter I was involved in more general inquiries connected with Blake. We got permission from the Governor of Wormwood Scrubs to bug the prison, because we thought that another of the inmates had been involved in the escape; one morning I went along to pick up a man from MI5, and smuggled him in to drill the cell walls and install our primitive listening device. It came as quite a surprise to find that he worked only part time for MI5, and had some other quite different occupation. The hidden microphone was not much help; but it did allow us to discover that when Blake left the prison, he had gone first to a safe house only a quarter of a mile away and stayed there for a couple of days before moving on. We went into that building in search of forensic evidence, and our discoveries there led us to suspect that he had made his way to Egypt, where he had worked during the Second World War, although later it seemed more likely that he had fled straight to East Berlin, where he surfaced again on 17 December.

The escape was seen as a major propaganda coup for the Communist camp, and led to the instigation of an inquiry under Lord Louis Mountbatten. I became involved in preparing the secret report on the affair, which included some highly disparaging remarks about the lack of security in the Scrubs, and made far-reaching recommendations for change. Altogether I spent nine months working on the case. Today, as I write in 2005, Blake is eighty-three and still living on his KGB pension in Moscow. In 2001 he had the effrontery to demand the return of £90,000 that the British Government had confiscated when the publisher Jonathan Cape brought out his memoirs in 1990.

Altogether, that was a fascinating assignment, difficult and frustrating though it was; and it was during my time on the Blake inquiry that I came across a man called Peter Imbert. He was then a Special Branch sergeant (first class), working from the Old Scotland Yard. The first time I met him, I thought, What a charming and pleasant man this is. My opinion of him has never changed. Now Lord Imbert, he went on to become Chief Constable of the Thames Valley Police, and Commissioner of the Met.

Back in Hounslow, I had a short spell of five weeks or so protecting the jury during the trial of the Richardson brothers at the Old Bailey. Because of the power and nature of the gang – the brothers were vicious characters involved in protection rackets, who tortured people and electrocuted them in the bath – there were worries that members of the jury would be tampered with. My particular job was to look after one of them – a schoolteacher who lived in Harrow – and a tedious task it proved. Four detectives, working in pairs, covered every two jurymen, and each pair was on duty for twelve hours at a time. We followed our charges wherever they went, including to court, either by car or on foot, and although we were not supposed to talk to them, we did in fact did get to know them. At night we slept in our cars outside their addresses. We ate when we could – pre-cooked meals in the station, sandwiches in our vehicles. I am glad to say that as a result of the trial the Richardsons were put inside.

While at Hounslow I was lucky enough to get another commendation, this time after a lengthy case that involved a series of burglaries carried out by one man over a wide area, from Brentford right through to Hounslow and Staines.

It was about nine o'clock one evening, and I'd just left the pub, on my way back to the police station with a colleague, when I happened to notice this fellow acting in what seemed to me to be a suspicious way: I saw him get out of his car and look around, as though casing the area. After a minute or two he realised we were watching him – and the fact that he picked us up so quickly heightened my suspicion. Prompted by a gut feeling, we stopped and searched him, and found he was carrying one or two things that could have been used for breaking into houses – a screwdriver, for instance – but nothing conclusive. In any case, we took him to the station, searched his car, found out where he lived, and went there. This led us to another address, at which he had a garage full of stolen property. Although quite a well-dressed fellow, he already had a lot of convictions for burglary, and also one or two for rape.

At that time my friend Terry Babbage had been having a very good run on a Q-car – a high-powered vehicle with a bell under the bonnet. The crew wore plain clothes, and were free to patrol wherever they liked, all over the division, a very large area that stretched from the western edge of Hammersmith out to Heathrow Airport, south as far as Richmond and Brentford, and in the north to the fringes of West Drayton. Their main objective was to make arrests.

For a month I went on the Q-car. The team comprised a driver, an aide to CID, Bob Cook, and myself as the detective constable in charge, sitting in the back. We moved around in an unmarked Rover or Jaguar, and frequently worked ten- or twelve-hour days. Everything went so well that we set a new Q-car record, with 110 arrests in a month. Not only were we responding to emergency calls: whenever some friend of mine – a CID officer in another station – had a suspect, he would pass the details to me, and we would follow up.

The detective chief superintendent of the division was then Ginger Hensly, a rumbustious personality who had spent much time on the Flying Squad and enjoyed a close relationship with a show-business agent who managed several leading pop stars. Whenever the CID held a dinner or dance at the Red Lion, Hounslow, Ginger used to ensure that one or other of his celebrity contacts turned up. One year it was Tom Jones, who came straight on after his show at the Palladium, and another it was Engelbert Humperdinck, Roy Castle and Tommy Cooper. All had a galvanic effect on proceedings.

By then I knew Ginger quite well, because earlier, when I'd been at Hounslow for only about four months, he came into the office one morning and said to me, 'Lad, have you ever been to a post-mortem?'

'One or two, sir,' I told him.

'But have you been to a *smelly* post-mortem?'

'No, sir.'

'Right, then. You're coming with me.'

Away we went to the mortuary at Kingston Hospital. Three weeks earlier, a young man had been chased along the tow-path by a gang of youths and in a panic had jumped into the Thames, thinking he would be able to escape by swimming across. When his body eventually came to the surface in a lock, inquiries revealed that on his last night he had drunk three or four pints of Guinness, and so had never had a chance of reaching the far bank.

Together with Detective Sergeant (First Class) Fuller, an intelligent and capable fellow, I was dragged to the mortuary in Kingston to witness the post-mortem examination. There on a slab lay this ghastly, bloated body, green and grey and black. It was in a truly appalling state, the face so puffed up that I could not even recognise it as that of a young man. Not only did the corpse look repulsive: it was also stinking beyond all description. When the pathologist stuck a knife into the distended belly, foul gas and liquid erupted into the air, and the stench redoubled. I held my breath and shut my mouth as tight as I could – for we had no masks or overalls or any other form of protection: we were supposed to be tough young detectives, immune to such horrors.

'All right, lad,' said Ginger jovially. 'What do you think of that? I *enjoy* these post-mortems! I enjoy every minute of them.'

I was sure he must be lying, but I felt so sick that I could hardly speak, and I didn't have the guts to tell him, 'If you enjoy this, God help you!'

Whatever Ginger's true feelings, the pathologist had to dismember the body, and I was obliged to stand there beside it, holding out glass vessels to receive blood samples and various unspeakable parts, for my specific role was to take the exhibits to a laboratory in the middle of London. It was a horrifying task. When it was over, I had one quick Scotch to take the taste out of my mouth, and smoked a cigar to clear the smell out of my nose and throat – a routine I have followed ever since after particularly unpleasant post-mortems.

That evening a posse of us went in search of the people who, we were fairly sure, had caused the young man's death. We arrested them in Richmond and dumped them in the cells, which, being pretty cold and unpleasant, generally encouraged prisoners to talk. Having worked all night, early next day I walked down an avenue of trees between Richmond rugby football ground and Twickenham Bridge, along with a certain detective sergeant. It was a glorious spring morning, with the sun shining through the blossom on the trees. I turned to my companion and said, 'Isn't this lovely? Doesn't it make you feel better, after everything we've been through?'

He glowered at me as though I'd shot him. 'What's the matter with you?' he growled. 'Are you queer or something?'

Because our prisoners admitted the offences when their case came to court the following day, we got convictions, not for manslaughter, but for affray.

Soon after that I went on a three-month course at the Detective Training School in Walton Street, in Chelsea. There, in one of the best such schools that exist anywhere in the world, we were taken through all aspects of detective work, including forensic science and inter-rogation techniques. The instructors were first-rate, and some lectures were given by outside specialists, all leading practitioners in their various fields, among them scientists and judges. The course was superbly run, and in a different league from the fossilised instruction I had endured at Hendon. Proceedings ended with three exams, which, in defiance of my normal trend, I passed easily.

After another short spell at Hounslow, I was told to move to our satellite station at Feltham – then known in the force as 'Filthy Feltham' because of the number of sexual offences that took place in the area. My sole colleague there was a detective sergeant, and as he was fre-quently off elsewhere on other duty, I often had to run the station on my own.

The CID office was in a small, prefabricated building, and one afternoon, as I sat there after lunch, I slipped off to sleep. By the grace of God I had an instruction book, which I was studying for the detective sergeant's exam, open on my knees, when in came Detective Chief Superintendent Bailey, the formidable individual in charge of the CID in West London. He thought he'd caught me sleeping – which he had, though I never admitted it – and he gave me the time of my life. I kept up the pretence that I'd been reading the book, and had just closed my eyes to concentrate; and although I'm sure he saw through it, he did realise that I was overworked, and took no action.

Filthy Feltham was a fairly tough place in those days, with some hard estates. Among the resident thugs was a well-known toughie called Gilleband. a big, red-headed fellow who was a perfectly nice citizen until he got drink into him, whereupon he became ultra-protective of his family, and of his own reputation as a hard man. One Friday night he went out and committed a GBH (an assault occasioning grievous bodily harm), almost killing a man, who ended up in hospital. When I came in to work on Saturday morning, I thought: Clearly, this guy's got to be arrested, but we have no resources – so how do we do it?

That evening I went down to the pub that I knew he frequented, and told the people there, 'Look. I want to see this individual, because he's committed a serious offence.' At first they just laughed at me and told me where I could go, but I persisted. 'All right,' I said, 'if he doesn't come and see me within the next day or two, I'm going to pester him. I'm going to ensure that his life's made hell.' Some of the regulars who drank in there used to buy and sell stolen property, and the last thing they wanted was a detective nosing around; so I told the publican I would keep coming into the bar every night of the week with colleagues until the villain was found.

Lo and behold, on Sunday morning – the very next day – Gilleband came into the police station and gave himself up. His surrender enhanced my reputation no end – not just among the hardies of Feltham, but also among my colleagues at the station. I'm sure if we'd gone down into his house and tried to pull him out, there would have been a major disturbance.

During my time at Hounslow I took the sergeant's exam. Because two or three of us wanted to go in for it, and none of us had a good pass rate in exams, Detective Inspector Jimmy Sewell got us together and said, 'You guys are not stupid. It's about time you passed this exam.' He gave us regular classes, and we really got down to studying law, procedures, regulations, courses of action in certain circumstances, the role of a sergeant, and so on. Once again, it was a question of learning the instruction book almost by heart, but Jimmy was such a good teacher, and drove us so hard, that I passed easily and came in the top fifty.

I was now eligible to go in for the accelerated promotion scheme. I went to a selection board at the Met, and, having got through that, visited Churchill College, Cambridge, for a three-day assessment, which included intelligence and numeracy tests, and interviews with senior police officers and civilian experts. I did not pass; but – unusually – I was invited to come back the following year, without going through another selection process – which I did, from Shepherd's Bush, as a detective sergeant.

At my second attempt I felt I was doing quite well until the final interview, which was with the Chief Constable of Hertfordshire, a Mr Clissett, who obviously disliked Metropolitan Police detectives. After being very aggressive and unpleasant, he ended by saying, 'The trouble with you people is that you take crime too seriously. You should be paying far more attention to motor-vehicle crime, accidents, fatalities and so on.' We never really hit it off, and once again I failed, the reason given being that I was 'too practically orientated'.

SEVEN

Flying Squad

For some time my ambition had been to join the Flying Squad – the mobile *corps d'élite*, originally known as the Ghost Squad, which had been created way back in 1919. To become a member, you had to prove that you were an exceptional thief-taker, and be recommended by someone in authority; then your name went on a list, and you had to wait. Luckily for me, my record, and a recommendation from Ginger Hensly, gained me entry.

The squad was then based in offices on the fourth floor of New Scotland Yard, the modern, glass-and-concrete building between Green Park and Victoria Street. It amounted to about 100 men, divided into teams of ten or eleven, each with a detective inspector in charge. Its operations were mostly informant-led: the teams depended on receiving tip-offs from people known as 'snouts', and each team generally had one member who was particularly good at cultivating relations with the informers. These people were paid small amounts of cash, but if their warnings led to the recovery of stolen property, or the prevention of a bank raid, the beneficiaries were usually more generous.

In the Flying Squad's main office there was a whole bank of telephone cubicles, fitted with head-shields to give conversations a degree of privacy – but members of the squad were supposed never to be in the building. Rather, their role was to be out on the streets, and men did indeed disappear on mysterious errands for two or three days at a time. Nobody ever told anyone else what he was doing. Somebody going out might murmur, 'I'm just off to see the other man,' and colleagues would nod wisely, pretending they knew who he meant, even though they hadn't a clue.

Everybody affected a certain style, smoking cigars, making cryptic remarks out of the corners of their mouths, and using rhyming slang. Members referred to the Flying Squad itself as 'the Sweeney'; 'the slaughter' was the place to which villains took a lorry-load of loot before slaughtering it – i.e., dividing it up into van-loads; 'the plot' was any scene of action: you would be 'on the plot' while watching a bank and waiting for the bad guys to arrive. Anyone out on a job described it, rather grandly, as being 'in the underworld'. Our head-quarters building was known as 'Coco' (short for the Commissioner's office) or the 'Blabber of Lard' – for 'Yard' – and the place outside where the Commissioner's car pulled up was 'the Flight Deck'.

My contemporary John Bunn never forgot how impressed he was, on his first day, when he was met by two detective sergeants walking along a corridor with a bit of a swagger and wearing identical blue Crombie overcoats, slightly off the shoulder, which were the Squad's unofficial uniform. Yet, in spite of their affectations, the senior members were hard men, mentally and physically. Like the instructors at Peel House and Hendon, several of them had fought in the war, and had seen colleagues shot or blown up: they showed us young aspirants the ropes, and although they hadn't got much time for anyone who made mistakes, we tended to look on them with awe.

I joined a team called the Fighting Six, so called because after a few drinks its members tended to do battle with each other, rather than with the opposition. We hurtled around London, either in speedy black Jaguars, or in taxi cabs, which were supposed to be covert. The taxis were ordinary cabs, fitted with meters, and it was well known that during an operation our squad driver would cruise round the block and pick up a few civilian fares while waiting to collect us again. Then he'd come back and buy us a drink. We also had observation vans, equipped with periscopes in the roof, with which we could keep watch on a target; but at that date the Squad had no real surveillance capacity of its own: we had no special equipment or training, so we used to back up the surveillance teams of the Criminal Intelligence branch and make any arrests that were necessary.

In a typical operation, an informant might be in touch and say that there was going to be a warehouse break-in on Saturday evening. We would set up observation points, with four or five cars strategically positioned, and then, when the villains arrived, a dozen or more detectives would swoop on them. Sometimes the predicted raid failed to come off, and we would spend days on end waiting: it wasn't very pleasant to be crammed into the back of a Transit van with six or eight other detectives for hours at a time.

I was on the squad for only nine months, and, being a mere detective constable, I was low down the pecking order, and generated no more than five or six jobs of my own. All the same, I had an exciting time, with plenty of freedom and loads of action. In those days, to be frank, the Flying Squad ruled by fear: if they put out word that they wanted to see someone, even the most hardened criminals would make an appointment and go into a police station.

On the domestic front, it would have made sense for me to move out of Trenchard House and find digs somewhere near the new job, but Cynthia was still living in Abbey Road. At one stage, before we were married, she went up to Lancashire to work as a fully trained staff nurse in Casualty at Blackpool General Hospital, which was near her home; and when she came across the Chief Constable of Lancashire, Mr Palfrey, he kindly offered me the chance of transferring to his force; but I preferred to keep working in London.

Eventually, in April 1966, Cynthia and I were married in the parish church at Stalmine. Numerous mates of mine came storming up from London, among them Johnny Batten, Brian Harwood and Tony Coppellotti (with his wife Kiki), and they were reinforced by dozens of old schoolfriends. The night before the wedding, we went into Blackpool and had a riotous stag party, which my father much enjoyed, and the great day itself was gloriously fine. Ours was a traditional white wedding, with bridesmaids, and for the reception, some 140 people repaired to a fine old country house-cum-restaurant on the bank of the river. Afterwards, we flew off for a honeymoon in Tangier.

Back at work, Cynthia got a job as a nurse at Kingston Hospital, and we bought a maisonette in Hampton, which made a convenient base for both of us, especially as my parents were living just down the road in Kingston. It now seems extraordinary that we could have survived on the little money we were earning, but at the time we thought nothing of it. Also, the police started paying overtime, and I did get a mileage allowance for running around in my own car as a detective. I had long since driven my old car into the ground – the cylinders lost compression – so I got a little Ford Anglia, with a large HP debt.

After nine months I was promoted off the Sweeney as a detective sergeant, and went to Fulham police station, on F Division, which covered Hammersmith and Shepherd's Bush, besides Fulham itself, and was run by a detective chief superintendent. I enjoyed my time there: Fulham was a nice patch, more like a village than it is now, and I worked under Raymond O'Connor, a precise detective inspector, who had come from the Fraud Squad and had also taught as an instructor at training schools. However, after only five months I was on the move yet again, because a certain detective sergeant in Shepherd's Bush was considered to have been less than honest in some of his dealings: he was moved away from the area, and I took his place.

I already knew Shepherd's Bush well, because I had spent a good deal of time there working on the Blake inquiry. It was quite different from Fulham – a seedy area, with few premises that could be called classy. Our office was a hard-working one, and we were extremely busy, with a lot of assaults that needed our attention. Besides serving the normal civilian community, we covered Wormwood Scrubs prison, and we spent a good deal of time there, for whenever trouble occurred in the prison, the authorities would ask us to go in and sort things out. Naturally, the inmates hated the police, and whenever we visited, we made sure we kept under the rat-rails – the metalwork balconies running round each floor outside the cells – because if any prisoner got a chance, he would empty his slop bucket on us. I once went in with a colleague to interview a man who had beaten up a fellow inmate very badly, and when a prison officer brought him into the room, he just wouldn't speak. All he did was spit in my face. I kept him sitting there for three hours, asking him questions, and in all that time, although he refused to utter a word, he didn't spit again.

In the station there were one or two larger-than-life characters: one detective sergeant had been there practically since the Ice Age. I was once again placed on the Q-car, Foxtrot One-One, which was famous for the unfortunate fact that its three occupants had been shot when they got out to accost a party of criminals outside Wormwood Scrubs. After a successful tour on that, I moved on to take charge of Tango

One-One, the area Q-car, which was run as a personal vehicle by the commander in charge of West London CID. We covered a huge area, from the West End out to Hounslow; we could go where we liked to answer calls and follow up cases that other stations gave us. Again we broke the Q-car record, with a total of almost 140 crime arrests in the course of only three months.

In the high-speed chases of those days, we never pulled back. At about eleven o'clock one morning in Kensington High Street, I was having a cup of coffee with the detective constable, when our driver rushed in to say there had been an armed raid on a bank. We jumped into the car, and we were away. The villains were in a black Humber Super Snipe, which went like a mad thing, on and off the pavements at 80 m.p.h. Out of the window flew a shotgun, with which the robbers didn't want to be associated. Luckily a uniformed car joined the chase, and *oomph!* – the Humber smacked into that, bringing it to a halt. Three men ran off, and we caught one of them.

Violence could erupt at any moment. On another occasion, called to an affray just south of Hammersmith Palais, we found a large-scale disturbance, as rival groups attacked each other with knives, broken glasses and staves. When we arrived at speed, we had to get tucked in straight away, before the uniformed branch appeared, because the one PC already involved was getting a hiding, and there was a person on the ground who probably would have been killed if we hadn't acted instantly. The three of us burst out of the car shouting 'Police!' and charged into the mob. The immediate result was that I was thrown through a plate-glass window, cutting one hand quite badly, but I came out, pouring blood, and rejoined the fight – an act for which I later received a commendation.

One of the cases I tackled involved a few curious manoeuvres. A man called Murphy had attacked someone in the street, stolen a considerable amount of money from him, and run away to southern Ireland. Armed with an extradition warrant – essential in those days – I went in pursuit, taking a plane to Cork, where I linked up with a detective constable of the Garda Siochana. The Garda had already arrested Murphy, at our request, but when we appeared in court, the judge pointed out that there was a small technical error in the warrant. 'I don't think it's quite right,' he told me, in his delicious accent. 'I'm afraid, Sergeant, you'll have to go home. And, Mr Murphy, we'll release you. You can go away now. And for sure the detective sergeant from Hammersmith won't mind coming back again.'

I knew that my boss in London was not going to be too impressed if I returned from Ireland without the prisoner. So, as I walked out of court, I said to Murphy, 'Listen, I'm on my way back to England. The best thing for you to do is come back with me, even without the warrant, and give yourself up. You'd better meet me at the airport. Otherwise, I'll be back over, and I will trace you, come what may. The plane leaves at 3 p.m. tomorrow. Be there, and I'll put a good word in for you in court.'

My friend from the Garda couldn't believe it. 'You'll not see him again – never,' he insisted. Yet the next day there he was. I had no power to arrest Murphy, but he came like a lamb, and when I gave evidence of his behaviour to the judge at the Old Bailey, he got two years, instead of the four he would have been given otherwise. Only after the event did I realise that, technically, I had breached the law in Ireland, by influencing the accused and persuading him to return. So I was wary of going over the water again.

Back in Shepherd's Bush, for several nights I was out in the Q-car with Detective Inspector Jock Colligan, an extremely tough and effective operator who had the nickname 'Little Wicked', and had spent some eight years on the Flying Squad. We had been asked to keep observation on a pub on the outskirts of Wormwood Scrubs, because an informant had warned that a criminal gang was coming to steal a lorry-load of goods. Beside the pub was a café, with a car park at the back.

After several nights spent watching, with no action, the raid suddenly came off. As three or four men ran to attack the driver of the lorry, we piled into the car park to arrest them. In the mêlée, one of our officers accidentally hit a colleague with his truncheon – and ever since, I have wondered what might have happened if we had all been armed: the man who was struck might easily have assumed that his assailant was one of the robbers, wielding a pick-axe handle (a favourite weapon in those days), and might have shot him dead in self-defence. Perhaps it was fortunate that the procedure for drawing firearms was still quite elaborate: first we had to get authority from the station officer for a specific mission, then guns had to be issued, and the weapons had to be loaded in the presence of the station officer, so that it took quite a while to get armed police on to the ground. When an incident was over, all firearms and unexpended rounds had to be handed back in, and if a bullet had been discharged, there had to be an inquiry.

During my time on the Q-car, I took the inspector's exam. Having had so many difficulties with earlier tests, I made up my mind, this time, to leave nothing to chance. So, between answering calls and arresting miscreants, I sat in the back of the car studying as hard as I could. The result was that I passed first time. This, however, did not mean that I was promoted immediately. I also had to go before a board, and it was several months before my promotion to detective inspector came through.

I was asked to run the F Division Crime Squad at Hammersmith, where I was in charge of a large number of young, inexperienced officers. As a detective sergeant, I had to make sure they did their paperwork, that they behaved themselves, that their morale remained high, and that they operated in a way that was effective, but did not allow their enthusiasm to run away with them.

During that period I learnt one of the most important lessons of my life: if you are leading any team, be it large or small, the most important thing is that your people should feel proud of doing their job. If you praise them, make them feel good about themselves, and give credit where credit is due, they feel they are being successful, and more success will follow, especially if a unit is starting to break records with numbers of arrests and reduction in crime. Because the police service is a bureaucratic organisation, and not very good at taking risks, it tends to fall down in the business of giving praise. It is something about which I've always had a bee in my bonnet. Praise must be given when praise is due.

Our job in the Crime Squad was to arrest as many people as we could. Our team, about eighteen strong, saw plenty of action, not least in the saga of the man who became known as 'the Beast of Shepherd's Bush'.

One night I was called to an incident in which a woman living in

Fulham had fought off a black man who tried to get into her car. I went down to take the details, and found she was an attractive blonde who drove a Mini. I didn't think the incident had any particular significance, so I put it down as an assault, rather than an attempted rape.

The next attack came on 17 August 1969, when a burly black man assaulted a twenty-one-year-old actress who drove back into London late, after appearing in a play at a theatre outside London. She too was in a Mini – a white one – and she had just parked outside her home in Sheen when a coloured man forced his way into the car, attacked her violently, punched her in the face and body, ripped off her pants, tied her hands with them, gagged her by shoving a road map down her throat, and raped her. He then took £10 from her handbag and decamped.

The victim reported the incident to the police, but in spite of extensive inquiries, we were unable to trace the attacker. In those days we were not very skilled at linking scattered crimes together. There was a method index at Scotland Yard, but we didn't have DNA or other modern aids. Besides, it turned out that the rapist operated across a very wide area – and the result was that we were slow to realise that the same man was responsible for numerous violent crimes.

A month later we had a visit from a woman who lived in Shepherd's Bush, and claimed to have been raped, in her own car – also a Mini. I had her interviewed by a woman police officer, and she told a lurid story: a black man had got into her car, forced her onto the back seat, spat on her private parts and raped her. Apart from other details, she said her attacker was incredibly strong.

Inquiries then revealed that, only about fifteen minutes before the ordeal she described, another young woman had been attacked by the same man outside her house in Gordon Road, Chiswick. She had just driven home and was parking her car when he came up, asked her the time and demanded sex. When she screamed, he thrust his hand over her face and held her down in the driving seat. Luckily, as she tried to fight him off and screamed again, her dog barked from inside the house, whereupon her assailant ran away. When she reported the incident at Chiswick police station, she remembered that a white Ford, driven by a coloured man, and with the licence plate ending in the letters AR, had overtaken her just before she stopped.

A pattern was emerging: the victims were young women (generally blondes), their cars were small (usually Minis), and, if the rapist was foiled in his first attempt on a particular night, he would try again within a few minutes. The hunt went into top gear. Our team was led by Detective Sergeant (First Class) Peter Cornish, a tall, slim, athletic-looking man, with a quiet voice that gave little hint of his acumen and authority (before joining the police, he had done national service in the RAF, and he finished his thirty-two-year career by becoming Commandant of the Detective Training School at Hendon). Armed with the information about the white car, he put out a call for the night-duty CID and uniformed officers to be on the lookout for a vehicle answering to the girl's description.

The following night, a white Ford Prefect with the registration number 3650 AR was spotted, parked in Goldhawk Road. Observation was kept on it till next day, when a powerfully built black man walked up to the vehicle. As he was about to get in, a colleague and I approached him – but when I took him by the arm, and found that my fingers wouldn't go halfway round his bicep, I quickly decided to say nothing about rapes. I merely remarked that he seemed to have a problem with his road-fund licence, which did not match his car, and that we would like to ask him a few questions. He had the arrogance to think we knew nothing about him, and he came to the station quietly enough.

He was David Ronald Lashley, a thirty-year-old electrician, amateur boxer and weight-lifter who had come over from Barbados five years earlier and married a white woman in London. He was powerfully built, all right, but not as tall as some of the women had claimed. Their reports suggested that he was as much as 6 foot 3, but in fact he was 5 foot 9: his breadth had made him look even larger than he was – as did the fact that he loomed over his victims when he leant into their car windows.

During interrogation he denied all knowledge of the attacks, claim-ing that he had been indoors during the times at which they had occurred; but when we searched his house, we found pornographic literature, indecent photographs and an imitation penis. Although he agreed that all these were his, he still proclaimed his innocence.

That afternoon an identification parade was set up, but he refused to take part – as he was entitled to do – and instead said that he wanted to be confronted by the complainants individually. We therefore arranged for each girl to be sitting on a chair, and for Lashley to approach her from the right, so that her first view of him would be similar to the one she had had from her driving seat. Both girls immediately identified him as their assailant. He then made the first of two statements under caution, and admitted both attacks.

Back in the police station after his first court appearance, Peter Cornish noticed blood on Lashley's wrist, and found he had gouged himself with the broken-off end of a spoon, whose handle he had snapped in half. When asked why he had damaged himself, he replied that he had been trying 'to make it easier' for the police. He then made a second statement, under caution, and admitted other offences, including one not known to the investigating officer at the time.

He was charged with five rapes, four thefts, two indecent assaults, and one assault occasioning actual bodily harm, and robbery. At his trial in April 1970 at the Central Criminal Court, he retracted his confession, claiming that he had been beaten up by the police, which was a total fabrication. He was convicted of three rapes, two indecent assaults and one robbery (the other offences were not proceeded with, but were ordered to remain on the file). He was sentenced to twelve years' imprisonment, but he was released after serving half his sentence, gaining himself early parole by going to the assistance of a prison officer who was being attacked by another inmate.

However, within a few months of coming out in March 1976 he resumed his predatory behaviour, raping and nearly killing a twenty-three-year-old woman, and then in February 1977 murdering Rosemary Jane Shepherd, an Australian, known as Janie, whom he strangled in her Mini, and whose body (we later discovered) he buried in Hertfordshire. This time, he was sentenced to eighteen years' imprisonment for the rape, and then to life imprisonment for the murder. It was hardly surprising that newspapers referred to him as the Beast of Shepherd's Bush. He was an exceptionally vicious and evil man, with an intense hatred of a number of people, in particular the investigating officers, whom he threatened with extreme violence in the event of his being released. Fortunately he is behind bars to this day.

Shepherd's Bush was an interesting ground in many ways. As a detective sergeant, I had to cover the weekend on my own, with responsibility for three areas: Shepherd's Bush itself, Hammersmith and Fulham. If I came on duty on Sunday morning, I *knew* that I would have to go and see four or five men who had been assaulted and had landed up in hospital. It happened every Saturday night, and inevitably in that area most of the casualties were Irish. When I asked them if they wanted to take any action against their aggressors, the answer was always the same.

'Bejaysus, no,' they would say. 'Get away witcha. We just had a bit of fun there.'

'But look,' I'd tell them. 'You've broken an arm, your ribs are cracked, your nose is all sideways . . .'

'Ah – it was just one of those things . . .'

One event that I regretted was the closure of Rowton House, a hostel run by the local council, in which homeless people had been sleeping. I had often gone there to make sure that none of the inmates were wanted by the law, and to shut it down seemed a thoroughly bad move, because the people who had been using it inevitably spilled back on to the streets.

During this period there had been various developments on our domestic front. Our first child, a boy, Nicholas, arrived, in dramatic fashion, in 1968, while I was at Hounslow. He managed the difficult feat of being three weeks overdue and, simultaneously, seriously premature. At about four o'clock one afternoon I suddenly got a call to say that Cynthia had been taken to hospital in Chiswick; my detective sergeant insisted on driving me straight there, and when I arrived I found that the baby had already been delivered by emergency caesarian. Because there had been some problem with the supply of nutrients to the foetus, he weighed only 4 lbs, and his head was so tiny that the palm of my hand would cover it. Nicholas spent his first few days in an incubator, and had it not been for the devoted skill of the hospital staff, he might not have survived (today he is a detective chief inspector).

In that kind of personal crisis the police service is at its absolute best: everyone I knew offered help and support, and I realised – not for the first time, but more powerfully at that moment – that especially in the CID the *esprit de corps* is tremendous.

Our second son, Alistair, also arrived rather suddenly, in 1970, when I was over in Ireland attempting to arrest our friend Murphy. He too was born by caesarian in Chiswick, but he had grown normally in the womb, and by the time I reached the hospital, he was flourishing.

I stayed at Shepherd's Bush for two and a half years. Not only was I on the Q-car: I ran the crime squad at Hammersmith for a period. One of the characters from that period was Tony McStravick, a highly intelligent detective, prematurely balding (but never seeming to look any older), extremely active and altogether most effective. We had a detective chief superintendent called Whitmarsh-Knight, an ex-Indian Army officer, with old-fashioned good manners, and one of the most gentlemanly figures you could come across – an unusual type among senior detectives, who were mostly hard-hitting and knew exactly what they wanted. We all became fond of Whitmarsh-Knight, but he had one serious drawback: every now and then he felt lonely and would repair to a pub, where he expected us to join him in discussing the problems of life. Because he had an ulcer, he drank nothing except brandy and milk, but he downed it in such quantities that it probably did him more harm than good.

Whether or not he had any home life, I never knew; but in those days we all just lived the job, and didn't see much of our homes. We worked ridiculous hours, and then went drinking: hard drinking was still part of the culture. On Fridays we would congregate in the detective inspector's office or the CID office and down a couple of bottles of Scotch before going on to a pub. The regime may not have done much for our health – especially as most people smoked heavily – but it did wonders in building camaraderie. Usually during the week we had seen some pretty horrible sights, and had been faced with unpleasant situations, and the Friday-evening sessions gave us a chance to wind down. The fact that we got together, talked as a group and took the mickey out of each other all helped to forge bonds, unburden ourselves and dissipate tension.

Also, in a strange way, some senior officers deliberately encouraged the drinking to see whether their subordinates could control themselves. In those pre-breathalyser days, people often drove home in no fit state to be at the wheel: the only legal test of sobriety was to see if a man could walk along a straight line – and frequent practice made most of my colleagues remarkably good at that. Rules were then very loose, and yet, no matter how boisterous the party had become, or how far gone people might be, anybody who did not turn up on time for work in the morning was immediately in trouble. (When breath-testing came in, drinking went out of the window, because anyone caught driving with excess alcohol in his blood automatically lost his job.)

Disreputable as it now sounds, that way of life had its advantages, not least because visits to pubs gave detectives numerous opportunities of finding out what was going on. In any community, everyone knew who we were, not least because we habitually went to work wearing suits and ties, which made us stand out in a crowd at a bar, and our evening sessions gave us the chance to make contact with members of the public. Frequently a publican or one of his customers would slide up to one of us with information, and there wasn't much happening on our patch that we did not hear about.

Aggravation was surprisingly rare: I remember only one incident, at a pub on the White City estate in Shepherd's Bush, where we had made some arrests a week or two earlier. We had hardly ordered our drinks before a couple of punters started an argument, threw beer over myself and a colleague and pitched their glasses through a mirror at the back of the bar. A few punches were exchanged. Then the publican confronted them and ordered them out; after they'd gone, we told him we would deal with the problem in the morning – and we did. We went round and arrested the miscreants, who were a little surprised, considering that the altercation had only taken place at 11 p.m. In court they pleaded guilty, and they received a £50 fine apiece.

I never let people get away with any misdemeanour – and that has always been a guiding principle of my career. If someone takes me on, I may deal with the problem on the spot, or I may tackle it later, but I never let the person escape unscathed. If someone thinks he can take advantage of an officer of the law, he soon believes he can run around the streets doing what he likes.

Relationships within the CID were, and are, finely balanced.

Although nobody wears badges, the rank structure is always present, even in the pub, and usually its maintenance is based on mutual respect. In those days the CID was a kind of exclusive club, whose members looked after each other as best they could, with a self-imposed discipline that was not exactly official, but always there. If somebody drank too much, or made a remark out of turn, he heard about it in the office the next morning.

The people who suffered most were probably our families, for married officers were rarely at home in the evenings, and all detectives were expected to be available for any job that might suddenly come up: if a murder or some other serious crime was reported a few minutes after they had got home, they had to be prepared to go out again at once.

In due course Cynthia and I moved from our maisonette into a house just round the corner, in Hampton. Our new home was white, with blue shutters, built in the 1930s; the rooms were quite small – there were only three bedrooms – and the whole place needed a lot of work.

The garden was small, but at least we could sit out in it during spring and summer, feeling that we had really arrived.

EIGHT

C 9

I was still enjoying myself at Shepherd's Bush when I got a phone call directing me to transfer to C 9, the Met's Provincial Police Crime Branch, based on the third floor of New Scotland Yard. I was slightly disappointed, because I was hoping to go back to the Flying Squad; but the detective chief superintendent in charge, Bernard Price, wanted to ginger up his branch and make it look more adventurous by drafting in some younger detectives who seemed to be going places.

I would not have joined C 9 out of choice; but in those days one didn't argue about postings, and C 9 was where I went. In spite of my doubts, I thoroughly enjoyed my time with the unit. The office was run by Detective Constable Lambert, who had won the Croix de Guerre in the Second World War, and knew everything that went on. There was a detective chief inspector called Duggie Creswell, and Bernard Price himself was a formidable officer, a tough old character, a former sergeant major, with long service on the Flying Squad and as an instructor at the Detective Training School.

It was an interesting branch, and a unique organisation, because we operated with officers not only from the Met, but also from other parts of the country, such as Hampshire and Kent, running a kind of liaison and arrest facility for the Metropolitan Police and all the different forces round about. In a way it was a fore-runner of the Regional Crime Squads. Until then I had worked entirely in London, but now I travelled widely outside the capital, learning about other forces, and seeing how good many of their officers were.

I went to C 9 as a detective sergeant (second class), and during my time there I was promoted to detective sergeant (first class) – a rank that did not exist within the outside constabularies. When I put

'DS 1' beside my name on a charge sheet, it used to raise a bit of a smile, because people thought I had invented it.

Soon after I had arrived at C 9, I was caught up in the nationwide racket that became known as the Hospital Fraud case. Cheque books were being stolen, and cheques with forged signatures cashed, all over the country. Most of the earliest thefts were from hospitals, where doctors were inclined to leave their jackets hanging in locker-rooms or offices, and by the simple expedient of donning white coats, the gang were moving around the hospitals unchallenged. Later, it emerged that some people were accepting money in exchange for colluding in the alleged theft of their own cheque books and guarantee cards.

The first credit card that doubled as a guarantee card had been introduced by Barclays in 1966. This prompted the other major banks to follow suit, initially by issuing cards that guaranteed the payment of cheques. The innovation was a huge advance for customers, who, until then, had been able to draw cash only at their own branch, unless they had some special dispensation. Unfortunately, the new system also proved a bonanza for crooks.

The maximum amount that anybody could draw at one time was £30 – but, provided the person signing a cheque could support it with a guarantee card, he or she could progress from one bank to another, cashing £30 at each one. Thus a single new cheque book could yield a haul of £900 – worth several thousand pounds in today's terms.

By the end of the 1960s the growth of cheque fraud had become exponential, and the banks were seriously alarmed. In London, the man grappling with the epidemic was Eddie Theobald, a fraud specialist at Barclays Bank. Until then, banks had been reporting frauds unsystematically to local police forces, and naturally no coherent pattern had emerged. Now, however, from cataloguing and monitoring stolen cheques at a national level, Eddie began to establish definite patterns, and deduced that the hospital racket was being operated by small teams of two or three people. Having stolen a cheque book one day, they would 'knock it out' the next, relying on the fact that the rightful owner would probably not notice or report its disappearance in less than twenty-four hours. Those who had colluded by handing over their cheque books and cards would undertake not to report the alleged theft until enough time had passed for the fraudster to misuse them.

Study of the forged signatures suggested that only a few people were involved, and that the Hospital Fraud group was operating mainly in large cities: London, Birmingham, Manchester, Dublin, Belfast, Edinburgh, Dundee and Aberdeen. Analysis of dates revealed that they seemed to move round their various haunts in the same sequence: the criminals were evidently creatures of habit, and it was this that led to their downfall.

Eddie had a hunch that someone who had stolen a cheque book would go by train, rather than fly, to his or her next destination, thereby gaining plenty of time to practise the signatures on cards just acquired. Therefore, after Dundee had been hit, he went to the railway police at King's Cross and asked them to let him know of any last-minute bookings on overnight trains to Aberdeen, made by two or three men. Sure enough, one morning the police told him that the previous evening three men had booked seats and jumped on a train straight away.

In Aberdeen the problem was being tackled by Detective Chief Inspector Ian Robbie. Eddie had already alerted him to the fact that the hospital gang were likely to visit his city again, and now he warned him that the fraudsters were probably at large on his patch. So it proved – but the call came too late to prevent them going from bank to bank cashing cheques.

Eddie had already reported the fraud to Scotland Yard, and given names of suspects deduced from analysis of handwriting; but although the Metropolitan Police were quite helpful, they declined to take up inquiries, because they had never been able to get a conviction on handwriting alone. In Aberdeen, however, Robbie was much more enthusiastic, because in Scotland it *was* possible to obtain a conviction on handwriting, and the evidence was increasing all the time. In one of the earliest cases it looked as though a customer who had reported his cheque book and card stolen had himself misused them. The bogus cheques ultimately found their way to Barclays central fraud team, who discovered that the handwriting on them closely matched that on the letter of reference that had introduced the account when it was opened. This suggested collusion, and gave Eddie two suspects – the account owner and his referee.

Undeterred by the near-miss in Aberdeen, and convinced that he was on the right scent, Eddie returned to the Yard a week later. This time he struck lucky: the man deputed to deal with him was myself.

Down at the front desk, in the foyer, I found a large young fellow, as tall as me, full of information and enthusiasm, and the two of us established an immediate rapport. At the time I knew nothing about finance, so I had to learn fast; but I was fascinated by this new challenge, and jumped at the chance to help.

By then not only Barclays, but all the five main clearing banks were involved; each of them had its own scrutinising process, run by officials known as inspectors (of whom Eddie was one), but because they were rivals, they had never talked to each other. I think I can fairly claim that we made a little bit of history by bringing together representatives of the banks round a table in Cannon Row police station. The meeting was chaired by myself and Eddie, who introduced me by saying, 'This is a detective sergeant from C 9 Branch of the Yard, who will take this on.'

Eddie then took one of his specimen letters to Aberdeen, where Robbie asked a forensic expert, Detective Inspector McPherson, to examine the writing on the letter of reference and the matching cheque. After two hours McPherson was certain that the same hand had written both, and he was prepared to stake his reputation on it in court. Eddie, as he put it, 'jumped for joy'.

Robbie then contacted me, and we began to arrest the ringleaders of the racket, handing them over to the police in Scotland, where they were remanded in custody for the time being. One of our problems lay in knowing how to charge the villains: the offences they had committed in Scotland represented only a fraction of the total fraud involved, and we needed some other means of proving identification besides handwriting. Luckily one of the trio arrested by Robbie decided to reveal all, so that when the three men received only suspended terms of imprisonment from the Scottish courts, they were handed over to Scotland Yard, where the work we had done in exposing the full range of their villainy ensured more substantial sentences.

Had one of them not confessed, a new technology, just emerging in America, might have been used to secure convictions. This was known as the ninhydrin process, which had been developed to highlight fingerprints on dollar bills. By reacting with moisture and grease from the skin, the chemical brought up fingerprints so clearly that they could be photographed. The process proved equally effective on the stolen cheques, revealing, in particular, the thumb prints, which most people leave by holding the book steady with their left hand as they sign.

The Hospital Fraud turned out to be far more widespread than anyone had realised. Some of the criminals were extremely unpleasant people, as well as sophisticated operators; besides committing repeated thefts, they had been approaching impecunious students, often at a pub in the Strand, and offering them £200 to go to their own bank, order a new cheque book, hand it over and wait two or three days before reporting it stolen. Nor were incentives always entirely financial: the young people were sometimes offered sex in hotel bedrooms, usually in Paris.

One of the racketeers, when arrested, had in his possession the key to a safe box in the Queen Victoria depository for valuables. In it we found numerous photographs of young people in compromising situations. Clearly the intention had been to use the pictures for blackmail in a few years' time, when the subjects had become respectable barristers, architects or whatever, with wives and families.

The first trio we arrested were by no means the only criminals involved in cheque fraud; but they were certainly the front-runners, and when we brought them in, they threatened us in various unpleasant ways. Rounding up more of the fraudsters involved travelling all over Europe – for instance, I went to the South of France in search of a woman called Monique Solengo.

In trying to trace this person, whoever she might be, I was enormously helped by the French national identification system, under which the police hold details of every citizen. We knew my target was somewhere in Nice, but although we had three addresses, they were all very speculative. I flew to the South of France, and when I gave her name to a detective at Police Headquarters, he immediately said, 'Oh yes – no trouble finding her.' He came straight up with her details, including fingerprints. Then he added, 'We have this information routinely – but this woman hasn't committed any offences.' Nevertheless, when challenged at her house, she admitted what she had been doing, and this enabled me to extradite her to England, where she was tried at the Old Bailey and found guilty.

The third man of the original trio had escaped our net for the time being. He had acted as a driver, transporting his accomplices from bank to bank. Then one day he rang Eddie Theobald at his office and said, 'I understand you're responsible for the arrest of my friends.' Somewhat unwisely, Eddie agreed to meet him in a pub, for a chat; but then, being nervous of confronting the man on potentially dangerous ground, he rang me. I was keen to see the fellow, as we had not been able to trace him, and I asked Eddie to change the rendezvous, to our advantage. Our man – also unwisely – agreed to meet him in the banking hall of the Barclays branch in Finsbury Park one morning: by the time scheduled for the meeting, I had two detectives circulating among the genuine customers, and our visitor had hardly sat down opposite Eddie at a desk when I myself walked in and arrested him.

The Hospital Fraud case was heard at the Old Bailey, and as a result of it, all the banks changed their procedures to make them more secure: the system known as 'frequency marking' was introduced, whereby each encashment was recorded on a page at the back of the cheque book. This was soon offset by greater sophistication on the part of criminals, but for a while there was a sharp drop in fraudulent activity involving cheque books and guarantee cards.

Another consequence was greatly increased cooperation between the police and the banks, not just over this particular kind of fraud, but in many fields: both sides kept to the discipline of their respective institutions, but met regularly to share experiences, often at the Samuel Pepys pub, down by the river in Cannon Street.

A further result was the setting up of a cheque fraud department within the Yard, designated C 1, and I continued with that type of work until I was selected for promotion as a detective inspector, having been commended on a number of occasions.

From C 9 I moved on to Marylebone Lane, which proved another fascinating assignment. Our territory, north of Oxford Street, reached all the way from Tottenham Court Road in the east to Marble Arch in the west, and up to St John's Wood in the north, where we had a satellite station, so that I suddenly found myself back on my old stamping-ground.

The CID office was highly active: there was one detective chief inspector, Terry Feeney – a tough, bright, charismatic character, dark-skinned, with long dark hair – but my particular workmate was Detective Inspector Bernard Tighe – a real character if ever there was one.

We dealt with every kind of problem, from small-scale burglaries to murders. The inhabitants ranged from the very wealthy to down-and-outs, and our workload was greatly increased by the fact that the IRA had started a bombing campaign on the mainland: what with real incidents and hoax calls, the atmosphere often became very tense. After one such attack in Oxford Street, just east of Selfridges, I was on the scene within a few minutes, and I was surprised by the wide variety of damage that the high explosive had caused: some windows and shopfronts had escaped unscathed; others, no closer, had taken a shattering blast.

Luckily the IRA had given a warning, in time for police officers to clear the area, and nobody had been hurt; but afterwards a ridiculous story emerged. When uniformed officers put a cordon across Oxford Street, a man came up and tried to insist on going through. The policeman said, 'Don't be silly. We've had a warning . . .' but the fellow persisted, saying pompously, 'There are no bombs around here. I'm a solicitor.'

'I'm sorry,' said the officer, 'but you're not going. Your life could be at stake.'

'I'm going,' the man persisted.

'In that case, the only thing I can do is arrest you.'

So he grabbed the solicitor, hustled him to a police van and climbed in with him. Just as he was about to secure his prisoner, the bomb went off. The van was rocked on its wheels, and in the ensuing chaos the solicitor ran off like a stag, never to be seen again.

A more traumatic incident took place in September 1975, when the IRA detonated a bomb in the foyer of the Hilton Hotel, near the bottom of Park Lane. A warning call was made to the *Daily Mail* at 11.55 a.m.; the newspaper immediately sent word to Scotland Yard, and three police officers were dispatched to investigate; but at 12.18, before they could evacuate the building, the device went off, killing two people and wounding more than sixty.

I had been the detective inspector on late turn in the Marylebone Lane station the night before, and I was still in the office when the bomb exploded. Together with a detective sergeant I sped down to Park Lane: we were the first detectives to reach the scene – and a horrifying one it was. The pavements outside the hotel were carpeted with shattered glass, not just from the Hilton itself, but from adjacent buildings. Inside, the entire foyer had been wrecked. One of the receptionists had been blown to pieces, and her remains were spattered on the walls and strewn across the floor. Our immediate task was to clear the area and secure the building, in case a second bomb had been planted close by, but the survivors and hotel staff were so shocked that it was difficult to make them move. We stayed until members of the Bomb Squad arrived and began their investigation, then withdrew.

That was horrific enough. Yet of all the incidents we dealt with, it is the murders that stand out most clearly. I can never forget being called to a street just north of Marylebone Lane police station, where a former public-school boy, then waiting to study at Oxford, had fallen in with a group of squatters occupying some substantial buildings on the southern edge of Regent's Park. They had met the young fellow in a pub, cultivated him and introduced him to drugs, particularly LSD. On that particular evening he had invited them into his parents' flat: they had all gone to the top floor of the four-storey building, and he, being high in every sense of the word, had thought he could fly. So at about two in the morning he had launched himself out of a window, ending up on the pavement below.

I was at home when it happened, but I drove straight in from Hampton, and by the time I reached the scene, his body had been taken to a hospital, where he was declared dead, and then to the mortuary. The post-mortem was horrific: during dissection the head simply fell to bits; and to this day I am disturbed by the thought of a life thrown away so pointlessly.

It took us four days to identify the people responsible for his demise: we knew that they had a room in the squatters' building, so at six o'clock one morning we slipped in, pulled them out and arrested them. Later we took a large number of officers to clear the place out completely. The squatters were convicted of supplying drugs, and each got between four and five years – though in my view they should have been charged with manslaughter.

Another unforgettable call-out came at a weekend, when a message reached me at lunchtime to say that a body had been found in an exclusive flat in Marylebone. The victim had been the *Evening Standard*'s restaurant and clubs critic: he had been stabbed through the chest a couple of times, and I was struck by the fact that although I reached the scene within two hours of the death, he was already starting to smell.

Later investigation revealed that he had been living with a most attractive Malaysian girl: when she found out that he had been deceiving her, she chased him with a knife. He had taken refuge in the toilet and locked himself in, whereupon she had opened and slammed the front door of the flat to make it sound as if she had gone out. A minute or two later, when he cautiously emerged, she was waiting, and stabbed him in the chest. Staggering out of the toilet, with blood pumping on to the walls from his severed aorta, he got as far as the lounge, where he collapsed on the floor, and it was there that he had been found, lying face down, with his head turned to one side, his face contorted and his eyes still open.

When I reached the scene. I didn't touch him, but waited for the forensic examiners and photographer to do their business. It was my practice to look round the room, and I found copies of letters that he had been writing – letters about his plans for the future, his hopes and fears. As a senior detective, I was used to being called to deeply unpleasant scenes, where people had died violent deaths; but there, in that tidy flat, I was hit by the realisation of how complex, transient and fragile life is. This poor fellow had been fully alive one minute, with many years ahead of him, but gone the next – a brutal reality that I found difficult to accept.

In due course the girl was traced and arrested. She claimed to have been defending herself, and pleaded guilty to manslaughter, but she went inside for seven years.

At Marylebone Lane, as elsewhere, the tough elements of our work were compensated for, to some extent, by the camaraderie within the station. At about 3 p.m. one afternoon in September, when Cynthia was coming to the end of her pregnancy with our third child, a message came through that she had been taken into hospital and had given birth to a daughter. I whizzed straight down to see her, found all well, and returned to the police station. Already the local publicans had congregated, together with Terry Feeney, the detective chief inspector, and all their officers. As I walked in through the front door, out came bottles of champagne and brandy, and everyone drank to the health of my growing family. That was how things were in those days – and it was then that I acquired the nickname 'Captain Beaujolais', from my liking for good red wine.

Another survivor from that time is the George Raft Appreciation Society, which holds annual reunion lunches to this day. As a joke, the detective chief inspector at Marylebone Lane sometimes used to put up behind his desk a picture of the New York gangster and film star George Raft (forever associated with the actor Humphrey Bogart), and anyone who worked in the police automatically became a member.

I eventually left Marylebone Lane when I was asked to go and run the Crime Squad at Paddington. In a way the assignment was similar to the one I had had as a detective sergeant at Hammersmith, although this was a bigger squad, and I was by then a detective inspector. There was an enormous variety of work to be done, not least because we were used as a fire-fighting unit in other areas, including Harrow, Marylebone and St John's Wood, and we also served as a back-up team in investigations whenever there had been a murder in the Division. As in earlier phases of my career, we were expected to chalk up large numbers of arrests on the street: it was back to the old system of being assessed from the number of people we managed to pull in. My own view was, and is, that quality also counts. Apart from the routine work, there was a chance to bring young detectives on, train them up, find out what potential they had. We saw ourselves as a bit of an elite unit.

One job given me by Terry Feeney was to investigate a travel agent in Marylebone High Street who had defrauded clients of very substantial sums and absconded to Australia. Through the Court of Appeal there he contested all the verdicts brought against him, and I had to go out in pursuit. I flew out first class on Pan American – one of the last police officers to enjoy the privilege, which was revoked soon after-wards. When I arrived in Sydney, my man had already been arrested, but my task was to present all the relevant papers and convince the Australian courts that there was a case to be answered in England. I lived in a hotel in the centre of Sydney, and made good friends with several local policemen, particularly Detective Sergeant Bob Frodgham, who later became a barrister. I was greatly taken with Australians in general, and my fondness for their easy-going ways has never diminished.

The accused, a homosexual, was in his early thirties, tall and exceedingly handsome, and he was being defended by a prominent QC, who cleverly blocked every avenue that we tried to open up. The result was that legal proceedings dragged on for over two months, but the compensation for me was that I was royally entertained by the New South Wales Police Service and had a most enjoyable time.

'What do you like?' they would ask. When I suggested sailing, they took me sailing on the winner of the Sydney-to-Hobart yacht race. When I said 'Flying', they put me up as supernumerary crew in an Ansett aircraft.

After six weeks I came back to England for a few days, to reassure Cynthia and the family that I was still around. Then I flew out again, and eventually we managed to grind the opposition down with the evidence. On the return journey I had to inform the captain of the aircraft that I was escorting a prisoner, and when we took off I had the handcuffs on my victim, because I didn't want anything to happen. The stewardesses were fascinated. One after another they came up to me and asked, 'Gosh, who's that good-looker you're travelling with?' When I told them, 'Actually, I'm taking him back for murder,' their faces dropped – but in fact he and I got on well: it was all a bit of a joke, and once we were airborne, I released him, and told the crew the truth.

NINE

Broadening the Mind

From Marylebone Lane I went on the six-month Inspector's Course at the Bramshill Staff College, in Hampshire, one of a class of twenty-six, all from different forces. The centre of the establishment is an Elizabethan mansion – one of the oldest buildings in England still in use as a place of learning – set in magnificent park-like surroundings. We lived in accommodation blocks not far from the house, and worked away at various topics, from leadership and psychology to legal studies. I played cricket for the college, but by then I had made squash my speciality: I organised the college team, and arranged for outside teams to come and take us on.

As usual, we eased the strain of concentration by downing a few drinks in the evening, and one summer's night two of us decided to have a race out to the island in the middle of the lake and back. A visiting chief inspector and I had already stripped off and were ready to go when someone told us that the lake contained enormous carp, quite large enough to bite vital equipment off human swimmers. That stopped us in our tracks – so we shook hands and went back for another drink. In retrospect, I'm sure the fish would have been no danger to us, but it was probably just as well that we called off our midnight swim, for we had already had a good many.

Among the men who ran the course was an exceptionally bright psychologist called John Brindley, and towards the end of the six months he told me I should think hard about going for one of the university scholarships that Bramshill awarded every year. At the back of my mind was a feeling that a spell at university would be an attractive proposition; yet I was already thirty-four, and for the past ten years I had been working as a hands-on, front-line detective, with the admirable but rather limited ambition of arresting as many criminals as possible. I doubted if I had the intellect or the application to get a degree.

Brindley was reassuring. 'Judging by what I've seen of you, I'm sure you'd manage it,' he said – yet when I discussed the possibility with Cynthia, I found she was strongly against it. She knew I had enjoyed every minute of my detective work, and thought I would never be happy having to buckle down to a desk in an academic atmosphere. Another consideration was the domestic upheaval that university would involve: we would have to move our three children, who were then ten, eight and five, not only to a different home, but also to different schools. That was one of the very few occasions on which my wife and I disagreed, but I felt I really wanted to see what I could do.

Having thoroughly enjoyed the Inspector's Course, I finished with the highest grade, and, urged on by Brindley, decided to apply for a scholarship. I knew that it would be several months before I heard whether or not I had been given an award, and when the course ended, I was posted to Heathrow as a detective inspector. At first I was in charge of the general office, under the command of Detective Chief Inspector Brian Baister (later President of the English Rugby Board), whom I had known when I was an aide to CID at Tottenham Court Road. Then, after a few weeks, I was asked to take over command of the Crime Squad at Heathrow Airport, where the Metropolitan Police were responsible for security.

The value of goods, equipment, personal baggage and bullion passing through the airport was so enormous that the place was highly attractive to thieves of every kind. Two years earlier, in November 1983, an armed gang had stolen gold bars, worth £26 million and destined for the Far East, from the Brinks Mat vault just outside the perimeter, and the passenger terminals were notorious as hunting-grounds for pickpockets.

The baggage-handling was riddled with corruption, and much of our work was directed at trying to cut down the pilfering: many of the thefts we dealt with were very substantial, for a third of the country's high-value goods came in through the Heathrow cargo area. Even though we were quite successful, we didn't have access to any of the high-tech equipment that came in later. Our method was to observe how long it took the baggage-handlers to unload a particular aircraft: if they overran the normal time, we could be pretty sure they were in the hold, pilfering, and we would race up the ramps in efforts to catch them. It was a job for young men – and no one moved faster than Detective Constable Fisher, who knew Heathrow inside out and took no nonsense from the loaders. Several of them threatened him – a tribute to his effectiveness – but he hounded them regardless. All in all, the airport was a difficult place to work in, not least because if we made arrests and had to take statements, it meant that a flight could not go, so that our activities had commercial repercussions.

During my spell at Heathrow there was an unfortunate incident: one of my Crime Squad officers became involved with Detective Superintendent Colligan, who had been my detective inspector at Shepherd's Bush. The pair were arrested when the wife of the millionaire Adnan Khashoggi had some jewellery stolen, and they were accused of inflating the amount, and trying to get money from her on an insurance claim. Both were convicted of corruption and given prison sentences.

Some five months after I had left Bramshill, the result of my application at last came through. To my delight, I found I had been awarded a scholarship to go to university. At once I was summoned to see Detective Chief Superintendent Pat Segrew, a dyed-in-the-wool Flying Squad officer, a legend in his time, who was the local boss. I expected him to explode with some rhetoric about it being an utter waste of time to go and listen to academic idiots preaching, so I pretended I was going to turn the offer down, whereupon he swung round in his chair, wiped the back of his hand vigorously across his upper lip, and exclaimed several times, 'John – you will go! John – you will go!' Much later, when I asked him why he had been so adamant, he confided, 'I'd have given my right arm to get that opportunity.'

Friends also told me I would be mad to decline the offer, so, in spite of Cynthia's worries, I decided to accept it. The only proviso from Bramshill was that I must pass all my university exams, during and at the end of my course: if I failed one, I would lose the scholarship at once. If all went well, the police would pay for everything, accommodation and tuition included.

My original intention had been to read history, but once I was back working in the police I thought that law would be of greater practical benefit. So my first application was to read law at Sussex University. At Brighton I was interviewed by Colonel Professor Draper, but I somehow made a mess of the interview, and did not get a place. That failure made me panic a bit, because it was already mid-June, and term would start in September, before which I would have to make whatever new arrangements we needed for moving the family and finding the children new schools.

My reaction was to apply to a scatter of other universities, all at once, and I was rewarded with offers of places at Leicester, Birmingham, Sheffield and Leeds. I chose Leicester, partly because when I went for an interview I found the place extremely friendly, but also because the authorities were able to allocate me a substantial, five-bedroomed house in the village of Oadby, west of the city.

So it was that in 1979 we rented out our own house in Hampton, and all went off to university. I was scared stiff, and almost paranoid about the likelihood that I would fail my first-year exams: if that happened, my scholarship would be terminated immediately, and I would have to crawl back to London with my career in ruins.

My apprehension was increased by my first tutorial, at which a number of very bright people were assembled, all of them at least fifteen years younger than me. Among them was Nick Green, who had got straight As in all his A-level subjects, was then only eighteen, and is now a leading QC, and an expert in European Law, and contributes articles to legal journals all over the world. Before we went in to the tutorial, we had been given a good deal of reading to do, and I belatedly realised that I wasn't as clever as I had hoped: on the contrary, I was surrounded by young people far brainier than me, and I was going to have to work exceptionally hard to keep my head above water. The others were perfectly polite, but I think they looked on me as some kind of oddity: an old man who had somehow strayed among them, and a policeman to boot.

In spite of that rocky start, I had three wonderful years at Leicester. The university campus, on the south side of the city, forms part of a large park, so that its setting is pleasantly green and spacious. The approach, if one walks out of the town and into the open, is very attractive. Especially before exams, when a fever of anticipation swept the place, the park seemed a haven of tranquillity, to which I would repair in efforts to settle my mind. I had developed a special method of learning, which used three senses: seeing, reading and hearing. Besides reading as much as possible I recorded essential information on tapes, which I would play back again and again. This used to drive Cynthia crazy, especially when I did it before going to sleep – but that was the most effective time for me, because when I woke up in the morning, everything was in my head.

Hard work was rewarded by good results in my first-year exams; I also became Captain of Squash, played cricket for the First XI and became involved in coaching the rugby team. The squash alone was a considerable commitment: I sometimes played two or three times a day, fast-walking the three miles to and from our home to the campus. I think I was fitter then than at any other period of my life. I also won the university competition for mooting – legal debating – and in general I could not have enjoyed myself more. The only occasions on which I took on my police persona were those on which we held mock courts, and one of the lecturers would ask me to take part in uniform, so that other students could cross-examine me. I passed all my inter-mediate exams, and ended up with a 2:2 degree. Although I know I could never have got a first, I think, with a bit more effort, I could have got a 2:1, but I was well satisfied.

One of the best features of my time at Leicester was the length of the vacations. Provided I kept passing my exams, the police did not want me back at any stage of my university career, and this meant that, for the first time in our lives, we Stevenses had wonderful opportunities of travelling together as a family. We took our ageing blue Volkswagen Passat estate on camping trips to France, Switzerland and Italy, and in spite of various mishaps – the brakes once failed as we were coming down off the mountains in the South of France – we had fantastic times. Nicholas was then twelve, Alistair ten and Susie seven, and from travelling and living at close quarters, we all got to know each other much better.

In Leicester Nicholas did very well at his new schools, but Alistair was too intelligent for the establishment in which he landed: before, he had been at a good private school, which kept him stretched, but now he finished whatever work he was given to do in the first five minutes of a period, and then, because he was bored, started getting into mischief. We therefore moved him to another school in the middle of the city, and there he took off. Susie was still small enough for me to take her to and from school on the back of my push-bike.

Altogether, I found my three years at Leicester immensely invigorating. Much of my own enjoyment derived from the tremendous support that Cynthia gave me: being the sort that just gets on with life, she overcame the problems created by our move, and formed another stable home. We made many friends, among both the students and the lecturers, and we liked Leicester so much that later I applied for a job as assistant chief constable (which I didn't get), because we would have loved to go back there.

But the most important result was that university opened my mind and gave me a new intellectual grasp. Cynthia felt that the experience changed me completely, making me far more subtle and analytical in my thinking. Until then I had crashed along, arresting people right, left and centre, thinking that the law was black and white. Now, suddenly more mature, I realised that things are often not as simple as they seem. Besides, the degree course left me with a strong enjoyment of law as a subject.

The police paid for every facet of my further education, and when I look back, I see how incredibly privileged I was to receive such bounty. Everything I have achieved in my career, I owe to the police's support at that point: for the broadening of my mind and for my further advancement, I have only them to thank. I later continued my law studies at Southampton University, gaining a Master of Philosophy (Law) degree.

Our return to the real world was dogged by organisational difficulties. One urgent problem was to find a good new school for Nicholas, and, about three weeks before my final term ended, we made the long trip south for an interview at a school in Sunbury. It was obviously an excellent establishment, and the interview seemed to go well, but afterwards we got a letter saying that no place was available. Cynthia and I then had one of our worst days, rushing round three or four other schools, desperately worried that a bad choice might affect Nicholas's whole education and prospects. In the end we managed to get him into Teddington School, where he did well, but making decisions from long range was exceedingly difficult, and it was an anxious time.

We also faced problems nearer home. The house we had in Leicester was larger and better than our own, so, from a distance, we tried to sell the one in Hampton – without success. We therefore had to return to our former quarters, only to find that the neighbourhood had gone downhill: the park at the end of the road had been vandalised, and the whole area was much less attractive than it had been when we went away.

On the career front, things were no easier. I had gone to university as a detective inspector, but during the first year I went up before a selection board and was promoted to detective chief inspector. When I left Leicester with a degree in law, the problem was: to what police job could I return? The Met was not renowned for looking after people who had been to university.

TEN

Kentish Town

Two weeks before we moved back to Hampton, I was surprised to be told that I was to work as head of the CID at Kentish Town, which was a good hour and a half's journey from home. This meant that my travelling time every day would be at least three hours. I made slight representations, but the answer was just what I expected: 'You've had three cushy years at university. Get on with it.'

That was what I did. On my first day I was summoned to the station in Albany Street to see Roy Habershon, the Commander of E Division, which took in Kentish Town, Hampstead and Tottenham Court Road. He had only a week to run until retirement, and his mind, not surprisingly, was on other things. He wished me good luck, and told me that Kentish Town was a very demanding place – but all he seemed really interested in was a company called Control Risks, which he was setting up with some friends as an advisory unit that would assess the security problems likely to be faced by entrepreneurs establishing businesses in various parts of the world. He wanted to know what I thought of the name, how the new firm should be structured, and whether I reckoned it would succeed. I said I felt sure it would – and indeed in time it did – but I found out precious little about my own new job.

Kentish Town had a very large CID office, and a Crime Squad over thirty strong. Its members were raring to go, and to take charge of it was an exciting challenge, since it covered a wide area, from King's Cross up to the fringes of Hampstead, and westwards to Paddington. One of my detective sergeants was Norwell 'Noz' Roberts, the first black policeman in London (who liked to style himself 'Nozzer the Cozzer, the High-flying Rozzer'), and another was my old friend and colleague Johnny Batten.

Because I had been out of circulation for three years, people naturally wondered who I was. I got wind of the fact that they thought, as one of them put it, I might be 'a bit of a tosser', so I reckoned I needed to show some pretty direct leadership. In my absence from the force some aspects of the law had changed, but the principles of good detective work had not. Thoroughness of investigation remained of paramount importance, and the task of a leader (in my view) was not to dominate, but to impart enthusiasm, let subordinates get on with the job, give praise where it was due, and encourage a feeling of pride in the unit. I knew that leading by example was very important, but at the same time, I never hesitated to give a man a rollicking if he had done something wrong or failed in his duty: it always seemed best to clear the air with some straight talking and then re-establish normal relationships.

The police station itself was a dump – a grim Victorian building, and one of the last to contain what was known as a 'tank' – one big cell that took all the drunks. The stench that emanated from there at weekends was unbelievable. As the drunks piled in, the single toilet would block and overflow, and the concrete floor would be awash with excrement, urine and vomit.

We soon had a chance for everyone to get stuck in. Down at Somers Town, near King's Cross, there lived a number of criminal families who had grown too confident and got out of control, pretty well declaring their independence from the rest of London. The place had become extremely violent. During my first two months a senior figure in that little mafia committed a serious assault, occasioning grievous bodily harm on a member of a rival gang, and we responded by arresting him for attempted murder.

That served only to stir things up in Somers Town. The Q-car, manned by a detective sergeant, a constable and a driver, was called to a pub: when the crew went inside to investigate, they were locked inside the toilets for three or four hours. The regulars thought this a great laugh; but when I came in to the office next morning and heard what had happened, I took a different view: this was serious business. They'd taken us on, and I decided that this was *not* going to happen again. That evening, and the next, I took the entire office staff down to the pub and infested the bar, some of us buying a mean half-pint, the rest nothing. 'Don't drink,' I told my detectives. To the publican I said, 'I want to know who locked our people in. Unless you tell me, we'll be coming in every night, and we'll ruin your business.'

Two days later a deputation from the pub came to the police station and agreed to square things up: from then on we never had the slightest trouble from Somers Town. That little episode set the scene: the office liked it – the whole of the station liked it – and from that moment we had an incredible run of success, with a detection rate of 160 per cent (besides current crimes, we were clearing up others that had remained unsolved from as long as two years earlier, including several murders). Such was our progress that the detective chief superintendent from Albany Street came over and said, 'Look, this is showing up everyone else. Slow it down a bit.'

When we had a raid to make, I used to lead from the front, but I was always glad if the party included Detective Constable Alan Slessor – a mountainous Scotsman, 6 foot 6 and 20 stone, known as ' Sless' or 'Slessor the Aggressor', because of his amazing ability to burst through doors without recourse to any form of battering ram or blunt instrument. He *was* the battering ram.

During this time there were two particular cases that led to a change in the law. In one, Detective Sergeant Bob Holmes had arrested two people for aggravated burglary and put them in the cells. Their solicitors went to the High Court and applied for an Act of Mandamus (which compels government officers to obey the court's directions), sanctioning their release. Next morning I sent for Holmes and asked him what was happening about the prisoners. 'Oh,' he said, 'their solicitors came in yesterday with this order.' He handed me some papers, and I saw to my horror that the documents demanded our presence in the High Court at 10.30 a.m.

'Hell!' I said. 'It's ten thirty already! Why aren't you there?'

'I didn't think it was anything important.'

'Well, get down there now!'

Away he went. I followed him down later in the morning, and we managed a certain amount of damage limitation. But the judge slated us for keeping the prisoners in custody, as well as for causing inconvenience to the court by turning up late. A lot of criticism came from Scotland Yard, much of it focused on myself and Chief Superintendent

Malcolm Sullivan, who later became a deputy assistant commissioner – but with his help I rode out the storm.

The other case also involved Bob Holmes, who arrested a burglar called Nigel Oldale after a nasty assault on an eighty-year-old woman in Camden Town. Oldale had heard that this woman and her son kept gold coins and jewels in her maisonette, so he went round, hit her with an iron bar, rushed in, ransacked the place, ran back down the stairs and kicked her out of the way as she was crawling along the hall. The old lady survived, but six weeks later Oldale gave himself up at Harrow Road police station, unable to live with what he had done.

When Bob brought him in to Kentish Town, he began talking about a series of burglaries in the Home Counties, where a gang were breaking into Victoria Wine stores and stealing cigarettes. As a result, we became involved with detectives from Hertfordshire: they were running a big operation, trying to lay their hands on these criminals, and wanted my lads to go out and work with their squad. But when I heard about it, I immediately said, 'No. We've got the icing on this cake. Let them come to us.' So that was what happened.

The outcome of those two cases was the end of what used to be called Judges' Rules, and the introduction of PACE, the Police and Criminal Evidence Act of 1984, which set out to strike a balance between the powers of the police and the rights and freedom of the public. I had mixed views about it. In certain ways it restricted us in the way we interrogated offenders, but it also gave greater credibility to what we said in court.

Our new divisional commander was 'Tug' Wilson, a former CID officer who had been on the Murder Squad. In the Albany Street police station worked a most effective detective superintendent, Basil Hadrell, one of the best murder detectives in the business – good-looking and a bon viveur. Unfortunately the two could not get on: they took a ferocious dislike to each other – so much so that during one murder inquiry, in Leeds, when Wilson had collapsed into bed after a drinking session, Hadrell dragged his bed out of his room, pushed it into the lift and sent it down to the ground floor with its occupant still on board. Wilson never forgave him.

One night I went over to Albany Street to make some report, walked into Wilson's office, and all at once found myself in the middle of a

ferocious row between the two. It began with purely verbal contradictions and disagreements, but the exchange quickly became
highly charged, and would have led to blows, had I not stood in the
middle and physically kept the combatants apart.

Everyone in the Kentish Town station worked very long hours.
Someone on early turn would be in the office by eight in the morning
and he'd still be there at seven or eight in the evening – or he'd have
gone round to our favourite pub, the Crimea, for a drink. Anybody
on late turn, theoretically from 2 p.m. to 10 p.m., generally ignored his
official start-time and came in first thing in the morning because there
was so much work to do. The terms 'stress' and 'counselling' were
unheard of: the only form of counselling we had was in the pub.

In spite of the pressure, the atmosphere in the station was lively, to
say the least, and everyone had to be on the alert, to make sure they
weren't being wound up. Agnes, the lady who ran the canteen, was
known as 'Rumour Control', because every syllable uttered in her
hearing found its way elsewhere. The temptation to wind her up was
therefore irresistible. One day Bob Holmes walked in with a colleague
and remarked casually, 'Poor old Sless ... Very sad.'

'Yeah, terrible,' Dave answered. 'Drink driving ... The Commander
turning up from the training school!'

'Yeah – for Alan to run him over ... Him lying there with a broken
leg.'

So they went on. Twenty minutes later, knowing nothing of their
conversation, I went to pay my bill in the senior officers' canteen.
Agnes turned round and said, 'I'm very sorry to hear about Alan
Slessor.'

'What about him?'

'Well, you know. The accident. Drink-driving outside the training
school. Running over the Commandant ...'

'*What?*'

Over the next two years in Kentish Town we achieved some notable
successes, among them becoming the first CID office to run a supergrass on our own (normally such top-level informants are dealt with
by the Flying Squad or another department at Scotland Yard). After a
large robbery, we tracked the criminal down and arrested him, and
found he wanted to tell us all about numerous kinds of organised

crime and robbery. His name was Martin Pither, and by special dispensation he was kept in custody in St John's Wood police station, as a kind of resident informant.

He began giving so much valuable information that the head of the Flying Squad, Detective Chief Superintendent Michael Taylor, came to see us. I said I wanted to keep running the supergrass; but a divisional CID officer had never done such a thing, so we came to a compromise: we would run the man to get as much out of him as we could, for the benefit of the division in Kentish Town. The other side of it would be run by the Flying Squad. But the arrangement led to allegations about malpractice and corruption, so a special squad was set up to deal with that.

For weeks on end our team debriefed Pither every day, collecting more and more statements about burglaries in which he had taken part: we would then go out on pre-planned operations and arrest the people he'd been talking about, bring them in, charge them and get them before the courts. Altogether his information led to 120 convictions. His reward was a reduced sentence of only three years, after which he was released with a new identity.

As elsewhere, criminal investigation was no respecter of holidays. One Christmas news came in that a dead body had been found in suspicious circumstances in a rubbish chute on the second floor of one of the big tower blocks. I decided I'd better have a look at it, in case there had been foul play. So it was that eight o'clock on Christmas Eve found me not at home with my family, but crawling around among stinking black bags and other unmentionable forms of refuse, lit only by the glare of searchlights. Later inquiries revealed that the dead man had been about fifty-six, and for some time had used the tip as a place for sleeping rough; a post-mortem showed that he had died naturally, of a stroke. But that first evening I had to make an assessment of whether the death could be murder or manslaughter. At first sight it seemed suspicious, as the victim had expired in a peculiar attitude: he did not look as if he had been sleeping, but he appeared to have thrashed around, and he had died contorted, as though after a fight. I had to poke around in the filth for three-quarters of an hour before I was satisfied, and before we moved the body we got a pathologist to come and have a quick look at it.

As always, a few drinks of an evening helped us relax. There was a party in the office every Friday night, and sometimes on Wednesday as well. As Bob Holmes was wont to remark, nobody liked eating on an empty stomach. After a session in the office we would repair to the Crimea, and no one imbibed more freely than Noz Roberts, whose capacity for absorbing alcohol was unbelievable. The one thing he could not drink was beer – but anything else!

His trick was to go right through the pub's optics, from one end to the other, getting a shot poured from every bottle of spirits into a pint glass, and downing the muddy brown mixture in one go. Yet he hardly ever seemed any the worse. He was normally so exuberant anyway that alcohol made no visible difference to him. An insomniac, he used to make do with two or three hours' sleep a night, and sometimes, if he was living in a section house, would come and batter on the doors of colleagues, forcing them to get up and join him for a session at five in the morning.

One evening, when just the two of us were having a glass, he divulged some of the experiences he had had when he joined the police. He told me how he had been ostracised and insulted and called a coon, and how people had dumped excrement in his locker. When he had been on probation as a uniformed officer, part of his route was through a fruit market; one day one of the porters called out to his companion, a police constable, 'Would you like an apple, and a banana for your monkey?' Noz turned round and said, 'Are you referring to me? Listen, I'll take my tunic off. You take your coat off, and we'll go round the back and sort it out.' The porter backed down, in front of all his mates, and Noz won the respect of the entire market.

It is a sad commentary on that time – the 1970s – that he met open racial hostility even within the police. Another day, in summer, he was giving directions to some American tourists on a street corner: an area car drove up, and when he asked the operator for help, the man just said, 'Eff off, you black bastard,' and drove away. Hearing such stories, I was all the more admiring of the way Noz had come through, retaining his dignity and his sense of humour, to be a thoroughly competent, useful detective and a most popular member of the office.

Not that he didn't have his lapses. One February night he and a colleague, Bruce Roberts, fell to drinking Scotch late at night in the

Kentish Town police station. By and by Noz dropped his cigar into a waste bin and set fire to the contents. The best solution seemed to be to tip the whole thing out of the window, which they did. Unfortunately they set fire to the bitumen covering on the flat roof outside, and within a few minutes the fire brigade was on the scene. Next morning, the whole office was blackened by smoke, and when someone asked what had happened, Noz said, 'You'll never guess. Some bastard came past and threw a petrol bomb in the window.' When I found him filling out a crime sheet with details of this fictitious attack, I stopped him and said, 'No! You can't do that. Say what happened.'

Our informants were so active that often a couple of detectives would come into the office on Saturday mornings and just sit there waiting for the telephone to ring. If it did, and some worthwhile tip came through, they chalked up a morning's work and put in for overtime; if nothing happened, they made no charge.

One of those crimes for which they waited took place in the mountains of Wales. We got wind of the fact that a robbery was being planned, but we didn't know exactly where or when it would happen. Then, sure enough, a gang tied up an old lady in a manor house and stole her pictures, but it wasn't until they were on their way back to London that they made the mistake of phoning a criminal who had been acting as one of our informants. He phoned us, and we arrested them at one in the morning in Notting Hill. The ring-leader turned out to be Delroy Showers, a big, powerful weight-lifter and a drug-dealer, who had two others with him. The Welsh police came to Kentish Town, desperately wanting to deal with them down there, but we'd arrested them, and they'd all confessed, so we dealt with them in London, and chalked up yet another success.

ELEVEN
Staff Officer

Our successes at Kentish Town put the spotlight on me, with the result that when David Powys, the deputy assistant commissioner at the Yard, was looking for a staff officer, he chose me. For two years I had enjoyed myself immensely in North London, and had no wish to join anyone's staff; but once the call came, there was no escape. When I got a summons to see Ron Stephenson, a famous deputy assistant commissioner, I went to the Yard expecting to be confronted by problems arising from the success of our supergrass operation. The reality was quite different. 'There's a job I want you to do,' said Stephenson. 'You're to go and work for David Powys. And by the way: this is not a matter for discussion. That's what you're going to do.'

It happened just like that. I didn't get any consideration, or any chance to demur. That was how things were done in those days. At the time I was cast down: the job was not one I would have chosen, especially as Powys, though gifted, had the reputation of being thoroughly difficult; but it was not long before I realised that I had been given a most privileged opportunity, working right at the centre of the Yard.

My new boss was immediately impressive: a bull of a man, big, square-jawed, powerfully built. He was very precise about how he dressed, and how other people should dress, and he was talented in many ways – brilliant on paper, with a sparkling wit, a wonderful mimic, and widely read. Every now and then he would come back into the office, close the door, and do a take-off of the person he had been with, until I had tears of laughter rolling down my cheeks. Also, he tended to assume the character of any historical figure whose life he was studying at the time. If he was reading a book about Napoleon, he would become a bit Napoleonic; if his subject was Nelson, he would turn rather Nelsonian. He was reputed to be a martinet, and his unpopularity in some quarters tended to rub off on me. But once I saw his qualities and got to know him, I became extremely fond of him.

One of my main tasks was to help with the servicing of the many hundred informants whom the Yard was running – in itself an immense task. It was my job to do research on all the new ones that we took on: I had to put in extensive work to find out their background and check their history. These contacts' real identities were known to only two people in the Yard – Powys and myself – and all of them had cover names, such as Jack the Lad, or Lazy Bones. Some were obviously crooks, but others held respectable positions in society.

In a safe in my office I kept a book in which I recorded their pseudonyms, their real identities and the amounts of money paid out to them, as well as details of why each person was being rewarded. Keeping that record up was a major task. Also, I used to have to go and get the cash from a bank and take it to the Yard: the sums varied from a few hundred pounds to (on one occasion) hundreds of thousands. Powys himself would count it out meticulously into small amounts, and while he did so, I would hover, with a £10 or a £20 note of my own in my pocket, in case, by chance, there was a shortfall in my counting. If there had been, he would have been merciless in his criticism. Then we would go out, usually in his car, and hand brown envelopes over to the informants, meeting them on street corners or in cafés, but never in a pub.

One of Powys's major innovations was the system whereby insurance companies started to pay informants centrally, through our office at the Yard. Until then, large sums given out by insurance firms had been handled individually by detectives, who approached the companies themselves and paid informants without supervision, so that corrupt officers had been able to siphon off a good deal of the money. Under Powys's reform, the money came directly to our office, and he and I alone paid it out.

My other main task was to check all the files that came through our office each day. There might be eighty or ninety, and some contained a mass of documents. Others were very sketchy, but I had to check each one and attach a minute to the cover before it went in to the boss. Files on unsolved murders demanded particular attention: in the short time available I had to try and spot anything that might have been overlooked in cases passed on to us by murder squads. Each assessment was the beginning of what might now be referred to as a cold case review. For the first few months Powys re-checked in detail everything I had done, but then he began to trust my judgement and accept decisions I took on his behalf.

Loving America and American ideas (and American ice cream), he crossed the Atlantic regularly, and went on the senior course at the FBI Academy at Quantico. From there he brought back the idea of offender profiling – of having psychologists look at traits inadvertently displayed by murderers at the scene of a crime, and analysing why people commit offences. Why *does* a person commit murder? Why does he use his chosen method? Does he leave a behavioural imprint, which the police can work on later? When Powys first came back from America with these ideas he was laughed out of court – not least by the assistant commissioner of the day, Gilbert Kelland, a very capable individual, quiet, deep-thinking and gentlemanly, who had led the fight against corruption for Sir Robert Mark.

After an initial period of testing, I wrote most of Powys's letters for him, even though he himself was skilled with words. He was the author of a couple of books, and in his correspondence he was meticulous about expressing precisely what he wanted to say – so that working as his staff officer was invaluable training for me.

The Commissioner of the day, Sir Kenneth Newman, had a habit of coming into the Yard at 6 a.m., and our job was to be there before him. David Powys said he couldn't have the commissioner coming to work before him, or leaving after him. This meant that my days were long indeed – sixteen- or eighteen-hour stints were nothing unusual – and sometimes Powys used to ring me up in the middle of the night with thoughts that had come to him in bed. Never was a man more dedicated to the police service: he ate it, drank it, breathed it, slept it. I found out from his driver that on occasion he would go out during the day so that he could have a nap in his car, but I, having no official car or driver, couldn't afford such a luxury.

As another consequence of working for Powys, I was often among the first on the scene of a terrorist outrage, because his style was to get down to the place where an atrocity had been perpetrated as quickly as possible. Thus, at about 11 a.m. on the morning of 20 July 1982 – a lovely summer's day – he suddenly put his head round the door of my office and said, 'There's been a bomb in Hyde Park. Want to come?'

In the car, on the way, he said, 'John, whatever happens, whoever you see, make sure you don't smile.' A few minutes later we came on a scene of appalling devastation in the South Carriageway, on the bottom edge of the park. A bomb loaded with four- and six-inch nails had been detonated by remote control in a blue Morris Marina, just as the Queen's Lifeguard, a detachment of the Household Cavalry, was passing on its way from Knightsbridge Barracks to Horse Guards Parade. Men and horses lay dead or dying, and over twenty people, as well as several horses, had been severely injured. The regimental farriers, who had sprinted from their barracks when they heard the explosion, were splashed with blood from head to foot on their bare torsos and long leather aprons. Debris was scattered everywhere, and human remains were being taken away. The atmosphere was desperately tense, for there was every chance that a second bomb might go off at any moment.

We were given a rapid report by the commander of the regiment, Lieutenant Colonel Andrew Parker-Bowles, who had seen his detachment off from the barracks a few minutes earlier. Hearing the explosion, he had raced to the scene on foot, and just as he arrived he had met a groom leading a severely wounded horse, which had blood gushing from a huge hole in its neck. Immediately he told the man to take off his shirt and stuff it into the wound – but that was impossible, for one of the groom's hands had been pierced by a four-inch nail, which was sticking out on both sides. Another man sacrificed his shirt and staunched the flow of blood. But for that prompt action, the horse would never have reached its stable. In fact, it survived and became a hero – Sefton – and lived to the age of thirty.

At the scene itself mortally injured horses were still struggling to get up. The only weapon to hand was a pistol belonging to a constable who had been on duty at a nearby diplomatic post, and as he had no experience of shooting horses, Parker-Bowles persuaded him to hand the gun over to one of the farriers, who carried out the grisly task of putting two horses out of their misery.

With commendable courage and presence of mind, the colonel then gave an order for the lacerated bodies of the horses to be left uncovered until press photographers arrived, to make sure that their pictures would expose the full horror of the attack. Then, mercifully, the corpses were shrouded with tarpaulins.

Hardly had we taken in what had happened when news came down from a police helicopter overhead of a second explosion, this time in Regent's Park. We fought our way through the choked traffic and arrived at another dreadful scene of death and destruction: a bomb had been planted under the bandstand on which the Royal Green Jackets were giving a lunchtime concert to an audience of about 120. Six soldiers had been killed, and twenty-four people wounded. Bystanders had rushed to help, but by the time we arrived, police had shepherded them away, in case another device went off.

Used as I was to seeing dead bodies, I found the massacre intensely disturbing. One of the young soldiers had been covered with a cloak, and when it was lifted, we found the upper half of a body, lying on its back, with wide-open eyes gazing at the sky, and the right hand raised, with clutching fingers spread outwards, apparently in supplication. Some of the other bodies had been blown thirty or forty yards, and were shattered, like rag dolls, but one soldier lay as if asleep, without visible damage.

The contrast between this man-made horror and the peaceful surroundings of the park, on that glorious morning, was almost too much to bear. Yet the police had to retain full control of the site. As we were leaving, Phil Corbett, the outstandingly capable head of the Anti-Terrorist Branch, who was the senior investigating officer, came up to Powys and said, 'Because you've been on the scene, sir, we need to take your shoes off you.' They were examined there and then, in case we had picked up any vital forensic evidence as we were walking about.

I admired Corbett for doing that. I think he was none too pleased that the deputy assistant commissioner had appeared on the scene – and I myself was surprised by Powys's eagerness to be present. But in time I came to realise that his interest was not ghoulish: he needed to make his own assessment of what had happened, so that he could report to the Commissioner and brief the media.

Within hours the IRA claimed credit for both attacks. At Scotland Yard, where a large team worked on the follow-up inquiry, our people were on close terms with the Royal Ulster Constabulary, and in 1987 a physics graduate named Danny McNamee was sentenced to twenty-five years for conspiracy to cause explosions.

TWELVE

Teacher

After I had worked with David Powys for eighteen months, he asked if I would like to go for a five-month stint as Visiting Professor of Criminal Justice, lecturing in law at the John Jay College of Criminal Justice, which is part of the City University of New York. After consulting Cynthia, I decided to have a go, and went for interview before Sir Kenneth Newman, who was then Director of the Police Staff College at Bramshill; but somehow – perhaps because I was half-hearted about it – I was not selected, only asked to re-apply. So my name went on a waiting list, and when I returned to Scotland Yard, Powys, unable to believe I had failed the selection process, accused me of not really wanting the appointment.

It turned out that I had lost nothing, for in due course I went to the John Jay College anyway; but in the meantime I was approached by Edgar Maybanks, the deputy assistant commissioner in charge of personnel and training, with an offer of joining the Bramshill staff as a lecturer in law. I soon learnt that there was something of a crisis at the college, because the man who had been teaching A level law to a group of 110 chief inspectors was returning to his force for good personal reasons in the middle of the three-month course, and a replacement was urgently needed. I came under a fair amount of pressure to accept the offer – and I made no objection, because one of the biggest tests in the service is to break through into what are known as the senior ranks, and I thought that to spend some time at the Staff College would be the best preparation for me.

I was selected to teach there while Sir Kenneth Newman was still commandant, but by the time I arrived at Bramshill, a new commandant in the form of Barry Payne, a former Chief Constable of

Kent, had just taken over – a less academic and austere individual than Newman, whom I always found quite difficult to talk to. I was anxious that a spell at the college should not get in the way of my promotion prospects, so I agreed to take the post only on the basis that I would go on the next available board for detective chief superintendent, whenever it was held: the fact that I happened to be teaching when the board came up would not rule me out.

The three-day selection process for Bramshill was quite intensive – psychological tests, interviews, practical exercises, team tests – and perhaps it was fortunate for me that the person who assessed us psychologically was none other than John Brindley, who had played such an important role in directing me towards university. Whatever influence he may have had, I was accepted.

David Powys and I parted company on the best of terms, with mutual regret. *He* knew that a two-year stint was long enough for me to be in that job, and *I* knew that I ought to be moving on. As a leaving present he gave me a portrait of a police officer, with the twelve qualities that an officer most needs – leadership, discretion, diplomacy, bravery, moral courage and so on – inscribed on it. I greatly valued that memento, and still have it.

At that stage the college at Bramshill had a staff of about sixty, a mixture of academic lecturers and police officers like myself, and there were always several courses running simultaneously. At the highest level was the Senior Command Course, for people who had been selected through extended interview to go on to be assistant chief constables or above; next there was the Intermediate Command Course, and then the Junior Command Course. This was the one on which I taught as a superintendent, taking chief inspectors through. Below that was the Special Course, for people going for accelerated promotion, up to inspector in three or four years. Yet another element was the Overseas Command Course.

All in all, Bramshill was a vibrant establishment, alive with intellectual and physical activity. A great deal of sport was played, and that suited me fine. At first I shared a flat with Superintendent Denis Meadus, from Hampshire, a fitness fanatic who never liked to be beaten at anything he tried: to start with, the atmosphere between us tended to be a little competitive, but we became firm friends. Later I was given a one-bedroom flat of my own, and because our house at Hampton was only an hour and twenty minutes away, I often went home at weekends, or else the family came down.

With scant time for preparation before I started lecturing, I had to work like a demon, briefing myself so that I could pick up the threads of the course halfway through. On my first morning I felt quite daunted as I walked into a large auditorium, to find sixty or seventy chief inspectors eagerly awaiting enlightenment. Nothing less than first-class instruction, and nothing lower than an A or B grade at A level, would satisfy them.

Among the group were quite a few I already knew, and it was my task to give everyone a more sophisticated understanding of the law than the fairly simple and practical version within which they had been operating. Subjects like contract law, tort, constitutional law, and the way in which law has developed were part of the syllabus, and new to the students, so that I was extremely busy.

In spite of the pressure, I thoroughly enjoyed myself, and I made two particular friends – Des Ladd, who had played cricket pro-fessionally for Kent, and Peter Sharp, who played for Sussex and ended up as Chief Constable of Hertfordshire. Stalwarts of the Bramshill team, we became known as 'the Three Musketeers' and played cricket on many fine grounds that summer – at the staff colleges of Camberley and Sandhurst, in the Hampshire League, and so on. Peter and I opened the batting, and whenever he saw me start to take hits from the opposition fast bowler, he (being a much more skilful player than I was) would come down the wicket and whisper, 'John, you really must learn to get out of the way of the ball.'

I learnt a great deal about how to give lectures, how to deliver speeches, how to show professional leadership; but apart from all the other advantages, I found it useful and enjoyable to sit with the syn-dicate of twenty-two officers that I ran, listening to the views of other forces. Until then, in my work. I had focused exclusively on met-ropolitan problems, but now I was hearing what went on in Wales, in the North of England, in Scotland, Northern Ireland and elsewhere. I was fascinated to learn about the lives of people in these far-flung forces – how they went about their work, how they interrelated with their communities, how they relaxed and enjoyed themselves. I began to realise that the Metropolitan Police, big though it is, had no monopoly of experience or talent: I saw that, love the Met though I did, there might come a time when I would wish to work elsewhere.

One of our most interesting visitors was a superintendent from Northern Ireland, Ken Masterson, a barrister with a first-class honours degree, who later became a deputy assistant commissioner at the Yard and Deputy Chief Constable of the Royal Ulster Constabulary. A quietly spoken man of exceptional talents, he ran the Junior Command Course, and with him came a fellow superintendent who had been a good deal less fortunate. I shall call this fellow O'Brien – not his real name: he had led a special unit of the RUC on an armed raid in Armagh, and as a result was in trouble over the shoot-to-kill policy. He was my first real contact in the RUC, and I shall never forget an evening I spent with him, hearing of the problems faced by the authorities across the water.

It was a strange occasion, for he was already on the move again: he had cleared everything out of the house, and was about to depart next morning for some other country – such was the threat against him. Yet he spoke with such clarity and honesty, telling me about tasks he had been given that he would have preferred not to undertake, that I gained valuable insights into the hard-core problems of sectarian hatred and violence in Northern Ireland. Until then my colleagues and I had tended to think of the situation over there in simplistic terms, but now I began to realise how complex and intractable it was. From O'Brien and from Ken Masterson, with his habit of cool, legalistic understatement, I learnt much that stood me in good stead later in my career. What came over most strongly from both men was the intense hatred that the RUC had for the paramilitaries; yet even at that stage I realised, from the nature of the war being waged against the RUC and the British Army, that some kind of collusion with the paramilitaries must exist.

One exercise that the college devised was a kind of psychological free-for-all, in which syndicate members were told to open up and say what they thought of each other, making face-to-face criticisms. I and other instructors were much against the idea: I felt it was detrimental, even dangerous, because it might destroy a man's self-confidence and wreck the camaraderie that had built up during the first half of the course. It seemed to me that, if it were done at all, it should be done by trained psychologists; but our objections were overruled, and it went ahead. Sure enough, it ended in quarrels and almost in fisticuffs, with people on their feet, yelling insults at the tops of their voices. I refused to let my syndicate take part in any more such sessions.

After six months at the Staff College, when I was still a detective superintendent, the Met kept their promise and allowed me to go on a board for detective chief superintendent. To my delight, I passed; but because I was at the bottom of the list, and officers were appointed to new positions from the top of the list as vacancies came up, I was grounded at Bramshill for another year. During that time David Powys twice came down from London as my guest – and he rapidly dispelled the image that people had of a cold, remote ogre. His wonderful sense of humour and gift for mimicry left my colleagues with tears running down their cheeks.

Then at last, through Barry Payne, who had been President of the Association of Chief Police Officers and Chief Constable of Kent, along came an opportunity to take up a visiting professorship at the John Jay College. I did not even have to go before a board.

I started in the autumn of 1984, hardly knowing what to expect. It was an experience merely to be met at JFK Airport and whizzed into the centre of New York. The visiting professor's apartment was on Seventh Avenue and Forty-fifth Street, opposite Manhattan police station, where they used to do the filming of *Kojak*, and from there I had to walk round to the college through a fairly rough area.

I took over from a chief superintendent called Les Poole, who helped me with a thorough briefing, but for a few days I felt as if l had been thrown into an enormous pond. The lecturing I had done at Bramshill now became extremely useful, because it had given me confidence in speaking to people, especially about technical and legal issues.

At my initial reception I asked the President of John Jay, Jerry Lynch, what was expected of me. 'Don't worry,' he reassured me, 'I'll introduce you to the faculty' – and he did. I soon became good friends with several of them, not least two who were former New York cops: John Cronin, of Irish extraction, a real character, and Eli Silverman, with whom I shared an office, and who is still a professor there.

In fact, I received very little advice or direction, but over the four months I spent in New York was left on my own, to create my own courses, within a certain framework. I set my own essays and marked my own exam papers, assigning grades and decreeing whether students had passed or failed. The range of students was enormous, because the John Jay College is an open university, so that anybody may apply to join: applicants varied from captains in the police and well-educated citizens with reasonably good jobs, to some who had difficulty reading and writing. Some worked in shops or garages, a few were assistants in libraries, and, at a guess, 70 per cent came from ethnic minorities. About a third were New York Police Department cops: naturally I warmed to them, and they warmed to me.

After my second lecture, during which I had talked about coloured people, most of the students dispersed, but two stayed behind – a big, strapping black fellow called Sylvester, very bright, and Gil Alvarez, an Hispanic cop, equally intelligent. They came up to me, and one said, 'Professor, we don't talk about coloured people over here. That's a term we don't use.'

'All right,' I said. 'How do I refer to people like yourselves?'

'Hispanic, or Afro-Caribbean.'

I never made that mistake again.

The Undergraduate Course presented me with few difficulties, but the Graduate Course, for people who already had university degrees, demanded a more sophisticated approach, and meant tackling subjects in a philosophical way. My undergraduate classes numbered fifty or sixty, and the graduate course only twenty-four, but on a few occasions I had to talk to the entire faculty, 200-strong.

Outside the college, I got to know the NYPD very well, and made good friends with the inspector (the equivalent of our chief superintendent) who ran the Manhattan Division and whose head-quarters were opposite my apartment. I had a drink with him now and then, and went out on live operations, once when President Reagan visited New York. As the motorcade went past the long, blank wall of a hotel, the President continued to wave enthusiastically. 'That shows you how good he is,' my friend remarked. 'He just keeps going, whether there's anyone there or not!' The NYPD's methods were a good deal rougher than ours. Whenever a major public figure came to town, they would put up crash barriers everywhere, and if anybody crossed one, they'd clobber him with their truncheons. If he tried to go any further, they stated, they'd shoot him.

I also went out on patrol in Brooklyn a couple of times with Gil Alvarez. One day there came a radio call of 'Suspects on premises'. The premises turned out to be a big apartment block, and as we left the patrol car to walk into the building, people started firing at us from the second or third floor. We dived under the car and called up reinforcements, but we never did find out who the gunmen were. Another day I set out with Gil at 6 a.m., and by 11 a.m. we had been to two murders – one of a homosexual whose boyfriend had stabbed him to death in their apartment, and the second a contract murder of a young woman who was going to stand as a witness in a drugs case.

Before I went to America, Cynthia had said that the only place in the world she *didn't* want to go was New York, because it was so dangerous. She had a point there, because in those days – the mid-1980s – it *was* very violent. But in the end she changed her mind, and brought the family over to stay in my apartment for three weeks before Christmas – and from the moment we all went into the Rockefeller Center, it became her favourite destination.

At Gil's request on a number of occasions I went to talk to the children at a school that had once been fashionable among film stars and others, but had since gone downhill. By the time I knew it, the staff needed armed guards on the premises. I found that these big, tough Brooklyn boys, up to eighteen years old, simply couldn't understand how British police could patrol without weapons, so I took them on, one by one, at the front of the class, in demonstrations of unarmed combat, to show them how one could deal with someone wielding a knife. This proved a great success, and we had a lot of laughs.

Then, when my family were over, I suddenly realised that my elder son Nicholas, who was fifteen, would be interesting to them, so I persuaded him to give a talk about what it was like being at school in England. It was no easy assignment for him to stand up and talk in front of a class of forty boys, all tough New Yorkers, who were fascinated and amused by his accent. But he managed it admirably: he got a good question-and-answer session going, and had the boys genuinely interested.

My colleagues were immensely hospitable. I played a good deal of squash with Neil Cronin, son of the professor and a dentist in the Rockefeller Center, and he invited us to spend weekends with his family down on Long Island. Over Christmas two of the other professors took us out into the Appalachian Mountains, where they had a house overlooking a lake, and we stayed three or four days as their guests.

Another formative experience was to walk round some of the roughest areas of the city, like Harlem, where huge, red-brick tenement blocks were standing empty except for a few squatters, who would come out and stare at anyone who went past. I went there with my big Afro-Caribbean friend from the NYPD, who had a gun in his pocket for emergencies; although we were both in civilian clothes, we never met the slightest aggravation – but if I'd gone to those places on my own, I don't think I would have come out alive.

My four months in New York were a revelation. I learnt a tremendous amount about police methods, and benefited by comparing them with what we did at home. I was also surprised by how unsophisticated the police were, and by their relatively low detection rate in murder cases (about 58 per cent, compared with our 90 per cent). My new colleagues were amazed by the fact that our methods are not more forceful: the concept of policing by consent is something they could not grasp. Every time we arrived at an incident of burglary, they leapt from their cars brandishing their weapons, even though the robbers had long since departed.

Yet by the end I began to understand the amazing cultural richness of the place. It was a city that never slept. There were down-and-outs everywhere. The place was alive with crime – several times on my way from my apartment to the college I passed shops that had been burnt out, and when I asked what the police were doing about it, found that only a single detective had been assigned to the case, and that no real investigation was taking place. Some parts of the city were completely lawless, mainly because the number of police on the streets had been enormously reduced, and the situation brought home to me the fact that if there are not enough officers on the street, you cannot deliver.

At the time, I had to admit, in some ways we were no better off in London. There we were in the throes of an IRA bombing campaign, and during 1984 we had lost more officers in London than they had in New York. At the John Jay College our faculty included a distinguished professor called Brendan O'Mara, who was one of the fundraisers for Sinn Fein and the IRA in New York. He made no secret of the fact that he wanted the Brits out of Northern Ireland, and habitually referred to the English as 'the oppressors'. All his thoughts and attitudes were rigidly conditioned by history. Not only did he visit Northern Ireland regularly: he also entertained members of the Sinn Fein and the IRA in New York. Normally I got on well with him, and enjoyed the odd drink: only when he started spouting Irish politics would I ask him to change the subject. Things improved a bit when the deputy commissioner of the Garda came over on a visit. We went out for a drink with other members of the staff, and he and Brendan got into a bitter argument, during which the deputy commissioner made some telling points about the IRA's murderous practices. Thereafter Brendan treated me with more respect, although he did not change his attitude to the IRA. In vain, I drove home the point that innocents, including some Americans, had lost their lives in recent atrocities: he seemed immune to the loss of life.

THIRTEEN
Heathrow

As always, a complete break from the Met created uncertainty about what job I could do next. Halfway through my time at John Jay College, Brian Worth, then Deputy Assistant Commissioner at Scotland Yard, wanted me to join the Murder Squad, up at C 1. Simultaneously, Colin Smith, Deputy Assistant Commissioner for the area covering Heathrow Airport, wanted me to go there. The tug of war was still in progress when I returned, but in the end Colin Smith won the argument – so to Heathrow I went, in charge of the CID on the airport.

I inherited a very large CID office, which included some eighty detectives, and a vigorous Crime Squad. Since I was last there, as a detective inspector running the Crime Squad, the boundaries of the local force had been changed. Earlier, the CID's area had taken in West Drayton and Staines; but by 1985 we were solely concerned with policing the airport, which had become much busier in the interim. The office, which I took over from Detective Chief Superintendent John Pole, was well organised.

One established member of the team was Detective Chief Inspector Trevor Griffiths, with whom I had played rugby. As we walked round for the first time, he said casually, 'Oh, by the way, we've got a bit of an operation running. There's a lot of pilfering going on, so we've managed to get a camera into one of the baggage-handlers' rooms. We've seen them opening luggage, taking out people's clothes, and so on.'

Trevor was not exaggerating. Pilfering at the airport had grown so notorious, and complaints from passengers so frequent, that the place was becoming known as 'Thiefrow'. I was immediately interested, and got Trevor to show me what was happening. By getting pin-holes

121

bored through the walls of baggage-handling rooms, the team had installed fibre-optic lenses and cables, through which they could keep surveillance without fear of detection, and they were recording what they saw.

Giving Trevor my total support, I increased the number of cameras until we were running surveillance twenty-four hours a day. Presently we realised that the loaders were divided into two camps, one of which was stealing, one not. It was extraordinary to be able to watch the thieves in action, day after day, night after night – and sometimes the sight made me feel physically sick. Their treatment of people's most intimate possessions was appalling.

As our evidence built up, we held lengthy discussions about what action we should take; we could have pounced any day, but we decided to run the operation long – so we carried on watching, filming, recording and monitoring for three months. We also set up arrangements to identify the thieves, follow them to their homes, find out how they were living, see what sort of people they were meeting and gauge their financial circumstances – so that when we judged the moment ripe, we could launch a major hit and take them all out at one go. Our investigations revealed not only that theft from luggage was rife, but also that a good deal of drug-smuggling was going on.

Waiting, as we did, carried two major risks. One was that word of what we were doing might leak out; another, that our total of active thieves was reaching such proportions that a mass-arrest was clearly going to wipe out a large part of Heathrow's baggage-handling capacity, and might bring the airport to a halt. We therefore kept information very tight, restricting it to half a dozen detectives.

There came a point at which I had to take major decisions. With the airport commander's agreement, I went to the hierarchy of British Airways and showed them some of the material we had recorded. The video tapes were clear as day and totally incriminating. Everyone was appalled. I also took the even more difficult decision to go and confront the local heads of the Transport and General Workers' Union. Many people warned me not to do so, as they thought I might provoke a walk-out and bring the whole airport to a standstill; but I insisted, and made a discreet approach.

Like BA, the union officials were horrified. There was no way they could refute the evidence I presented: there, on videotape, were their own men opening suitcases with skeleton keys, removing anything they fancied, and closing the bags again. One man was filmed holding up a patterned jumper for size – and later, when he was arrested, he was actually wearing it. I told both union and airline that we wanted to seize all the people at once, search their houses, follow up, and get them into court as quickly as possible – and neither organisation demurred. To confirm that I had the full backing from my own people, I also went up to Scotland Yard and laid our plans before Deputy Assistant Commissioner Wyn Jones, a young and lively operator, who gave me his unconditional support.

With the help of BA we also introduced fibre-optic cameras into the baggage-holds of various aircraft – something that had never been done before – so that we could continue our surveillance on board, where the loaders supposed nobody could see them. We discovered that they had refined a sophisticated system, whereby they would bring the luggage through the security checks in tugs and other vehicles, and run it through to their receivers. What amazed us was the amount of cash being smuggled – and then stolen. Passengers from Ghana, especially, were hiding huge sums of banknotes in their hold baggage, thinking the money would be safe: when it disappeared, of course they could neither claim it back nor prove that they had lost it – and for the thieves, it was easily laundered.

When everything was ready, we set the date of our strike in June 1986. On the morning we deployed almost every single policeman based at Heathrow: I myself briefed 120 detectives and uniformed officers, and sent them off on raids that began at five in the morning. I remained in the station, monitoring the operation, and coordinating the interrogation of people as they were brought in.

The operation was a phenomenal success: the known addresses were searched, property was recovered, and every one of the seventy-two people we arrested was found guilty of theft, conspiracy to thieve, or handling drugs. Some of the handlers had managed to amass astonishing amounts of property. One man we interrogated lived in a small terrace house in Hanworth, but owned a hotel in Florida. Another was said to keep a yacht at Malaga, a house down there which now would cost one million pounds, another house in England, and a top-of-the-range Mercedes – all on £20 a week. When asked how he had acquired so much, he had the nerve to reply, in his Cockney accent, 'I've been very lucky in the gambling houses.' Others lived on a similarly lavish scale.

The best thing of all was that nobody – but nobody – threatened to go on strike. Because I had created a bond of trust with the unions and the airline, both backed our action publicly, and the airport carried on in a normal way. This taught me one of the most important lessons I ever learnt: if you take someone into your confidence over a major problem, you do create a risk, but if it comes off, the reward is enormous. Another vital lesson was that the kind of evidence we collected was irrefutable. Neither the union nor the airline could challenge it.

Harder to deal with, in a way, were the pickpockets who infested the terminal buildings. Our specialist in sorting them out was Detective Constable Steve Richardson, who spent countless hours loitering among the crowds of passengers, trying to pick out the professional thieves, many of whom were South American. He found that they tended to be smartly dressed, often in suits, so as to blend in with the crowd, and that they gave themselves away only with their eyes, which flickered back and forth, on the lookout for potential victims (and for police officers). They targeted Arabs and Africans in particular, knowing that such people often carried substantial amounts of cash, and it was extremely difficult to catch them red-handed.

The other major problem we had to face was the possibility of terrorists hijacking aircraft. In 1985 terrorist activity was rife in many countries: during the first six months of the year there were seventeen incidents of hijacking, worldwide – as many as in the whole of the previous year. On 14 June Shia gunmen hijacked a TWA airliner after take-off from Athens, ordered it to land at Beirut, and for the next sixteen days held the American passengers hostage, demanding the release of 700 prisoners in Israel. On 23 June an Air India 747, en route from Canada, vanished into the sea 120 miles west of Ireland, presumably destroyed by a bomb, for which Sikh extremists were blamed. There had already been massacres at Rome and Milan airports.

High-level meetings at Scotland Yard led to decisions that we should harden up and refine our preventative measures at Heathrow. One result was that we carried out exercises in cooperation with the Blues and Royals (Household Cavalry), who intermittently sealed off the entire airport with armoured cars, so that we could check who was coming in and out at any time of particular threat. We also decided to arm the airport police with Heckler & Koch sub-machine guns – the first time that police in this country had openly walked around with automatic weapons in their hands.

On 25 June, in a show of strength, armed troops patrolled the terminal buildings and boarded an Air India jumbo carrying automatic weapons. Tanks and other armoured vehicles took up position on the tarmac. These precautions evoked some sharp criticism – not from the Yard, but mainly from ACPO (the Association of Chief Police Officers), and in particular from the organisation's chairman, Sir Kenneth Oxford, the Chief Constable of Merseyside, who was renowned for plain speaking, and on this occasion thought we had taken leave of our senses. At one meeting he turned round and said bluntly to me and Commander Pat Carson, 'You've gone right off your trolley. You're overreacting. This should never have happened.' Carson would have none of it – yet the Commissioner of the Met backed us.

The reason for our actions was simple and specific. As the world's busiest airport, Heathrow was, is, and will always be, a key target, and we knew through intelligence that members of terrorist groups were about to reconnoitre it for a possible attack. Later, representatives of two groups did indeed come to Heathrow, but when they saw the defences, they decided it was too hard a nut to crack, and turned their attention elsewhere. Thus our precautions were fully justified, although our critics naturally did not know this.

Our defensive measures included frequent exercises carried out in conjunction with the SAS and other Army units – 'combined operations', we called them – and we held numerous hostage-rescue practices down at the western end of the airport. Inevitably, there came a day on which our skills were fully tested. I had been at Heathrow about six months when an American Airlines 747 landed there, with the crew reporting that in one of the toilets someone had scrawled a message claiming a bomb was hidden on board. The captain parked the aircraft right out in the middle of the airport, and I was the first person up the ramp. We evacuated the passengers as fast as we could and bussed them away, then searched the plane, but found nothing.

On the morning of 28 March we learnt that a Lufthansa jet had been hijacked in midair, on its way from Frankfurt to London. A young man had burst into the flight deck holding something under his jacket that looked like a gun, and claiming that he had explosives strapped round his waist. Having made various not very coherent demands, he stationed himself behind the cockpit door and ordered the captain to land at London. The crew thought he was English, but were not sure, as he was making little sense.

The 737 came in, taxied to the west end of one of the runways and stopped. Within a few seconds our full police team drove up to within fifty yards or so. Stuart Higgins, the uniformed chief superintendent, and myself then walked in under the nose and began to negotiate with the hijacker, talking to him through a telephone line plugged into the belly of the fuselage.

He spoke so incoherently that it was not at all clear what he wanted, but we knew that the important thing was to keep him talking until we could make a more accurate assessment of the threat he posed. On another line we were in touch with members of the crew, and as time passed they came more and more to the view that he was bluffing, and was not carrying weapons at all. In all, our negotiations lasted two and a half hours – an eternity for all the passengers trapped inside, with the plane growing steadily hotter and more uncomfortable.

While this was going on, a quite different thought was playing in the back of our minds – that the Prime Minister, Margaret Thatcher, was even then supposed to be taking off on her way to an EEC summit conference, together with the Home Secretary, Leon Brittan. Because of the crisis, we swiftly arranged for her aircraft to depart from Nort-holt instead, but, as usual, she wanted to know exactly what was going on, and she twice sent Brittan across to find out what was happening.

Eventually we took the difficult decision to storm the plane, because the crew reckoned there was a 90 per cent chance that the hijacker was unarmed. On some pretext we got him to agree that we could bring a set of steps up to one of the doors, and as soon as that was in position, we sent in one of our armed teams to overpower him. I ran up the steps after them and, the moment they had frisked the fellow, arrested him.

To launch the team like that was a calculated risk. If the hijacker had blown the plane up, there would have been numerous casualties, and we would have been blamed for the disaster. But we had weighed all the pros and cons as best we could – and our decision proved right. As we thought, the young man had no weapon or explosive. Once he had been taken off, the pilot brought the aircraft in to the centre of the airport, and the passengers at last were able to disembark.

It turned out that the hijacker was a twenty-four-year-old from Bristol, and when I took him back to my office to interrogate him, I found he was in a state of mental confusion: it seemed that his aim, as much as anything, had been to attract attention. While I was interviewing him, Leon Brittan appeared for the second time in search of news, and I was able to assure him that everything was under control. The young man got little sympathy from us: he was charged with hijacking, under the Civil Aviation Act of 1982, and received a prison sentence. Lufthansa, in contrast, were extremely grateful, and later took the highly professional Stuart Higgins and myself out for a celebratory meal.

One day we had a visit from Geoffrey Dear, then Chief Constable of the West Midlands, who brought his Police Authority down to show them what we were doing, and to pick up any tips that he might apply to Birmingham Airport, which was in his territory. That very evening, just after Dear's party had left, who should appear but Peter Imbert, then the deputy commissioner. This seemed a curious fluke, as both men were then in the running for the post of Commissioner (Imbert got it).

FOURTEEN
Senior Command Course

Towards the end of my time at the airport I decided to apply for extended interview for the Senior Command Course, which an officer has to pass to go beyond the rank of detective chief superintendent. The interview took place over three days at Brighton, and the chairman of my selection panel was Geoffrey Dear, who had become the Chief Constable of the West Midlands. I managed to achieve a high pass mark, and that meant I was due to go on the course at Bramshill.

Before that, however, an inspection was carried out at Heathrow by John Smith (later Sir John, Deputy Commissioner of the Met). Towards the end of his tour he came to my office, sat down and said, 'I know you're due to go on the Senior Command Course in a couple of months' time, but meanwhile a vacancy is coming up in Hampshire for an assistant chief constable.'

'Yes . . .' I said cautiously.

'Well, I think you should consider applying for it.'

I was taken aback, because it was most unusual for anyone to be appointed assistant chief constable without having done the senior course. On the other hand, I knew that Smith was a close friend of John Hoddinott the deputy chief of Hampshire, and I realised that this must be a serious approach. Nevertheless, having thought the proposal over for a few days, I came to the conclusion that I stood no chance of gaining the job. Then, about a week later, Smith approached me again and said, 'In fact, John, it's not just one post. There are *two* posts going, and I really do think you should put in for one of them.'

That decided me. I did apply – but so did twenty-three others. Both the posts were for assistant chief constables: one would be in charge of operations, the other directing personnel and training. Everybody knew that one of the applicants was John Wright, the outstanding head of the CID in Hampshire, and that he would almost certainly get the operational role: this meant in effect that the other twenty-three of us were competing for the second job.

In any case, the Senior Command Course started. It was one of the largest ever held, with thirty-six officers taking part, and included people from other forces. Among those from far-flung beats were the Chief of the Gibraltar police, and YP (as he was known to his friends), the assistant commissioner from Hong Kong, who later became the Commissioner there. This made a lively mix. But in only my second week at Bramshill I found I had been short-listed for the Hampshire post, and went down to Winchester, where the interviews were held in the Town Hall, just up the hill from the cathedral.

I had low expectations of success, and after I had been before the board I sat gloomily in a room with a dozen others, waiting to hear the panel's verdict. Nobody was more amazed than me when, at about four thirty in the afternoon, out came the Chief Constable of Hampshire, John Duke, and said, 'Mr Wright and Mr Stevens, come back in. You've got the jobs.'

Then an extraordinary thing happened. Cynthia, out shopping at that moment in Kingston, suddenly stopped, somehow receiving a message that I'd been successful. When I rang to give her the good news, she knew it already. We were both astonished, for she had never had a telepathic experience before – but a very clear one reached her that afternoon.

Having landed the job, I quickly went down to a doctor near the cathedral for a medical, then back to police headquarters, and joined Duke and his colleagues in a nearby pub. When I asked Duke, 'What about the Senior Command Course?' he replied briskly, 'Carry on with it. Don't worry about that. We'll pay half the fees, and the Met will pay the rest.'

Back at Bramshill, amid tremendous celebrations, I met Keith Povey, the only other assistant chief constable on the course, who became a firm friend, and the Chief HMI (the Chief of Her Majesty's Inspectors of Constabulary). Naturally I was itching to start in my new post, but the course proved a delight, not least because a high proportion of the students were detectives. We studied leadership, political issues and financial matters, visited various places and wrote extensive research papers: off duty we had a lot of laughs, did the odd bit of drinking and indulged in some horseplay. After a while we realised that one of our number was telling stories about us to the staff who ran the college: when we managed to identify him, Keith blew his cover quite effectively in front of the staff.

Among the course's major attractions were visits to other countries. Keith went to Hong Kong – lucky fellow. I drew the short straw and only managed Holland, but even that proved fascinating. During two weeks in Amsterdam I saw at first hand the results of the Dutch decision to legalise all drugs: I witnessed many unnerving sights, but one experience above all has stayed with me ever since.

Together with a couple of my colleagues, I was taken by senior Dutch officers to the Balmermeer, a big housing estate, where we went into a prefabricated hut tucked under an overhang of the motorway. Living there were people taking crack, cocaine – any drug they wanted – and sitting in one corner was a quite pretty young girl, alongside her pimp. As we watched her injecting herself, I turned to one of the Dutch officers and said, 'What's her future?'

My mentor seemed quite unconcerned. 'Oh,' he said, 'she's come in from the country. She's on drugs and into prostitution. She'll probably be dead in two years.'

That squalid scene still haunts me. This is *not* the way policing should be done, I thought, and I've never changed my mind.

Equally riveting was a tour we made round the centre of Amsterdam, surveying the effects of legalisation. The liberal authorities had stationed barges on the canals, where addicts could live, take drugs and inject themselves within the law. The trouble was that the junkies raised mayhem around the station area, causing disturbances and carrying out robberies, and they became so provocative that in the end vigilante groups went in and fired the barges. For us visitors, it was horrible yet fascinating to see the consequences of a free-for-all drugs policy exposed in such detail.

An entirely different but equally useful project – part of the course – was a survey of Newcastle, Gateshead and Sunderland (Northumbria Police). Our brief in the north-east was to analyse why there had been no riots in the area. There had been plenty of major disturbances elsewhere – in Brixton, Toxteth, Bristol and other places – but none in the north, and a group of eight of us went up for two weeks to find out why. We split into smaller groups to tackle various jobs, and then came together to write up our reports.

I already knew something of the area, because my father had based his airline business there, but this visit gave me fresh insights into local problems. We soon discovered that relations between the community and the Northumbria Police were exceptionally good.

We interviewed the leader of the council in Newcastle, Jeremy (now Sir Jeremy) Beecham; we studied crime levels and instances of public disorder in an area of high unemployment, toured various districts to get a feel for the attitude of residents, and generally assessed how the police and local authority were working together. We came to the conclusion that they had forged an exceptionally good partnership, and that this was the reason no riots had taken place.

That was the most important lesson I learnt from our northern tour – the necessity for police to work closely with local councils. The other revelation was the value of allowing small teams of police officers to concentrate on particular areas: I saw how important it was to leave each team in place for a reasonable length of time, let its members get to know the community and work with it. Those principles of policing have stayed with me, and I applied them successfully when I went back as Chief Constable of Northumbria.

All in all, I enjoyed the Senior Command Course immensely, and derived great benefit from it. Towards the finish the chief officers from Scotland Yard came to an end-of-course dinner. The Commissioner of the day, Sir Kenneth Newman, was a very good police officer, but he was not renowned for his small talk. Unfortunately, I found myself sitting next to him at dinner. He was on my left; on my right was John Duke, and opposite was Peter Imbert, then Chief Constable of the Thames Valley, whom I knew well.

During the first course Sir Kenneth lived up to his reputation and did not say one word. I kept making half-hearted overtures, but they hit a blank wall. Then, during the second course, he at last opened up with a real conversation-stopper: 'I don't know why they didn't use plastic bullets at Broadwater Farm,' he said. I remember thinking, Well, if the Commissioner doesn't know, who does? He never mentioned the

fact that I was going to Hampshire, let alone offered any congratulation. The contrast between him and John, 'the Iron Duke', was
astonishing, John being naturally convivial and a keen imbiber.

During the course I occasionally went up to Heathrow, to hone my
pilot's skills on the flight simulator. One night, as we drove up, I was
feeling a bit odd, with a severe pain in my abdomen. I thought nothing
of it, because I had hardly ever been ill, and I expected the discomfort
to pass off. Next morning we were supposed to be visiting the Home
Secretary, but for once I didn't feel like getting up, and I continued to
lie in bed. Presently I had a visit from Detective Chief Superintendent
Brian Reynolds, from the Met, a good friend who occupied the room
next to mine. He stuck his head round the door, and, finding me still
horizontal, said, 'Aren't you coming?'

'No,' I said. 'I just don't feel right. I think I've got flu coming on.'

'You do look a bit pale,' he admitted. 'Maybe you'd better stay put.'

Off went the course to London. As the morning dragged on, I grew
worse and worse, and at about ten I felt a sudden, agonising internal
explosion, and suspected that my appendix had burst. The next thing
I remember is crawling out into the corridor, and one of the cleaners
screaming when she saw me, because I looked so awful. An ambulance
whisked me into hospital, but the surgeon did not operate until the
evening, because he wanted to make sure that it was appendicitis,
rather than a burst ulcer. The delay gave me an incredibly unpleasant
day – for acute appendicitis it was – but the operation was successful,
and I spent the last week of the Senior Command Course in hospital,
recovering.

In spite of that setback, I ended the course with an outstanding
grade. I was lucky in two respects: one, that there were no unpleasant
characters on the course, and the atmosphere was always friendly; and
two, that I made firm friends with many on the course. That was to be
of great use to me later, as twelve of them became chief constables.

FIFTEEN

Hampshire

I left Bramshill feeling that the world was really going rather nicely. In the meantime Cynthia and I had bought a house at Swanmore, in Hampshire, about half an hour's drive over the downs from Winchester.

'Push him,' my father told Cynthia. 'Go for something a good size.' We took his advice, and in the quality of our accommodation made a quantum leap: we acquired St Helens, a five-bedroom house with a lovely garden extending to an acre – a total change in our lives. Once again the worst difficulty came in moving our children to new schools. Because there was a bit of an overlap, I had to commute to work from our old home for the first two weeks. Nicholas, our elder boy, had already left school, and we got Susie into a school in Southampton; but our second son, Alistair, had to travel to and fro between Hampton and Winchester until we moved.

After convalescing, I started my new job at police headquarters in Winchester. I quickly fell in love with the city and its cathedral: sometimes during my lunch break I would go into that great building and spend time there, letting my mind wander.

One major sadness at that time was the death of my father. His fascination with flying had never wavered: he sold BKS for a handsome amount, but soon found that he was bored, with nothing to do, so he joined another company, Invicta, a smaller airline based in Kent. After a while there he moved to Airbridge Carriers, a cargo firm; he still held his commercial pilot's licence, and held a licence to fly Tridents.

He and my mother had bought a substantial house in New Malden, not far from our own home in Hampton, so we saw a good deal of them before we moved down to Hampshire. Then in 1986 my father fell ill with gall bladder trouble, and was taken into the hospital at Kingston Hill for an operation. Things went badly wrong: he developed blood clots, and although he was sent by ambulance from the private hospital to Kingston Hospital and put in intensive care, it was too late. He died aged only sixty-two – but at least he lived long enough to know that I had been appointed an assistant chief constable in Hampshire.

In only my second or third week with the force, John Duke asked me to go with Cynthia and represent him at a social occasion in the New Forest. I had never done anything like that in the Met, and when I arrived at a large village hall packed with two or three hundred people, and found myself required, as the guest of honour, to make a speech and hand out certificates to scouts, I suddenly realised that being a chief officer in a county force was something entirely different. As a commander in the Met – the rank equivalent to an assistant chief constable – I might have been responsible for running the Flying Squad, and I would have had a very heavy work-load, but I would never have been invited to social events like the big annual agricultural show at Ringwood and numerous boat jamborees at Southampton.

Another agreeable discovery was that we had a great relationship with the Navy at Portsmouth: although the docks and the Navy each had their own police, it was our CID who had to investigate any serious crime such as a murder. Yet another of our tasks was to carry out periodic inspections on the Isle of Wight. There were only two main means of reaching the island – the ferry or a plane – and somehow bush telegraph always conveyed advance news of an impending visit to the inhabitants and to the local police. There was a kind of dare, that no chief officer of police could gain access to the island without local policemen getting wind of his coming: no matter how or when we travelled, they knew we were on our way.

Personnel and training were not the areas I would have chosen: I had been involved in training at the Staff College, but the personnel side was something I had to learn. Apart from anything else, the constabulary was a large one, with a force of 3,600 officers and its own brand-new training school. At the top was the Chief Constable, the formidable John Duke, backed by his deputy John Hoddinott and three of us assistant chief constables, one in charge of administration, one of operations, and myself.

I soon saw that Hampshire was an outstandingly good force, and working for it was a revelation. Duke was a tall, imposing ex-miner from the north-east, who had taken elocution lessons to eliminate his accent. Not for nothing was he known as 'the Iron Duke'. Although never much good on paper, he had a remarkable tenacity of purpose, and once he had made up his mind on an issue, never changed it. He had a reputation for being very tough indeed, but he possessed big skills: he was an innovator, and prepared to take risks, a man who knew how to work the Police Authority and get the best out of it.*

By cultivating the Hampshire Authority, Duke managed, among other successes, to get the funds for a new training school – one of the best in the country. This splendid facility, at Netley, on Southampton Water, was based on what had been an old mental institution and a hospital used for receiving casualties as they came back from the trenches in the First World War. The school was set in beautiful grounds, and included ranges for firearms instruction, as well as areas for training our people in the maintenance of public order. There were two ranges, one underground and one in the open, and all trainees did a lot of coupled shooting – letting off two rounds in succession at close quarters – as well as firing at more distant targets. We worked up new forms of instruction in the use of weapons, designed to help officers assess potentially dangerous opponents in tight corners – the first steps towards the more sophisticated psychological training that came later. The aim was to see if people could handle a firearm in difficult situations.

I myself had been authorised to use weapons for twelve years, having gone through the necessary training at Shepherd's Bush. Even so, I was surprised to find how rough it could be to come under physical attack from a determined opponent. You might be armed with a .38 revolver or a self-loading pistol and blank ammunition, but you had to decide whether or not to fire in self-defence. One of the most important lessons I learnt was that a weapon can sometimes be more of a hindrance than an asset: if a powerful assailant is grappling with you,

---

* The Police Authority is the body which appoints the Chief Constable and his assistants. The members are not themselves police officers, but local politicians, magistrates and other dignitaries. Since the police service is accountable to the Authority, it is essential to have the Authority on your side – otherwise you are in real trouble.

trying to wrest a gun from your grasp, you have to take rapid decisions about how best to deal with him.

Public order sessions could also become pretty violent. A hostile crowd, impersonated by maybe twenty or thirty officers drafted in from nearby police forces, and sometimes including myself, always enjoyed letting off steam; but the mob could seem seriously menacing when they yelled abuse, wielded sticks and started hurling bombs in the form of bottles full of petrol. We taught abseiling, built mocked-up streets, drove cars about and threw everything we could at the trainees, to make sure that if ever they were pitched into the middle of a riot, they would know how to bring it under control. Occasionally people got hurt, but I took the view that unless the training was realistic, it would not produce the results we needed.

I saw that in Hampshire, as well as outside the county, the Chief Constable was regarded as a distinguished figure, and that a good deal of the respect accorded him brushed off on his assistants. He had a rare ability to conceive and implement new ideas: for instance, he was the first to issue officers with woolly pullies. During the miners' strike, which began in March 1984 and lasted a year, Hampshire was the only force that constantly moved its officers round the country by plane to wherever regional support was most needed, and Duke was there on the tarmac at Southampton Airport to greet his men when they came home.

All five of us – the Chief, his deputy and his three assistants – used to meet at nine o'clock every morning in his office, without fail, unless one of us was away (if you were missing, he never asked where you were, because he trusted everybody to make the best use of their time). While he puffed continually on cigarettes, keeping the window open so that the smoke would go out, we would discuss what we proposed to do that day and how we were going to tackle the problems confronting us.

Much of Duke's success derived from the skill with which he handled members of the Police Authority and sold them his vision: for most of the time he was extremely diplomatic – although sometimes he could also win a point by turning tough. Not long before I arrived, Hampshire officers had carried out a big raid on travellers in the New Forest because they were causing so much trouble. Duke sent police in to confiscate all the vehicles that were not in good enough condition to be on the road, and tell the occupants they weren't staying any longer. There was no rough-house, because enough officers took part in the raid to prevent any trouble, and many local people were delighted by the action the force had taken. All the same, the raid raised quite a rumpus in the Authority, especially among Labour members from Portsmouth, who gave Duke a hard time during their next few meetings. He, however, was so skilful at fielding complaints that he soon managed to defuse their hostility.

The way he dealt with the Authority at the monthly meetings which took place in County Hall was an absolute revelation to me, and I saw how important it was for the Chief Constable to establish a good relationship with his opposite numbers: unless he achieved that, he would not get much done. In this respect John Duke excelled.

About an hour before each meeting started, we ourselves held a conference, deciding who would say what. Then, as he discussed matters with members of the Authority, he was always punctilious in the extreme, invariably addressing them as 'sir' or 'madam'. Although he was not much liked by the Labour members, he really hit it off with the Chairman, Captain Michael Boyle, a plump, moustachioed former Irish Guards officer, known to his friends as 'Docker', who had a yacht, a Rolls-Royce, a large country house and excellent champagne. Duke saw how to manage Boyle, and Boyle saw how to manage Duke, and the result was a partnership that made Hampshire one of the best forces in the country.

We had another major asset in the form of John Hoddinott, the deputy chief constable – one of the clearest and most deep-thinking officers of his generation. Guided by him, we had time to discuss things in detail and to plan what we were doing in a way that seemed to become impossible later. We met every day, exchanged ideas, and derived mutual support from each other – a method of working that I later developed in Cambridgeshire and Northumbria, and also at Scotland Yard. I have always found that style very beneficial, because people feed off each other and spark each other off.

Among Duke's innovations was the introduction of the Optica light surveillance aircraft – a strange-looking contraption (which appeared in the James Bond film *You Only Live Twice*) with a bulbous Perspex cockpit and propulsion provided by a large-diameter fan at the back. Shortly before I arrived in Hampshire there had been a fatal accident, when the engine lost power and the plane stalled into a field, killing the pilot and the observer. As a result of the crash, the Optica was under suspicion, and one of the tasks Duke gave me was to assess its safety and potential, working with the chief pilot, Chief Inspector Bob Rupprecht. So it was that I had the pleasant task of putting the little plane through its paces.

The Optica was a delight to fly: it was quiet, slow and man-oeuvrable – it could potter along with the flaps down at 45 knots – and it had tremendous visibility. Our proving flights cleared its reputation, and it came back into operational use – only for it to break down again, when Bob took off from Gosforth and one of the fan blades failed. Luckily he managed to nurse the aircraft back and land it on the field, but again the viability of the design was in doubt, and when the company who had built the plane went into liquidation, that was the end of it. That was sad, because the Optica was a brilliant concept, and a most useful asset: we worked out that it could do 90 per cent of what a helicopter would achieve, at a twentieth of the cost.

Another task that Duke and ACPO gave me was to chair a committee dealing with offender profiling. A series of crimes in Surrey had been linked with others elsewhere, and certain aspects made it look as if all the offences had been committed by the same person, or possibly by two or even three people, who were travelling by train to find their victims, then strangling and raping them. They started by attacking women in parks, jumping out in front of them; then, it seemed, one after another the chief criminal's two associates dropped out, whereupon he carried on alone, and after one woman had reported him, he killed the next three.

In the early stages of the investigation Detective Chief Superintendent Vince McFadden, who was in charge, feared that the case might never be solved, because the crimes were so widely spread over the eastern counties. The police therefore arranged for a psychologist from Surrey University, Professor David Canter, to study the murders and see if he could deduce what character traits the murderer might possess.

This idea – the psychological profiling of offenders – had been advocated by David Powys while I was working with him at the Met, and had been developed in America, but no one in this country had ever really taken it forward. Now Canter, with help from two detectives seconded to him, analysed the railway cases and came up with some remarkable predictions – for instance, that the murderer would be found living within half a mile of the spot at which he had committed his first offence. His reasoning was that the offender would be mentally conditioned by physical boundaries – a motorway, a railway line and a main road, in the middle of which were housing estates – and that he had committed his first crime there because he was comfortable in that environment.

Vince therefore identified what, as far as he could deduce, had been the first crime. This had been committed in West Hampstead, so he studied potential criminals who lived in that area. Canter further predicted that, once the man had made several attacks, he would realise that, if he continued to operate within the same boundaries, he might well be caught. He would therefore extend his activities elsewhere. This, too, fitted the sequence of murders, and led Vince not only to concentrate even more closely on the man's home territory, but also to try and identify how he had travelled from West Hampstead to the scenes of crime. The railway was the obvious means: had the man worked on the railway?

Other clues helped build a picture. The find of a size six shoe – very small for a man – suggested that the murderer was fairly short, probably no more than 5 foot 3. From remarks made to surviving rape victims we knew that he had ginger hair, and that he had some experience of martial arts. He had tied some victims' hands behind their backs by the thumbs with Somyarn, a kind of paper string made in Scandinavia that had gone out of production a couple of years earlier, and he had once blocked a footpath beside a railway line with a length of white plastic monofilament designed to lace up bags of cattle-feed.

In the end it was normal detective and forensic work that led to one individual, John Duffy, who, sure enough, lived in West Hampstead: the police put him under twenty-four-hour surveillance, and although he did not commit any more crimes while being watched, he did visit all the scenes of his earlier attacks, clearly in search of more victims.

Eventually the evidence collected from his various homes proved over-whelming, and he was gaoled for life; but the help given by Professor Canter, and the profile he built up, certainly narrowed what might have been an impossibly wide search.

So successful had the psychological exercise been that it was decided to extend the work by bringing over American experts and forming a committee that included them and Canter, with myself acting as chair. After a meeting at Surrey Police headquarters in Godalming we decided that the initiative was well worth pursuing: Canter was commissioned to carry out further research, and we set up a series of protocols to give ourselves a framework within which to operate. A second member of Surrey University, Dr Jennifer Brown, who had come to Hampshire to deal with other psychological issues, became secretary of the committee – and that was the beginning of the offender profile research work, which lasted for ten years and proved extremely interesting. At first we made fairly rapid progress, but problems started when other psychologists became involved, and there was conflict between them and Canter, who, though highly intelligent, tended to dismiss other people's ideas peremptorily, and often rubbed them up the wrong way. Later he and I, together with a couple of other colleagues, went to Moscow to discuss offender profiling with Russian scientists and police officers. They told us, among other things, that they used physical ugliness as an indicator of criminality, but all went well until one night when one of the group started trying to sell us doubtful antiques – at which point I said, as politely as possible, 'I think it's time we went to bed.'

John Hoddinott made no secret of the fact that he wanted to be Chief, especially when Duke's health began to decline, and there was sometimes friction between them, although John was always a loyal deputy. Eventually Duke had a stroke during one of our meetings: he left the office, went into the toilet and didn't come back – so we had to go and get him out. A worse difficulty was to smuggle him out of the building without anyone else knowing what had happened. He was passing in and out of consciousness, so five of us carried him downstairs to a waiting ambulance, which took him to hospital.

He recovered from that setback, but then, shortly after he retired he suffered a worse stroke. Together with Brian Davis, the assistant chief constable in charge of administration, I went to see him in hospital. To our distress, we found that although he could obviously understand what we were saying, he could not speak.

John Hoddinott took over, and when he was appointed Chief Constable, I tried for the post of deputy that he had just vacated. In due course the job went to Michael Mylod – and the fact that I had failed to get it reinforced my belief that I should move on to another force.

Hoddinott encouraged me to stay on in Hampshire, saying how much he enjoyed working with me, but I was determined to push ahead and go for a deputy chief's position.

The mainspring of success in Hampshire was the team at the top, and its team captain, the radical Duke, supported by the clear-thinking Hoddinott. It was their skill in managing change that made any innovations acceptable, both inside the force and out. One positive result of my time with them was that I worked out a style that I thought I should follow if ever I became a chief constable. The first essential was regular consultation with the senior team, and another was listening to what the force wanted. A third indispensable ingredient was the vigorous, and if necessary ruthless, pursuit of issues that I knew were right and that I knew would produce better policing. Delivery on the streets was all important.

Presently I was faced with a difficult career decision. I was offered a place on a year-long course at the Royal College of Defence Studies – a high-level affair designed primarily for officers in the armed services who were destined for senior command. The offer was tempting, since the course would include opportunities for travel all over the world, and would give me an insight into the defence arrangements made by many different countries. After some deliberation, however, I decided to stick to my plan and go for a deputy chief constable's job.

SIXTEEN
Deputy Chief Constable

My first target was a vacancy in Wiltshire, for which four of us were short-listed. I knew my chances were slight, because one of the other candidates, Alan Elliott – a friend who had been on the Senior Command Course with me – flew back from America especially for the final interview, and as he was very friendly with the Chief Constable, Wally Girven, the dice were clearly loaded in his favour.

The interviews took place in the senior officers' mess in the Wiltshire headquarters: I went in first, and shook hands with the chairman and other members of the Police Authority, and everyone seemed friendly enough. But when Alan came in, the chairman gave him a positively glowing welcome, hustling straight across and exclaiming, 'It's really good of you to come all the way across from the States!' The rest of us exchanged secret smiles, feeling sure we could see which way things were going – and sure enough, Alan was the winner. I am sure that was the right decision.

The next job I went for was in Cambridgeshire, where the Chief Constable was Ian Kane, a tough former leader of the Special Patrol Group in the Met, with a great reputation on the rugby field and a liking for a pint – a real, no-nonsense police officer. His deputy Alan Radcliffe – a big, powerful, square-built fellow who had also come from the Met – was an expert in public order, and had dealt with various disturbances and demonstrations at the American air base at Molesworth, when protesters were evicted from an unofficial camp. The vacancy was caused by the fact that he had landed a job in the Cayman Islands.

At that stage I didn't know Ian Kane, but because he was quite friendly with John Hoddinott, I decided to have a go. John encouraged me. Kane would be a good man to work for, he said. Cambridgeshire was a good force, although a small one, with 1,200 police officers only about a third as big as Hampshire. I therefore applied for the job – but so did a lot of other people. In those days there seemed to be a glut of senior officers putting in for the top posts.

In Hampshire there had been twenty-two applicants. This time there were twelve, with some talented starters among them. There was Keith Povey, who later became Chief Constable of Leicestershire, Chief HMI and a lifelong friend. Ted Crew, who became Chief Constable of the West Midlands; and David Blakey, later Chief Constable of West Mercia and President of the Association of Chief Police Officers. Besides them, another three or four also reached the rank of chief constable. Up against such opposition, I didn't fancy my chances.

The interviews were quite different from those in Wiltshire or Hampshire. We met at the Police Headquarters, near the hospital in Huntingdon, and at the dinner the night before we all moved round from one table to another, so that members of the Police Authority could talk to as many candidates as possible. On the interview board, besides Ian Kane, was Jack King, the Provost and Bursar of Wolfson College. Today he is a good friend, but I did not know him then, and he really tried to stir me up by talking about 'the arrogance of the Met'. 'How would you ever deliver here, coming from a background like that?' he demanded. I knew he was just trying to wind me up, because Kane, the local boss, was another Met man, and so was Alan Radcliffe, whom I was hoping to replace. Even so, I had to keep my wits about me in the effort to remain calm.

The interview proved a tough one, lasting over an hour, and the questions were wide-ranging. Why was I trying for Cambridgeshire? What were the strengths of the country force? What was its financial position? (That was an awkward one, because the force, although effective, was not well-funded at that stage.) Luckily I had spent weeks boning up on these very subjects. I had found out in advance that the deputy chief constable was in charge of administration, personnel and training, strategic planning and discipline, besides liaising with the Police Authority – in other words, that he was a one-man show, and that his knowledge had to be extensive.

After that grilling, half a dozen of us gathered in the deputy chief constable's office and sat waiting to hear the result. Then I was called back in, and I was amazed to hear that I was being offered the job. It really was a big surprise, because I had made up my mind that one or other of such talented competitors must get the prize.

Promotion meant yet another domestic upheaval: we had to leave our lovely house in Hampshire and look for new accommodation in a place I hardly knew. Nicholas, our eldest son, was on his way round the world, looking at prospects in the building trade, and Alistair was starting on an English degree at Leicester University; but Susie was just coming up to her O levels, living at home, and would need the best school we could find for her.

We were sad to leave St Helens – and when we began trying to sell it, we found that the market had gone very slack. As a stop-gap, I went to live in the officers' mess at RAF Brampton, the Headquarters of Support Command, where Ian Kane had a good relationship with the Air Chief Marshal. For me, Brampton was seventh heaven. Not only was I lucky enough to live in a comfortable mess for several months and get to know some of the officers: I also had numerous chances to go flying, in Jet Provosts, in a Canberra, in helicopters, and (once) in a Jaguar fighter-bomber.

The family's girls were not so lucky. For the time being Cynthia had to stay in the south on her own. In Cambridgeshire, the only dwelling that became available was a police officer's house just outside the village of Bluntisham, in the Fens. The place was old, small and basic: there were mice under the floorboards, and the central heating was erratic, to say the least. When heavy lorries came grinding up the road that curled round the hill, they made the whole building shake. But we managed: Susie had her room upstairs, and we transformed a ground-floor room on one side, which had been used as the police office, into a bedroom for Nicholas when he returned from Australia.

The one amusing feature of life there was the fact that people often thought the house was still the local police station: they would stop on the main road, walk up the short approach, and ask the way to their destination, or try to get their firearms certificate renewed. One weekend a woman appeared asking for help in rescuing her cat, which had got stuck up a tree – so naturally I went along.

When we agreed to take the house, we did not expect to be there very long; but as things turned out, we lived there, on and off, for nearly two years, and although in the end we did manage to sell St Helens, we made no money on the deal, barely getting what we had paid for it.

I had no break between jobs: I went straight from Winchester to Huntingdon, and arrived at a moment when the Cambridgeshire force had just been through a major reorganisation. Reassessment of the changes was in progress, and, unlike in Hampshire, where the top team had been five strong, here we had only three – chief, deputy and assistant – so that there was a lot of work for me to do.

Geographically, the force is challenging: there are two big centres of population – Cambridge itself, and Peterborough – and a large area very thinly populated – the Fens. It was to the university city that we ourselves gravitated, and we ended up buying a house in Huntingdon Road. The force had no purpose-built training school; but within the headquarters compound there was a set of offices that we used for a bit of training, and there I initiated leadership courses for sergeants and inspectors.

I found Ian Kane quite different from John Duke. Duke was tough, but he was absolutely determined to get on with the Police Authority, and, as I say, handled its members with the utmost courtesy. Kane, in contrast, might just switch off if someone asked a question that he did not like. Rather than prevaricate or contradict, he would simply not answer. This habit was naturally disconcerting for members of the Authority, and for journalists who came to interview him – but it was quite a useful tactic, which, I have to admit, I have used myself on rare occasions.

Kane and his deputy had put into practice several new ideas, not least what was called 'activity analysis', which involved assessing per-formance in terms of money spent. In Hampshire we had met the Police Authority in County Hall; but here we met at Police Head-quarters. My particular responsibilities lay in maintaining the link with the Authority, in drawing up strategic plans, and above all in supervising the finances. Along with Norfolk, Cambridge was one of the least well funded forces in the country, and as there was little chance of increasing our budget, we had to look for every way of using what money we had more effectively.

These contrasting tasks widened my experience, which I knew would stand me in good stead if ever I became a chief constable, and I enjoyed my time in Cambridgeshire. However, I had been in the post less than a year when there came an entirely new call on my time: a request to go and work in Northern Ireland.

SEVENTEEN
Northern Ireland

Ian Kane's office was next to mine, and we shared the same toilet, which was off a short passage linking the two rooms. Occasionally, if nature happened to call us both at the same moment, a minor traffic jam would occur – and he, as the chief, always had precedence. One beautiful autumn morning, 12 September 1989, as I emerged from my office, he said casually, 'Oh, by the way, Hugh Annesley wants to speak to you.'

The message instantly put me on edge: Annesley was Chief Constable of the Royal Ulster Constabulary, and there had recently been a tremendous furore in the Northern Ireland press about alleged collusion between the security services and Protestant paramilitaries, principally the Ulster Defence Army.

'Sir,' I said to Kane, 'can you tell me what it's about?'

'No,' he replied. 'I'd rather you spoke to Hugh Annesley first.'

That was typical of Kane: he was always absolutely fair, and did not want to prejudice any decision I might take.

I knew Annesley slightly, as I had met him when, as Assistant Commissioner, Crime, he had chaired the panel holding the Senior Command Course extended interviews at Bramshill. Now I rang him, and he lost no time in putting his proposition.

'You obviously know we've got this problem,' he said. 'I want to set up an independent inquiry to establish exactly what's happening. It should only take four or five weeks. Would you be prepared to undertake it? And could you get a team together?'

'Well, sir,' I said, playing for time, 'may I think about it?'

It was hardly the best moment for me to be faced with a momentous decision. Cynthia and I had moved into our little police house only

147

the day before: we had no carpets on the floors, we were using packing cases for chairs and tables, and the central heating wasn't working properly. Although Cynthia accepted that my career must come first, she was never happy when my work kept me away from home for extended periods, and now suddenly she had landed in alien surroundings, far less comfortable than the ones she had been used to – and immediately she was faced with the possibility that I might disappear, to work in a hostile and dangerous environment.

'What do *you* think?' I asked Ian Kane. 'Are you prepared to let me go?'

'Yes,' he replied. 'For you, with your CID background, it's a real opportunity. I think you'd do a good job over there.'

'All right,' I said. 'I'll speak to Cynthia.'

I rang her, went and saw her, and explained what I had been asked to do. I said I thought it would be a great challenge, and extremely interesting, and if the job only took four or five weeks, it wouldn't be too bad for either of us. As always, she backed me and trusted me to make the right decision.

Back in Ian Kane's office, I said, 'Look – yes: I'm prepared to do this. But I want to make sure I take over with me absolutely the best people I can get. The Ulster situation is obviously very difficult – headline news every day – and I'm going to need people of the highest calibre.'

He agreed – and my thoughts flew to some of the most able people I'd worked with: Vince McFadden, head of the Surrey CID; Detective Superintendent Laurie Sherwood, who had been in the Met and had come on to Cambridgeshire, and others. Kane said, 'Right, I'll ring the chief constables of the people you want. I'll also speak to John Smith at the Met, to make sure you get the support you need.'

'In that case,' I replied, 'I'll do it.'

For the first time in my life I had the opportunity of selecting people whose abilities I respected, and who, I knew, would do a superb job. When I began ringing round, I got an almost universally enthusiastic response: of the ten people I called, only two declined to join the party – and I did not blame them, for at that time Northern Ireland was seen as an exceedingly dangerous place. Police officers were losing their lives. Protestant and Catholic citizens were being murdered.

Whenever anybody agreed to come, I asked him or her the same question: 'Can you select one or two of the best people you know, and get them on board as well?' So the call went out for a total of nearly thirty. As soon as I knew I had the necessary backing, I rang Annesley and told him I was on. He then said, 'I want to get this started straight away. Will you come over tomorrow?'

On the evening of 14 September Laurie and I flew to Belfast. Because we didn't know quite what we were going to have to do, prudence was required, and we decided to go via Luton, rather than Heathrow, travelling under assumed names. I was Mr Pollock, and Laurie was Mr Rogers. To make sure there would be no snags, Laurie had telephoned the Special Branch at Luton and warned them that he and the Deputy Chief Constable of Cambridgeshire would be flying out incognito. 'Can you make sure that your guy on the desk there knows what's happening?' he asked.

Somehow the message failed to get through. The officer on duty stopped us and wanted to see some identification. Of course, we hadn't got anything that matched our pseudonyms: no passports were needed for visiting Northern Ireland, and we weren't on a deep undercover mission, but simply wanted to keep our real names off the passenger list. When Laurie suggested the duty officer need not bother, he became very suspicious. Then Laurie asked him, 'Did you not get a message from Cambridgeshire about people coming through?' – whereupon he turned bright red and hastily ushered us past, by which time everyone else in the line was staring at us.

In the departure lounge we ran into Ken Masterson, who had been the director of the Junior Command Course at Bramshill while I was there, and now was an assistant chief constable in the RUC. When I said, 'Hi, Ken,' he shot me a look with his twinkly blue eyes and said quietly, 'I don't think I should be speaking to you, John. You've got a very, very difficult job to do there. It might turn into something bigger than you think.'

It was not a very auspicious start – and things got even worse when the aircraft, still on the ground, filled with smoke. The captain closed the engines down and asked everyone to keep calm, saying, 'We think it'll clear,' and after a while it did; but because we were setting off to plan a secret inquiry in Northern Ireland, we were ready to see sinister possibilities in any slight irregularity.

At Belfast we were met by Detective Sergeant Grahame Foote, who had looked after John Stalker while he was in Northern Ireland, acting as his liaison officer and bodyguard. A splendidly calm, laconic character in his late forties, he now became my driver and personal protection officer: tall, very slim – almost gaunt – with receding dark hair, he drove his big Ford Granada at 100 m.p.h., leaning far back in the seat, with his revolver in the well beside him. I couldn't have found a more loyal or efficient helper. (I had considered arming myself. Having retrained on firearms to marksman level, I had carried a gun during my time at Cambridge, but I never took it to Northern Ireland, because I had no permission to do so. Instead, I left it with the driver at Luton or Heathrow, and relied on Grahame when I got to the other side.)

That first evening we saw Hugh Annesley, who was exactly as I remembered him – tall, charming, articulate, with a gentle southern Irish accent. He told me he was under heavy pressure, mainly from local politicians, to commission an independent inquiry; he confirmed that our task would last little more than a month, and that our brief was to investigate the theft of montages from the charge room and administrative offices at Dunmurry police station.

The montages were A4-sized posters, each carrying photographs of six or eight individuals and basic information about them, which had been produced by the Army and police for briefing their men on patrol about suspects on whom the authorities wanted to keep an eye; but some of them had been stolen by Protestant paramilitaries, who considered that anybody appearing on them was automatically an IRA terrorist, and could then be shot. '*It is said*,' Annesley told us, putting emphasis on those words, 'that it was probably police officers who stole the montages, and it's constantly been on the national news. No doubt you need offices, transport and so on . . .'

Laurie and I checked in at the Culloden Hotel, and over a beer we began to realise how complex our task might turn out to be. We already knew in a general way that the affair had ruffled a good many feathers; but until we reached Northern Ireland we didn't realise quite how hot the subject had become. Television and newspapers were absolutely full of it: the credibility of the RUC and the security services in general was under intense fire, and suddenly we could feel the heat all round us.

It struck me that the decision to issue the montages at all was a difficult one: the documents might help the security authorities gather intelligence about terrorists, but if they fell into the wrong hands – as they had – they would be tantamount to death-warrants for anyone whose photo and details appeared on them. Yet it was not our business to criticise past actions of the RUC: rather, our remit was to find out who was colluding with whom.

Next morning we had an appointment with the Assistant Commissioner, Crime, Wilfie Monaghan, who was going to be our link with the RUC, and would sort out our accommodation. We met him at ten o'clock on another lovely autumn morning – a delightful man with sparkling blue eyes and enormous charm, immediately amusing, quick in speech and in his movements. As we entered his office, we had hardly closed the door behind us before he said, 'John, you really do need to know that you've come into a can of worms.'

That phrase lodged in my mind, and it has nagged at me ever since. 'From a personal point of view,' Wilfie told us, 'I want to make sure that you succeed, because our force cannot afford another fiasco like Stalker. I give you my word that we'll do whatever is necessary to help you get to the truth.'

A can of worms? What was he talking about? At that stage Laurie and I had no clue. All we knew for sure was that no independent inquiry before ours had ever succeeded in unravelling the truth about what was going on in the Province, and reputations had been destroyed. Clearly, we would have to be fairly penetrating and tenacious in our inquiries.

Wilfie began talking about where we should establish our operational base. He told us of two or three possible locations, one of which was the place from which Stalker had worked. For obvious reasons I didn't want to go there. We then suggested that we might work out of the Army camp at Hollywood Barracks – at which Wilfie said starkly, 'If you go in there, they'll burn you down.' We laughed at that, but not with much conviction. The third alternative was a place called Sea Park, a secure complex, extending to seventeen acres, in which the Belfast Police Authority had its headquarters. Wilfie also gave us some of his best CID officers to assist.

In the meantime, Hugh Annesley and his publicity chief, Bill

McGookin, decided that I should make a brief appearance on television; so, together with Laurie, I went in front of the cameras outside the RUC headquarters in Knock Road and said that I had come to do a job of work on behalf of the Chief Constable. 'We will do what is necessary,' I promised. 'We'll go where the evidence takes us – and now I had better get on with it.'

Short as it was, the clip made headline news, and my phrase 'where the evidence takes us' was picked up everywhere – but after that we decided that we would say nothing else to the media. We would just press ahead with our inquiry, and let the results speak for themselves. The only other appearance I made on television came a few weeks later, when I allowed a camera to film me as I sat at my desk and read documents. But our reticence did not keep us out of the newspapers or off television. Far from it: over the next weeks and months there was constant derogatory rumour, speculation and innuendo about what we were doing; but, rather than try to counter the propaganda, we simply kept our heads down and got on with the job. I decided that actions would speak louder than words.

For the first two or three days, before the rest of the team came out. Laurie and I went round assessing the various sites for our base, and our clear choice fell on Sea Park. Much work was needed to set up an incident room there: telephones and computers had to be installed, and secure communications with the mainland put in place. We also had to decide – with the agreement of the RUC – where the team should stay, and we selected the Tedworth Hotel in Bangor, partly on Grahame Foote's recommendation. 'Bangor is safe,' he assured us cheerfully. 'We haven't had a bomb there for six months.' In his terms that indicated total security, but to us it was hardly reassuring.

With preliminary arrangements in place, Laurie and I flew back to Luton, spent the weekend sorting out our domestic affairs, and then, on the Monday, flew into Belfast with the rest of the team. Our hosts repeatedly told us to be careful about our own security, and on our first night in the hotel at Bangor we had a lecture from Grahame and others about the dangers of the environment. Not surprisingly, one or two of the team were very nervous: after my short television interview, all the political parties and paramilitary organisations knew we were in town, and some of them bitterly resented our arrival. The atmosphere was extremely unpleasant, but, knowing that my team would need leadership, I was determined not to show any lack of confidence. Privately, however, I did feel professionally challenged by the scale of the task ahead.

As British police officers working across the water, we had none of our normal powers. In particular, we had no power of arrest: having taken legal advice, we learnt we could detain people only through the RUC. That was where Wilfie Monaghan came up trumps: we found we could trust him totally, and although warnings were leaked before one or two of our operations, anything organised by him remained absolutely secure.

As part of our induction, we were given a presentation by the Army, in the headquarters at Lisburn, during which one of the staff officers, a colonel, and his top team told us categorically that the Army never ran agents of any kind in Northern Ireland. In that respect, then, we thought we knew how things stood.

We started collecting evidence by doing basic detective work – finding documents and fingerprinting them. Many had been photo-copied, and forensic examination revealed that several had been copied on the same machine. We therefore seized photocopiers, and found (for instance) that two documents had been photostatted on the copier at the Shankill Road headquarters of the UDA.

As our inquiries progressed, hoax calls started to pour in. Then a soldier serving in Germany wrote anonymously to the *Sun* newspaper, enclosing a montage, and saying that it was easy to get hold of these things. Forensic examination of his cover note revealed his address, indented in the paper (but invisible without special equipment), which he had carelessly written on a sheet of paper on top of it. We therefore sent people over to Germany, arrested him and brought him back to Belfast. Quite quickly the trail led to other people who had been involved in the thefts, and we recovered several of the stolen posters.

Soon, however, we realised that there was more involved than had at first been apparent. The key to our breakthrough was analysis of fingerprints on the montages and other captured documents. This was organised by Detective Superintendent Jim Barkas, a member of the team and an old friend. We sent the material back to Scotland Yard, where, with the agreement of John Smith, the assistant commissioner, crime, a special team was set up to deal with them. The bulk of the work – paid for by the RUC – was done by an expert called Roger Shern. The systems in use at the Yard were far more advanced than anywhere else in the world, and ahead of those of the RUC. At the Yard the unit had an eighteen-stage method for detecting prints, and this often yielded evidence of which the RUC had found no trace. Identification of handwriting was carried out in Birmingham, and all the ESDA testing – electrostatic examination which reveals the indentation produced by handwriting, even if it is invisible to the naked eye – was done in Surrey.

Our fingerprint evidence goaded the RUC into more efficient action. Until then, their officers had tended to interrogate a prisoner superficially and come out saying, 'It's a waste of time. He doesn't know anything about so-and-so.' Now we could give them a copy of a document and say, 'See what he knows about *this*.' Out would come the officer again. 'No – he denies he's ever seen it.' 'Then ask him how his fingerprints come to be on it.'

The identifications from prints enabled us to make more arrests. It turned out that two of the suspects accused of taking the montages were Ulster Defence Regiment men, and as our own intelligence base built up, we got more and more information about UDR involvement. During the third week of our investigation I decided that we were going to go a step further and do some searches, first to discover where the rest of the montages were – we had been told that certain people were holding them – and second, to find the guns that had been used to assassinate some of the paramilitaries' victims.

After the shooting of the Catholic Loughlin McGinn in August 1989, word had gone round that he was not part of PIRA, the Provisional IRA – whereupon the head of the Ulster Defence Association, Tucker Lyttle, had immediately countered with, 'Oh yes, he's definitely a PIRA man. We know that from the security services, and the montages prove that this man is wanted.'

This inadvertent disclosure showed us that, beyond doubt, the UDA was suspect. We therefore set up more searches, and began to find 'int dumps' (intelligence dumps) where the terrorists had cached little stores of documents and photographs, often in conjunction with weapons, sometimes in derelict buildings, sometimes in the lofts of inhabited houses. These dumps gave details of opposition players they wanted to attack. Furthermore, different dumps sometimes contained particulars of the same person: we would find an original P-card (personality card), with photograph and written details, and then a photocopy of it elsewhere. This showed that somewhere there must be a central source from which the information was being disseminated.

One morning we mounted a large-scale search operation, backed by armoured cars and a whole fleet of RUC Land-Rovers. I myself briefed about 250 RUC officers, and as I was walking through the yard of the station at Castlereagh with Jim Barkas and Laurie Sherwood I said, 'This looks like something in the Second World War.' Jim turned round and said, 'Yes, John, and you've started it!' Although said as a joke, the remark sent a shiver through me. I was not as confident as I appeared, and was aware of the anger that our actions would arouse.

I had certainly started something. For the RUC to be searching the homes of members of the UDR – another arm of the security apparatus – was unheard of. For me, a still more disquieting element was the fact that some senior RUC officers had tried to block our plans to make the searches, pointing out that this would be a very dangerous step to take. 'After all, we're fighting a battle against the IRA,' they said, 'and the UDR are supposed to be helping us.' A further consideration was that our action would infuriate the Protestant leader Ian Paisley. Altogether, it was a difficult issue, which ended only when I went to see Hugh Annesley and told him that what we were about to do was essential. He backed us, which could not have been easy.

So the searches went ahead, and they proved our point: our main quarry was weapons, and some of the illegal firearms that we found had been used to shoot people portrayed on the montages, as well as other Catholic targets. One was the 9mm-P Browning that had fired most of the rounds that killed the prominent Belfast solicitor Patrick Finucane, who was gunned down by a hail of bullets on his own doorstep on Sunday, 12 February 1989. Another had been used in the murder of Loughlin McGinn. The documents we discovered along with the weapons yielded much useful intelligence.

It must be remembered that we had no assistance in our intelligence-gathering – a business that we were learning fast. It was fingerprints that gave us our breakthrough: from the identifications that came back from the Yard, we started to build up our own intelligence base.

We were working extraordinary hours – often sixteen a day – and we seemed to be making big advances in a very short time. Nevertheless, the days flew past: Hugh Annesley had assured me that our job would be over in a month, but October, November and December came and went, and we were still only getting into our stride.

It took us months to crack the question of where all this mixture of intelligence and propaganda was coming from. Then up came the fingerprints of a man called Brian Nelson. We decided we would like to have a look at this Nelson, but when I spoke to Wilfie Monaghan about it, I could see he was in difficulties. He referred me to Brian Fitzsimmons, the Acting Head of the RUC's Special Branch, and, together with Vince McFadden, I went to see him. I had already met Fitzsimmons several times, and at one point he had told me he was getting criticism on the grounds that he had allowed us to build up our own intelligence system and network. This was true – but what people didn't realise was that we were using fingerprints, rather than intercepts or word of mouth, to increase our knowledge, so that we knew for sure, rather than from rumours, who had handled what documents or photographs. By that stage we had a list of about a dozen people whom we wanted to detain.

When we told Fitzsimmons that we had found Nelson's fingerprints on stolen documents, we were met with a blank refusal to cooperate. Fitzsimmons became evasive, to say the least. 'We can't help you with this man,' he told me. 'We don't know where he is.' This was very disturbing, especially as members of the RUC's CID had been working with us and giving us assistance.

Our suspicions about Nelson intensified when we sent people round to various RUC collators' offices, to look through their intelligence card system and see what it contained. At the Grosvenor Road station we found a card bearing Nelson's details, describing him as 'Chief Intelligence Officer for the UDA/UFF' (Ulster Freedom Fighters). When our man asked for a copy of the card, it was whipped away, and he was told he couldn't have it. He promptly rang our incident room and spoke to Vince McFadden.

'You stay where you are,' Vince told him. 'Don't move till I get down there.' He went straight over and demanded a copy of the card. He was told that a senior RUC officer had vetoed the request. Persisting, Vince eventually went high enough up the chain of command for someone to authorise a copy.

So we found out who Nelson was, what he had done, and his address. We learnt that he was a convicted criminal who had been sentenced to seven years for torturing a mentally and physically retarded Catholic. The fact that he had picked a soft target gave some idea of how vicious he was.

Yet it seemed that he was not entirely without remorse. In 1986, after he had helped the paramilitaries target a man called Harry Fitzsimmons, who was shot and gravely injured, he became disgusted with himself. Feeling no better than the terrorists around him – and no doubt also alarmed that the world was closing in on him – he went to Germany, where he worked at laying floors. A year later the Army's secret Force Research Unit lured him back to Northern Ireland with the promise of a substantial retainer, and he helped target another Harry – Harry Maynes, a cab-driver – by agreeing to act as the trigger-man (not the one who does the actual shooting, but the one who drives out to ensure that the victim is where he should be, and then comes up to give the CQA – Close-Quarter Assassination squad – the thumbs-up). For various reasons the operation had to be aborted, but there was no doubt about Nelson's involvement.

Now that we had fresh evidence of criminal activity on his part, we planned a major hit for the following Monday morning: at dawn we would seize him and eight or ten others. I cleared the operation with Hugh Annesley, and geared up an RUC team to come with us and make the actual arrests. Among our assistants were some of the excellent people from the CID who had been feeding us information. Everything was set for a major showdown at dawn – but on the day before (as I recounted in chapter One) we found that reporters had got wind of the raid, so we put it off for twenty-four hours; and then on the night of 10 January our incident room was burnt out.

EIGHTEEN
Digging In

From the start, our existence in Belfast had been anything but comfortable. At one stage, because of threats relayed to us by Grahame Foote, I had had to move to a different hotel every three days, and the sense of danger was ever-present. After the fire we all went to live, as well as to work, in the RUC's heavily fortified police station on Antrim Road, where the whole perimeter was sealed with barbed wire, or by walls topped with wire, and there were reinforced-steel gates at the entrance. One of the instructions we received was that we should never turn right as we went out of the gates, because the road led to an area designated dangerous. In other circumstances the instruction would have sounded fairly innocuous, but to people who had just been driven out of their former headquarters by an arson attack, it served to heighten tension still further.

As always, my foremost concern was the welfare of my people, who were frequently at risk: from the information that reached us intermittently, we knew that there were terrorists who, if they got the opportunity, would take us out. The moment at which I became most seriously alarmed was the one when we discovered an alliance between Protestant paramilitaries and the IRA – a sinister combination, which we came across when we were investigating the murders of John McMichael, the head of the UFF, and James Pratt Craig, the high-living boss of the Southern UFF. We found that Craig had been meeting PIRA people and carving up territory for the purposes of blackmail and extortion: it was alleged that he had propped McMichael up to be shot by PIRA. In the end his intrigues did him no good, because he too was killed by PIRA, who put a bomb under his car.

Among our team, nerves were further frayed by anxiety about what might be happening at home in the absence of the head of the household. For operational reasons weekend leave often had to be cancelled at short notice, and sometimes our people were stuck on duty for three weeks at a time. Even when somebody did get back on a Saturday, he hardly had time to wind down before he started worrying about his return by the 8 a.m. flight on Monday morning. Another factor was the stress on the families themselves: inevitably they were anxious about what might happen in Belfast, and their anxieties were reflected in members of the team.

Everyone remained totally loyal, but one or two became quite twitchy from the stress of operating in such an unpleasant environment; and the pressure was naturally increased by the fact that it was the security forces – the vast majority of whom were the good guys – whom we were investigating.

Our accommodation was far from ideal, and our existence was highly claustrophobic. There was no question of going out for a meal, or even for a drink in a pub – for pubs were among the most dangerous places in the Province – and we had to rely on our own company for entertainment. Occasionally we would bring in a Chinese meal, but when we did, we ordered from a different restaurant every time.

The station's décor was abysmal, and the heavy windows of armoured glass would hardly open. I had a small cell of a bedroom for myself, but everyone else lived in little rooms coming off a central corridor. We had a common room, a room where we could do some cooking, and one other where we could sit together. At first we sometimes went down to eat in the RUC mess, but later we tended to buy food in the canteen on the ground floor and take it up to our own quarters on the second – a move prompted by a big press story to the effect that after we had done searches at Castlereagh, we had gone into the RUC canteen there, only to find the company singing 'We Didn't Start the Fire', the popular song by Billy Joel.

The only occasions on which we went out of the police station were to search for terrorists, and we always moved with heavy protection (at one stage the RUC told us we could not even go in and out of the station except in armoured cars). We found it ironic that the typists and civilians who supported us were paid danger money, and were ferried in and out by enclosed, armoured Land-Rovers.

As for telephones – we knew that any call might be intercepted and overheard, and the contents published in some newspaper. Even when somebody rang his wife, he couldn't tell her that he was catching the five o'clock flight: each family devised a code of its own for passing this kind of information, and kept the secret formula to itself, so that if somebody listening in cracked one code, he could not crack them all. Every single action we took had to be thought out in advance: was it really necessary? And what reaction might it produce? One of the conditions of employment for members of the team was that they did not mix with the public, or with each other in a public place.

We could never tell who was listening, who was watching. We once sent a car into a Protestant area to get a statement from a widow after the murder of her husband. The vehicle – an armoured but unmarked Granada – parked outside the woman's house, and very soon, while our party was inside the house, two boys appeared at one end of the street, then two at the other. Soon there were three and three. The driver of the car reported that he had been spotted, and we had to deploy a large number of soldiers, just to pull our people out safely.

Even when interviewing terrorists, we could not proceed in a normal police manner. We told them as little as possible, because every bit of information they gleaned might be of use to them in the future. Anti-terrorist legislation overruled the codes of practice laid down by PACE (the Police and Criminal Evidence Act of 1984), so that although PACE had been in use for some time on the mainland, in Northern Ireland it was only just coming in; but we were dealing with PACE prisoners, and it was clear that they were operating by a different set of rules.

The strain of living and working in Belfast was increased by all the small aggravations contrived by people who resented our presence. One wet night, as we were setting off for a break on the mainland, our aircraft was rolling towards the end of the runway for take-off when it came to a halt. Because of a bomb-warning, which turned out to be a hoax, we all had to get out into the pouring rain while a search was made. Our suitcases came out too, and they also were soaked. Eventually we went back on board and took off – but it was the only time that we had ever known such a thing happen.

Another Friday night, as we were returning in convoy to the barracks in Antrim Road to pick up our bags for a weekend trip to the mainland, we came on a big dust-cart ablaze outside the main gate. Sharp right turn, round the back of the compound to the other gate, and what should we find, but two clowns in balaclavas framing about in the street, one with an Armalite and the other with a hand-gun. We had no option but to carry on and go straight to the airport, leaving our luggage behind.

Our activities received an amazing amount of attention in the media, and the UDA put out a constant stream of propaganda in attempts to ridicule and belittle what we were doing. Even when we had convicted twenty or thirty people, they still tried, to an extraordinary degree, to denigrate our activities. We were achieving nothing, they said. We were arresting the wrong people. Our inquiry was a complete waste of time and money.

As part of their campaign they sent some montages to the *Sun* newspaper, and plastered others across walls in Loyalist areas of Belfast: on one hoarding they stuck up a picture of me at my desk, taken from the brief TV interview, with the slogan STEVENS READS WHILE ULSTER BLEEDS. In thinking that they could see us off, they failed to realise that, far from undermining our morale, their insults were merely deepening our resolve to get to the bottom of the morass.

As I say, the sole result of the fire was to increase our determination still further, and before dawn on the morning after it, in company with detectives and uniformed officers from the RUC, we went out and arrested our suspects. Tucker Lyttle turned out to be a relatively gentle person. In interrogating him, we were inhibited by the fact that he had a heart condition, so that we had to have a doctor examine him frequently, to make sure that he was fit to carry on. Unlike the real thugs of the movement, the trigger-men, he had met politicians and liked to talk at high level: he fancied himself as a kind of Protestant Gerry Adams. He certainly enjoyed talking to Laurie, which he did at length, to our considerable benefit.

That Nelson eluded us for the time being was a major disappointment, but I insisted that we should continue to pursue him. Through our local CID contacts we heard that he had decamped to England because he was a double-agent, and working for some organisation based on the mainland. This made us exceedingly angry. We had been hot on his trail, frustrated only by some of the security forces' refusal to cooperate.

Confronting Wilfie Monaghan and Brian Fitzsimmons, I said, 'I'm sorry, but this man's got to be arrested, wherever he may be. If necessary we'll send people to the address where we think he may be in England, and pick him up there. Then we can bring him back over.'

It was clear that both men were caught in an extremely awkward position – but they could not tell me why. All Wilfie could say was, 'Well, we'll see what we can do. But this is very difficult.' I could see that he was struggling, but I couldn't tell exactly what his problem was.

In any case, we were soon tipped off that, after a short visit to the mainland, Nelson had come back to Belfast, and in due course we brought him in. He was not an inspiring specimen: in his late thirties, tall, thin, with mousy brown hair, wearing glasses, a chain-smoker and a heavy drinker, highly nervous, always shaking, obviously living on the edge. As soon as we arrested him, he wanted to talk, to impress on us that he had been acting on behalf of the British Government; so I asked Vince McFadden to start taking a statement – a process that dragged out over nearly two months, and yielded a document of 650 pages, purporting to describe what Nelson had done. As Vince set to work on it, urgent messages began to reach us from members of the Army, saying they wanted to come and see us, to explain what they were doing, and we no longer had any doubt that we had stumbled on something extremely dangerous and difficult.

Once again I confronted Brian Fitzsimmons and demanded to know what was going on. From him I took statements in which he maintained that Nelson had been acting on behalf of the Army, not of the RUC, and when I told him about one or two things that Nelson claimed to have done, he came back with, 'Well, we certainly didn't authorise *that*.' This made things still more difficult, because at that stage the RUC allegedly had supremacy in Northern Ireland, and should have been in full control.

I next went and saw John Deverell, the head of MI5 in Belfast, and he told me that Nelson had been run by the British Army, rather than by MI5. This provoked a sharp disagreement between the RUC and the Army about what Nelson really had been doing, and about who knew what. When Vince McFadden interviewed one senior officer and took a statement from him under caution, he admitted that Nelson *was* an agent for the British Army, part of their set-up, and had been used to target people.

Just at that stage Nelson himself revealed that, as Intelligence Officer for the whole of the UDA, he had been charged with the task of setting up a process for targeting Sinn Fein and IRA terrorists, including some of the men who had already been killed. In other words, he had been tasked by both the British Army and the Protestant paramilitaries with the job of pulling all the intelligence together, to make the UDA a far more effective killing group. He was privy to information that should have been confidential to the Army, including index numbers, people's backgrounds and movements. Feeding his information into a computer, he had produced dossiers that he called 'intelligence packages', which he gave to the killers so that they could go out and shoot people who *they* thought were members of Sinn Fein or the IRA.

Even worse, he had been running an index system of blue cards, on which he entered details of people whom he picked out from the mass of information reaching him. Each card bore a photograph and basic facts about an individual's existence – his address, occupation and so on – and the selection of names was Nelson's alone. If your name was in the system, and a UFF man came along asking for a target, Nelson might easily take out your blue card and hand it over – so that he was actually choosing the people who were going to be shot. Sometimes paramilitaries would come with the vaguest notions and ask, 'What people do you have in the Ardoyne area?' Again, he would hand out cards of his choice.

While plying this lethal trade, Nelson and his masters, the FRU, had been slack about keeping records. Once, when paramilitaries asked him for details of fourteen men who were standing for election as Sinn Fein councillors, Nelson could find blue cards for only ten of them. He therefore had to go to his system, dig out details, and make up cards for the missing four. He then told the FRU what he had done – except that he gave only ten names, and claimed that he couldn't remember the other four. Within a short space of time those four had been shot dead, including the lawyer Pat Finucane, but the other ten are alive to this day. In other words, the FRU had been inexcusably careless in failing to protect the four who lost their lives. The killers themselves were no more careful. Several times, in the int dumps, we found blue cards identifying men who had been shot, and the murderer had not bothered to destroy the evidence, which had his fingerprints, and Nelson's, as well as Nelson's handwriting, on it.

Nelson had also handed out cards to members of the UVF, a different loyalist organisation, twenty or fifty at a time – and again he kept no record of the names. The FRU had no agents in the UVF, and nobody was protecting those people.

That was bad enough, but soon something still more dreadful emerged: it turned out that on two occasions Nelson had got the wrong person, and that paramilitaries had gone out and shot men who had no links of any kind with the IRA.

After his arrest we asked him where his intelligence base was. He said he had pulled all the documents together and given them to his Army handler in the base at Lisburn. Next stop Lisburn, then. But when Vince asked to see the dossier, the answer from the Army was, 'Well, we're not sure we can give it to you.' Again I went to see Hugh Annesley and told him, 'This is now a murder inquiry. We must have this material.' Annesley rang up the General Officer Commanding, and he, after taking legal advice, agreed that it must be handed over: otherwise he could, in theory, be charged with obstructing a murder inquiry.

Vince and I went to collect Nelson's dossier from Lisburn, and brought it back to our base on Antrim Road. The number of documents was colossal. We began to analyse them and work through them for fingerprints, each of us taking batches of them to Scotland Yard whenever we went back for a break.

By then our inquiries had created obvious difficulties in the relationships between the Army, the Special Branch and the RUC, and I myself had become more determined than ever to find out what those relationships *were*. I spent hours talking to Brian Fitzsimmons and the Special Branch, and to senior RUC CID officers. We also had continued strong support from Alistair Fraser, the Northern Ireland Director of Public Prosecutions.

Before that – we reminded ourselves at bad moments – no inde-

pendent inquiry in Northern Ireland had ever secured a single conviction. And yet here we were, with our total of convictions climbing
from the twenties into the thirties. But for the outstanding loyalty and
skill of the RUC detectives who worked with us, we would never
have achieved half as much: they shared our values, and like us were
dedicated to upholding justice and the law, and to getting criminals
locked up. One of the best was the red-headed Detective Superintendent Maurice Neely, who died in June 1994 when a Chinook
helicopter flying from Belfast to Inverness crashed on the Mull of
Kintyre, killing twenty-five senior intelligence, army and police officers, among them some of the men who would have been important
witnesses in our inquiry.

One task that Annesley had asked me to carry out was to produce
recommendations about what action could be taken to prevent any
repetition of the fiasco we had uncovered. The aim was to shore up a
shaky system that had, in effect, collaborated with terrorists, for whatever reasons. I therefore wrote a report and handed it in to the Chief
Constable. He then proposed to hold a press conference, against the
advice of the Director of Public Prosecutions, who thought that any
announcement might influence further trials that were imminent.

Once again there was conflict between the legal system and public
interest, but Annesley insisted that it was essential to hold the conference, so that the public of Northern Ireland could know that the
Stevens Inquiry had done the job it had set out to do, and, more
important, that it had made more than a hundred recommendations
for improved procedures in the future. The disagreement went on for
so long that at one point, the night before, although all the arrangements were in place, we almost pulled the press conference; but after
last-minute discussions, which included senior people in London, it
was decided that we should go ahead.

The event was packed out, and attracted worldwide coverage. We
handed round a résumé of my report, and gave the press half an hour
to digest it, before the conference proper began. The atmosphere was
highly charged, and the event was of special interest to Ian Paisley and
other Protestant leaders, because parts of my report criticised the
Ulster Defence Regiment. In its defence Paisley initiated a 'Stevens
must go' movement, and a campaign proclaiming 'Save the UDR'.

In the heated atmosphere of that time, people failed to see that our argument was neither with the UDR nor with the RUC, but with a criminal minority. We were not arguing with anybody. We were simply pursuing the scent wherever the evidence took us, and we were encouraged to carry on by the strong support we received from some quarters: at the Tory Party conference, for instance, the Prime Minister, Margaret Thatcher, said that the rule of law appertained as much to Northern Ireland as it did to the rest of the United Kingdom, and that the fact needed to be recognised.

At the front line, in Belfast, it was the determination, the professionalism and the *esprit de corps* within our team that enabled us to keep going in the face of innumerable difficulties. Yet in the background, as a form of insurance, I had two small groups of advisers on whom I relied heavily for back-up and support. One consisted of Ian Kane in Cambridgeshire, John Hoddinott in Hampshire, and two other senior police officers, whom I used to contact and meet whenever I needed to discuss some difficult problem. I knew that, working and living in such a fraught atmosphere, I might easily get things out of proportion, and it was an immense help to be able to call on cool heads elsewhere.

Besides them, I had recourse to Captain Michael Boyle, who had helped me so much as Chairman of the Hampshire Police Authority, and who (I knew) had strong connections in Northern Ireland. One evening, when our inquiry had been running for a few weeks, I happened to bump into him in London, and asked if he could help me get together a committee of seven or eight people in Northern Ireland, to give me advice on local matters. He responded by passing on my request to a friend in Belfast, and he in turn lined up a small team of prominent citizens, with whom we started to hold regular meetings, sometimes at a hotel, sometimes in a private room at the Police Club, near Sea Park, and sometimes at the Masonry centre. (This last venue gave rise to a rumour that we were all Masons, and that we had formed some kind of secret society. One of our members *was* a Mason, but I was not.)

Vince and Laurie came to the meetings with me – and very useful gatherings they were. At one point our team was going through a particularly rough patch, specifically over the UDR and some of the arrests we had made. In the midst of these problems our support group met for lunch at the Police Club, and towards the end I asked the six eminent citizens present what they thought of our activities. 'I want your honest opinion about what we should do,' I told them. 'Do you think the inquiry's a waste of time? Should we slow down? Should we pack it in? Or what?'

I fully expected to be told that we were overreaching ourselves and that we had better ease off a bit, even that we should go home. Not at all: one member, a Protestant, an ex-soldier, and well known in the media, looked me straight in the eye and said, 'There is only one thing we've got to say to you, and it's this.' As he paused, I thought, What is coming now? Glancing at Laurie and Vince, I saw that they were equally apprehensive. But the man went on: 'You have only one option, Mr Stevens, and that is to *do your duty.* Your duty is to uphold the law, and carry out what you've been asked to do. If you do that, and do it well, no one is going to criticise you.'

We left that lunch uplifted, enormously reassured, and I realised as never before what tremendous moral power independent advice can give you. Ian Kane and John Hoddinott were wise and unfailingly supportive, but they were professionals, and naturally on my side. In contrast, the group in Belfast were important people in their own communities, but in no way beholden to me or my team – so that their endorsement of our activities was immensely encouraging. For me, that was a defining point in our inquiry. From that moment I had not the slightest doubt about where we were heading: to use that old-fashioned phrase, we were going to do our duty, and go wherever the evidence led.

To be fair to the Army, I think many officers were bemused by what was going on, and the liaison officers attached to us did their best to help. The undercover unit on which we had stumbled, the FRU, was wrapped in secrecy: it kept its activities well removed from those of the regular Army, and it reported only to the GOC (General Officer Commanding). Its existence was not known to most of the rest of the military. Nevertheless, a few Army personnel *did* know about it, for one or two private telephone callers and contacts told me simply, 'Get on with it.'

Besides, people were still being killed. The morning after we carried out our big search operation with all the vehicles, an RUC superintendent got into his car and was blown to bits. In other words, while our investigations were doing visible damage to the Ulster Defence Regiment and the Army itself, the IRA was still murdering people. It was obviously galling for the British soldiers that, while the IRA openly claimed to be fighting a war, they, the military, were not allowed to fight back with every means at their disposal. It is easy to imagine the conflict of emotions that such a tangled situation created; but our view was that we had been given a job to do, and that we must ensure that the rule of law was upheld.

Copies of my first report went to the Chief Constable and the Army. All 110 recommendations were accepted, as was the report itself. We got some excellent press coverage, notably in *The Times*, which ran an editorial saying we had come up with a 'counsel of excellence'. In contrast, one article – which I knew had been generated by a small group in the Army – began talking about 'a Pyrrhic victory', and claiming that we had achieved nothing.

Once again they made a fundamental mistake. In trying to rubbish us, they merely spurred us on, not understanding the determination of our team. That said, we were beginning to suffer, physically and psychologically, from the accumulated strain, and a small number of people dropped out. I myself started to get severe pain in my back, and although at the time I didn't think it was the result of stress, I later came to believe that it was.

Our best therapy was to go back to the mainland for a weekend: as soon as we touched down at Heathrow, we could relax, and we evolved a ritual whereby we would repair straight to a local pub and have a good drink together. As Laurie put it, 'The moment we stepped off the plane, we felt that a great weight had been lifted off us.' Yet the full effects of the ordeal did not become apparent until the inquiry was over. Then, with the team back in England, not a single one of them escaped unscathed: several had phantom heart attacks, dropping in the street, and others came out in boils. Some, like Pat Tosney, were so shattered that they had to leave the service. I still feel guilty that I did not appreciate the scale of their problems earlier, and that I did not do more to help solve them.

Quite apart from the pressure and danger of work, I also had to deal with the fact that Cynthia was stuck in an uncomfortable little house on the edge of the Fens, with no friends around, and Susie travelling to and from school every day – a tiring journey of twenty minutes by car from home to Huntingdon, and another hour by coach. I went home for quick visits whenever I could, and – extraordinary as it now seems – I somehow managed to keep my work in Cambridgeshire going. I was determined that people there should not forget about me, and Ian Kane was most complimentary about the way I kept my hand on the tiller, especially at times when he was absent. Susie not only managed: she did spectacularly well, getting A grades in all the eleven O-level subjects that she took. (She later read law at Manchester University, where she got a first-class honours degree.)

In Northern Ireland, towards the end of the inquiry, there was a big warming towards us. By then we knew that our real allies were the local CID, whose members felt that they had sometimes been obstructed while investigating murders, that the Special Branch had kept too much to themselves, and that a new system was needed. They also knew by then that their relations with the Army had been by no means straightforward – and it was, after all, they, the CID, who had to investigate politically motivated murders. All this had made the CID keen to help us, especially as they knew that the recommendations I made – for the greater use of forensic science and the updating of equipment – would benefit them, and these were improvements that Hugh Annesley was determined to achieve.

One mark of approval came when Wilfie Monaghan invited me to stand in for the Chief Constable and give the closing speech at a ceremony in the canteen in Omagh, when a senior RUC officer, Detective Chief Superintendent George Jackson, was retiring. He was well-known in the service as 'the man who never carried a gun', for he had always chosen to go about unarmed, on the basis that if he did have a weapon, he might end up shooting somebody, and it would forever be on his conscience.

George had been severely criticised during the Stalker Inquiry, because when he turned up at a particular incident, and was told by a junior Special Branch officer to go away, he had done so. The result of that rebuff was that, when I first arrived in Belfast, he was very hostile: obviously he thought, Here we go again, and he wanted nothing to do with us. Nevertheless, as the months went by, some of his fellow CID officers were seconded to our team, and, as they came to realise that we were pursuing the truth to the best of our ability, an effective partnership developed. As I have said, in time we trusted them absolutely, and they trusted us, and their knowledge of the Belfast scene benefited us immensely.

All this meant that, at George's retirement ceremony – a buffet supper in the bar – I could deliver a heartfelt speech of thanks, and I shall never forget how, in that long room inside the fortress, 150 RUC detectives rose to their feet and gave me a standing ovation as I concluded my tribute to him, to them and to their work. If ever I had had any doubts about what we were doing, they were banished by that roar of approval and gratitude.

Next day George appeared in our offices on Antrim Road, to say goodbye. I happened to be out, but he went up to Vince and repeated the story of how he and his colleagues had been slaughtered in earlier reports. 'But when *you* put in *your* report,' he said, 'I know we'll get a fair crack of the whip.' With that he left, and as he turned to go, tears were rolling down his face. What an extraordinary man!

Nelson went for trial in 1992. Once he had pleaded guilty, and been sentenced to ten years on five counts of conspiracy to murder,* I took the decision 'Out', and back we came, leaving only a hard core of officers to tidy up. In all, we had arrested ninety-eight people and convicted sixty of them, and shone light into a lot of dark corners. Afterwards, I was several times asked why we had not carried on and probed further into various murky areas. My answer was that we had not gone to Belfast to solve the problems of Northern Ireland. Rather, we had worked to specific terms of reference set by the Chief Constable and agreed by the Secretary of State, and once we had done what we were asked to do – namely, to investigate collusion – we pulled out.

Laurie arranged for everything in the offices to be bundled up and loaded into two Ford Transit vans, which were driven out to the

* He was released in 1998, but died of heart failure and a brain tumour in 2003.

airport. There the vehicles rolled straight into a Hercules aircraft, were flown to Lyneham, in Wiltshire, and then driven to Cambridgeshire – the most secure way of making our departure.

It is hard to believe that all that began sixteen years ago – especially as my later inquiries, designated Stevens Two and Stevens Three, have continued ever since. Every scrap of the material we seized has been retained, either in its original form or in copies, and the amount is staggering: so far it amounts to thirteen and a half tons of paper and 1,295,000 pages of documents. Because of the nature of the material, the protection of it is an enormous responsibility. The Inquiry has become the largest and most complex of its type ever undertaken.

Stevens Two, was precipitated by further allegations of collusion, made in a BBC *Panorama* television programme, which claimed that the State was still killing people, and in particular that Nelson's handlers had supplied the paramilitaries with information, such as the name and address of Terence McDaid, who was murdered by Loyalists in 1988. A further allegation was against Nelson's solicitor, who represented him both in the criminal trial and in civil proceedings brought by the Finucane family against the Ministry of Defence, and against Nelson as their agent, for complicity in the murder. The solicitor was supposed to have told the Crown solicitors that if his client ended up in the dock in a civil court, he would tell all: he would say that he had told his handlers everything about Finucane – the opposite of what the FRU had been claiming.

Yet another accusation was that a person from the security forces had instructed Nelson in how to blow up an oil dump – in other words, that there had been collusion of the highest order. Nelson had already been reported for his involvement in the destruction of the oil dump, and he had been charged with (but not convicted of) aiding and abetting the murder of McDaid; as he was already in prison, the new allegations were against the FRU, rather than against him.

For this second inquiry I again hand-picked a team, including some of the people who had worked on Stevens One, but this time they were based in an incident room in Northumbria, and commuted to and from Northern Ireland as necessary, staying over for two or three days at a time. As on Stevens One (as it was now known), the detectives found the work intensely tiring – not so much from the length of the hours they were putting in, but more from the feeling that they were operating in a dangerous environment and being watched all the time. Most of the people they interviewed were extremely guarded, Army officers especially. Again, we worked to the Director of Public Prosecutions, whose directions ensured that we could proceed effectively.

Stevens Three began in 1999, when I was called back to Belfast yet again to investigate allegations that the security forces had connived in the murder of Finucane; and although we had examined accusations of collusion in connection with Nelson, now we were asked specifically to re-examine the Finucane murder, and to ensure that everything possible had been done to identify the killers.

Stevens Three started with a preliminary meeting in October 1998; then, together with Vince, I went over in January 1999 to get our terms of reference from the Chief Constable of the day, Sir Ronald Flanagan (now Chief Inspector of Constabulary), and a team of twenty-six travelled to Belfast in March 1999. Once again they were based in Sea Park, where our original, burnt-out offices had been completely refurbished – new ceiling, new carpet, new furniture, new computers – and I frequently crossed the water to direct operations.

By then, following the cease-fire of 1994 and the initiation of the peace process, Northern Ireland was a different place. All the road-blocks had been removed, and army patrols no longer prowled the streets. Besides, we knew our way around, both topographically, and as far as police systems were concerned, which made it much more difficult for people to pull the wool over our eyes. Also, we had made a lot of friends, and we had built up a good rapport with RUC officers who had been juniors when we arrived nearly ten years earlier, but now held senior rank. Their positions, and the trust they had in us, meant that when we asked them questions, they responded quickly and with useful information.

By the time we arrived, Detective Sergeant Jonty Brown of the RUC CID had claimed that an unemployed man called Kenneth Barrett, who lived in a hard area of West Belfast, had admitted Finucane's murder. Yet this claim was far from straightforward. Brown had been questioning Barrett on other matters, and then had said, 'If you ever think of trying to help the police put a stop to this carnage, give me a ring.' Barrett duly made contact again, and because terrorist activity was involved, Brown brought in a Special Branch officer for the next interview; Barrett then said he could help with a number of matters, including the recovery of weapons. But in the course of the conversation he said enough to convince Brown that he, Barrett, had indeed been one of the gunmen who shot Finucane.

The difficulty was that, in law, Brown had been talking to an individual to get information, for which the man would be paid, and since Barrett was not under caution, what he said was inadmissible as evidence. Brown then complicated matters still further by saying he had been undermined by the Special Branch, who took over Barrett as an agent. He claimed that his conversation with Barrett had been covertly taped by the Special Branch, and that when he went to the SB office, he had heard his own voice booming out of a recorder.

In all these claims and counter-claims, it was very hard to know what to believe. But one obvious step for us was to check if Barrett's fingerprints turned up on any of the documents recovered from Nelson – and they did. As a result of this, and of his admissions to Jonty Brown, he was arrested and interviewed by our team. Now, however, he admitted nothing, and when his file went in to the DPP, the evidence was deemed insufficient to charge him.

Free again, Barrett started talking to the press, and indeed to anyone who would listen, clearly admitting that he had played a part in the Finucane murder. To monitor his utterances and obtain evidence, I authorised a covert operation, creating a phantom company and putting out a carefully worded advertisement seeking a driver; sure enough, Barrett got the job and began talking to men who he thought were fellow employees, but in fact were covert police officers. The rules forbade them to prompt him or ask questions about his background; but – as was intended – he got the idea that the people he was working for were drug barons: when on duty in England, he often had to take them to Heathrow or collect them from there. To impress them, he started laying out his pedigree and his career, and in particular he told them he had been involved in the Finucane murder.

In due course he was arrested again. The covertly obtained evidence reinforced that gleaned over several months by the *Panorama* team: so the case built up.

While we were investigating Barrett, we also became interested in a man called William Alfred Stobie, an ex-soldier then living in West Belfast. A former UDA man, he had been a quartermaster for the UFF, and at one stage had been in possession of the 9 mm machine pistol used to shoot Finucane, which was one of a number of weapons stolen from the UDR's Palace Barracks by a colour sergeant called Fletcher and sold to the UFF.

That, on its own, was an extraordinary episode, verging on farce. An alcoholic, up to his eyes in debt, with his marriage gone to pot, Fletcher was suffering from depression. Let Vince tell the story: 'One morning he goes into the armoury, of which he was in charge, borrows an army van, loads it with weapons and drives to the barrack gates. As he's going through, the guard shouts at him to stop. He's convinced that he's about to be arrested, but all the man says is, "Your back doors are open, and the weapons are about to fall out."

'Having left the van in a park, Fletcher goes to the Woodvale Club and puts out word that he has weapons to sell. One of the people who turns up is Ken Barrett; a price is agreed, the party goes off and transfers the weapons to two cars, which drive away, one piloted by Ken Barrett's brother Jim. There's a discussion as to whether or not Fletcher should be shot, but he is let off, and paid off, because it's thought that his death would discourage further weapons sales.

'Fletcher then goes down to Dublin, checks into a hotel, goes out drinking. The maid makes his bed and finds a .38 revolver under the pillow. When Fletcher gets back to the room, the Garda are sitting there saying, "*Do* come in. You're arrested." He's then taken back to a Garda police station and admits stealing all the weapons.'

In Belfast the van was found burnt out, and Fletcher was brought back to be dealt with in court. Meanwhile, the RUC had established that Stobie, also, had been deeply implicated in the Finucane murder. He, too, was a Special Branch agent, but also a quartermaster for the UFF, servicing and repairing guns. He claimed to have warned his SB handlers that a top PIRA man was going to be shot, and moreover, that the man was Finucane. When we took up the investigation, we found messages in the SB system confirming that he *had* rung in with that warning, and that on 9 February – a few days before the Finucane murder – he had been asked to supply a 9 mm pistol. Later recorded messages from him said, first, that the 'package' was about to be handed over, and then that it had not been. Again, it was impossible to establish the truth, but the evidence strongly suggested that Stobie knew that Finucane was going to be shot, and that he had supplied the murder weapon. (After the shooting, a number of other weapons were recovered from him, and they *had* been involved in terrorist activity.)

In due course we had Stobie arrested and charged with conspiracy to murder Finucane, and also with possession of firearms. But before he could appear in court, Neil Mulholland, a former reporter in whom he had confided, and who was our principal witness, fell ill. We had to accept that he had suffered a nervous breakdown, and was unfit to appear in court. Our case then folded: Stobie was released, and went home to West Belfast, with an undertaking from the UFF that they would let him live in peace.

A debate about Stobie, and his status as an agent, then started up in the press, and he was foolish enough to stand up and say he thought there ought to be a public inquiry into the Finucane shooting. That would have meant that any suspect in any way connected with the murder would have been dragged in for questioning: just what the UDA didn't need. So on 12 December 1991 they went and shot him in his driveway. That was the end of Stobie, and of our inquiry into him.

There were plenty of other entanglements for us to unravel. One was the claim that the FRU, who had run Nelson on the Protestant side, were also running PIRA, Catholic agents, and that in particular the FRU had been handling the PIRA man known as 'Stakeknife'. The FRU were under fire for allegedly having brought about the deaths of some thirty agents by feeding them to PIRA, to protect Stakeknife.

The issues are so complex that, as I write in the summer of 2005, Stevens Three is still in progress, and even though I retired at the start of 2005, I am still running the inquiry. A public inquiry is due to open in October. Our investigations have already yielded a number of other reports: those which go to the Chief Constable of the RUC are relatively short – maybe 150 pages – but those that deal with criminal investigations and go to the Director of Public Prosecutions in Belfast run literally to trolleys full of documents. After receiving each report, the RUC has set up a core group to examine any recommendations and to implement them. The public inquiry is due to open in October 2005, and will take place in Northern Ireland; but how long it will last is anybody's guess.

As I write, there are 1,015 sets of fingerprints outstanding, which we have handed back to the RUC. We identified over 2,000 people from their prints, and on Stevens Three, in trying to investigate the Finucane murder, we have identified eighty-seven.

Over the years some members of the team have had doubts about whether we were right to stir things up as we did. Yet everyone who comes to see us – parliamentarians, lawyers, researchers carrying out reviews – all go away strongly endorsing the course of action we followed: the universal view is that we were right to pursue the truth and bring to light what was going on. Criticism has naturally come from the terrorist organisations – but the good thing is that it has come from *all* of them, since this proves that it was criminal activity, rather than any one terrorist group, that we were targeting.

NINETEEN
Northumbria

My occasional returns to Cambridgeshire gave me much-needed breaks, and I found that, back in England, the mystique of working in Northern Ireland, and appearing on television there, had given me some kind of star status. During one open day that we held at Police Headquarters in Huntingdon, as I was walking round with Ian Kane, the Chief Constable, a number of people came up and asked for *my* autograph, not his. I said, 'I'm sorry about that, sir', and Ian, with his usual quick response, whipped back, 'It's going to cost you a drink later on!' I had no problem with that, because he had given us the most tremendous support throughout our time in the Province, and he knew that I knew we would not have succeeded without him.

By the summer of 1991 I had spent some time evaluating the experience I had gained over the past few years, and now I was wondering whether I had it in me to become a good chief constable. I felt, or at least hoped, that I had something to offer, so I thought I had better apply for a new job.

There were numerous vacancies coming up – plenty of choice – and the first post I applied for was in Surrey, where we had once lived. I was short-listed and went for an interview, but the job was awarded to David Williams, who had a natural advantage, in that he was already deputy chief constable of the county. Although disappointed there, I continued to look around, and three more vacancies came up more or less simultaneously. One that I fancied particularly was in Northumbria – partly because the force there was a big, substantial one, which had been commanded by Sir Stanley Bailey for nearly fifteen years, and partly because I had been up and had a look at the area during the Senior Command Course. I had seen then that the force was very progressive in terms of community relations – and in any case I was familiar with the north-east, because my father's airline had operated out of Newcastle. I had always loved the city and that part of the world.

I knew that Frank Taylor, Chief Constable of Durham, was going to put in for the job, and rumour had it that since he was already on the border of Northumbria, and an experienced hand, he would get the post. Even so, I decided to apply, and to put in for Humberside and Cumbria, as a fall-back.

Of the three, Northumbria was obviously the jewel in the crown. Bailey had been a highly successful chief constable, a leading innovator in crime prevention: he had been knighted and had become President of the Association of Chief Police Officers – a substantial national figure. I respected him immensely. Yet he himself accepted that the time had come for change, and that the force needed development.

The act of applying made me think hard about what I had to offer. I realised that there was no point in going for the job unless I could bring some special skills to bear. One of the main lessons I had learnt over the years was the crucial importance of integrity. Northern Ireland had taught me that integrity was vital, and that along with it you must have a certain amount of honesty: you must let people know who you are and what you are – because there is no point in taking a job if you are not the person you appear to be. Nobody who tries to operate under false pretences lasts very long.

I had also learnt that I must be completely focused. My experience in both Hampshire, where I had had responsibility for personnel and training, and in Cambridgeshire, where I was in charge of the strategic development, training, finance and discipline of the force, had given me confidence in that kind of work. As for Northern Ireland – I believed that merely managing to survive in that environment had hardened me up, and I hoped I had developed skills of leadership. Working in a difficult political atmosphere, heading a team from four different police forces, had taught me a certain degree of patience, and shown me that on occasion one has to play a game of chess or poker, concealing one's intentions and cards until the right moment.

I hoped I would be able to put over some of these thoughts when I went for interview in Newcastle. As usual, proceedings kicked off with a dinner, at which I tried to engage members of the Police Authority in conversation; and because I already had some local knowledge, I felt things went fairly well. After the meal Frank Taylor went back to Durham, but three of us got together in a pub to compare notes – myself, Paul Whitehouse, who became Chief Constable of Sussex, and Wally Boreham, who was then Chief Constable of the Ministry of Defence Police – and we all agreed that Frank probably had the job sewn up. Not only did he have a good reputation as Chief Constable of neighbouring Durham: he already knew the local authority members. I felt that all I could do was to give the panel my best, and that I had nothing to lose.

Next morning came the interviews, which were cast in a form new to me. Instead of being asked individual questions by members of the panel, each of us was given a list of questions and required to answer them in order. The questions were wide-reaching – What are the main problems you see in a force like Northumbria? What steps would you take to improve things? What are your views on community policing? Why you? – and I found it difficult to tackle them one after the other: I would have preferred to get some feedback from the panel after each reply. As it was, they just sat there without making any comment.

I had worked out a game-plan, whereby I tried to concentrate on issues on which I had something to contribute. I managed to bring in the Northern Ireland inquiry, and described what we had achieved or failed to achieve there. I also mentioned my time at Heathrow, where I had taken the risk of telling the unions in advance that we were about to arrest eighty of their members. I had done enough research to see that there were areas in which the Northumbria force needed changing, and I took a chance in saying so: in particular, I said, there was a need for some very hard-edged policing, to reduce the amount of organised crime and the disturbances among the rival gangs of hardened criminals who styled themselves 'the Untouchables' in Newcastle.

Nothing I said provoked the slightest reaction. It was thoroughly unnerving to sit there talking, and to get no response. For much of the time one or two of the panel were looking down, as they took notes, but I made every effort to hold the attention, and the eyes, of the rest. At least I knew I wasn't boring them.

After forty-five minutes I came out feeling drained, and sat down to await developments. The next man in was Frank Taylor – and it seemed to me, in my state of apprehension, that his interview went on for ever. Three-quarters of an hour passed. A whole hour. What on earth could he be talking about? At last, after an hour and five minutes, he emerged.

We had been told that the four of us would be short-listed into two, or possibly one. If one was chosen, he would go in front of the Police Authority, as a formality, the following morning. Imagine my astonishment when they came out and said that I was the only person they wanted to go before the Authority the following day. I was dumbfounded. I know Frank was bitterly disappointed, because he had already staked his reputation on the outcome, and was prepared to leave his own force and move next door. I discovered later that he had simply gone on too long with his answers.

The other candidates departed, and I was left on my own in the hotel. At about six o'clock I called Cynthia to say I had landed the job, and we had a few minutes' excited speculation about what it would mean to us. Then I walked down the hill from Gateshead, over the swing bridge across the Tyne and into Newcastle, thinking, *What have I done here?* This is just unbelievable! My state of shock persisted when I had a meal on my own, and even in the morning I was still so muddled that I mistook the time at which I had been told to report. I arrived slightly late, to find Colin Smith, the HMI, running around, wondering where I was: he thought I had lost my nerve and pulled out.

However, all was well. My appointment was confirmed, and Stanley Bailey, who was due to leave about three months later, came down with his wife to congratulate me. As I drove back south that night, I heard on the radio that a 'terrorist expert' was going to be chief constable – and later I learnt that the interview panel had liked what I told them about our work in Northern Ireland. But apparently what made the biggest impression was the way I had dealt with the unions at Heathrow.

Never have I felt more frustrated than when trouble broke out in my new domain before I was in a position to deal with it. After years without any serious upheaval, riots erupted in Meadow Well and the west end of Newcastle in September, right in the middle of the three-month gap between my being appointed and taking up the reins.

The riots were not racially motivated: trouble was sparked off by a car chase. Youths twocked a car (took it without owner's consent), and when pursued by a traffic car into the Meadow Well estate, crashed into a lamp-post, set themselves on fire and killed themselves. Locally based criminals, who had become used to officers keeping out of the area, decided to take matters into their own hands, so they set up barricades, burnt down a club for youngsters and generally went on the rampage. Gang fights broke out, shops were looted, houses and cars torched. The disturbances went on for four days. Nobody was killed – although one Asian shopkeeper was seriously injured – but the level of violence was such that the police had had to pull out.

Quite rightly, the outgoing Chief Constable had stayed at his post, but I shall never forget having to drive back down to Cambridge from Newcastle, where I had been for the listing of new assistant chief constables, and hearing on the radio that Sir Stanley was about to make a statement on national television later that morning. It was difficult to drive away from what was obviously a crisis, which badly damaged the confidence of the force.

All I could do for the moment was to get Superintendent Wilf Laidlaw to update me on what was taking place. Sir Stanley stayed until the last day of his time: when I turned up at seven that evening, he said, 'It's all yours at midnight,' and I started first thing next morning.

I arrived in Newcastle on 20 September 1991. The force was at a low ebb: it was 125 police officers and 100 civilians below establishment, and everyone was still smarting from the Meadow Well riots. We had already appointed one assistant chief constable, David Mellish, who came from the Metropolitan Police, but we also needed another, and we settled on David Smith, from Lancashire. On my second day I took the pair of them down to the Wooden Doll, a favourite pub of mine, overlooking the Tyne in North Shields, for a drink and a chat. On the way back I suggested we went through the Meadow Well estate, to get a feel for what had gone on there. So my driver took us down. At the edge of the estate we came across a police car, and the chief inspector on duty stopped us, telling us that outsiders weren't allowed into the estate in case they got into difficulties. I realised that to go through might cause a problem there, so we told our driver just to keep round the edges.

Next morning someone came and told me that the chief super-intendents of the force had got together at one of their regular meet-ings, and intended to criticise the new Chief Constable for making an unannounced visit to the Meadow Well estate with his two new assistants. I was not impressed. I sent back a message asking that whoever had made these remarks should kindly come and see me, so that I could give them a warning that I did not need people to tell me where to go in a force of which I had just taken command.

They should also realise, I said, that I was used to danger, having worked for two years in Northern Ireland. Furthermore, they should know that the two assistant chief constables who had just been appointed were equally irritated. I knew that this was the first attempt to resist any change that might be coming, and gave the following message: 'You need to know this. I'm telling you – do not do that ever again. I shall be in charge of this force in five or six weeks. I shall be the Chief Constable. You will never dictate to me about where I go or what I do or don't do.'

We never had another critical motion from the chief super-intendents. But the incident showed me that change, as always, was not going to be easy. I was determined that the force would be led by us, the chief officers. One of the chief superintendents, Alan Brown, eventually became an assistant chief constable and an absolutely key agent in the reforms, but at first he would not apply for the job, because he didn't like the way the force had been moving, and didn't feel inspired to stay in the police until he was sixty. He wasn't confident that the top team would support him in some of the changes that he thought should be made, and he was contemplating finding other employment elsewhere. It was a great stroke of luck for me and for Northumbria that he approved of the ideas I started proposing, and changed his mind.

Once again my career move led to domestic difficulties. For the time being we could not sell our house in Cambridge, because Susie had still to take her A levels and needed a home not too far from her school. In Newcastle I therefore lived in a bungalow converted from a prefabricated office block sometimes used by the police for interviews,

Early days: *Top* At the Metropolitan Police training school in Hendon, 1963 (I am in the second row from the front, second from left); *Below* Three years later, at the Metropolitan Police detective training school (I am in the second row, third from right); *Inset* Pay was hardly generous. I had to sell my old Vauxhall Velox (in the background) when I wanted to get married and buy Cynthia an engagement ring.

(i) in office and Station until Refreshments 12.00 - 1.15pm. Then to Thornbury Road, Hounslow re enquiry into larceny

'A' there engaged until 3.00pm when I arrested John Gannon for larceny. To TD with prisoner and engaged in charging until 7.00pm, when I purchased

(ii) an extra meal at TD 7.00 - 7.20pm. Then to patrol with D/S Draycott until 8.30pm when I entered Wimpy Bar, High Street and purchased a further

(iii) meal, then to further patrol of TD Section generally until 10.0pm off duty. Info Gazette read.   12 hours.

TUESDAY the 5th OCTOBER '65.

On duty at TD at 9.00am and engaged in office till 9.45am then to Brentford Magistrates Court where engaged till 11.00am then to Wimpy Bar, High

'I' Street, Hounslow where I purchased refreshments for an informant re local crime. Then to TD at 11.30am and engaged in office till Refreshments 1.00 - 1.45pm, then engaged in office until 2.15pm then to Lampton Road re enquiry returned to office at TD at 3.15pm and there engaged till 5.0pm off duty.
Info Gazette read.   8 hours.

Pages from my Criminal Investigation Department diary, which was filled in daily. Expenses had to be authorised twice over.

EXPENSES	£	s.	d.
Bf	10	0	
4 - 10 - 65.			
Extra meal		4	0.
Further meal		2	0.
5 - 10 - 65			
to Brentford return		2	0.
Incidental		10	0

SUMMARY FOR THE WEEK ENDING
THE 5 - 10 - 65.

		£	s.	d.
ARRESTS. 2.	INCIDENTALS	1	0	0
ASSISTS. 1.	TRAVELLING		2	0
TOTAL HOURS DUE. 171	REFRESHMENTS		6	0
EARLIEST DATE INC. 15.10.65.	TOTAL.	1	8	0
HOURS INCURRED. NIL.				
HOURS TAKEN OFF NIL.				

SEEN:

DET INSP'T

CHECKED:

DIV DET SUPT'T

DIARY
CRIMINAL INVESTIGATION DEPARTMENT
OFFICER PC 604 DC STEVENS.
DIVISION E
DATE From 20th JULY 1964
To

Above 'First in and last out' of the Armagh Road police station. With Vince McFadden on the final day of Stevens One, the Northern Ireland inquiry into alleged collusion between paramilitaries and the security forces (my first inquiry as chairman).

Below The Commissioner in the dock at No 2 Court at the Old Bailey: giving evidence in my defence in a criminal case brought against Paul Condon and me by the Health and Safety Executive.

Above Riot control was an issue early in my time as Commissioner, as this May Day 2000 picture shows; *Inset* I had earlier that year donned riot control gear at the opening of the specialist training centre at Hounslow; *Below* In the autumn of 2001 I made several trips to the United States to visit Mayor Rudolf Giuliani and Howard Schaeffer, the Commissioner of the New York Police Department, who was a fellow-graduate from the same senior FBI course, which I had taken earlier.

The Commissioner is in the unique position among senior policemen of reporting to three masters; the Metropolitan Police Authority, the Mayor of London and the Home Secretary. *Left* Here Ken Livingstone and I give one of our regular press conferences; *Middle left* My relationship with David Blunkett (centre), when he succeeded Jack Straw as Home Secretary, had its ups and downs; *Bottom left* I had first known Charles Clarke, who succeeded Blunkett, when he was Minister of State at the Home Office.

Below My successor as Commissioner, Ian Blair, had been Deputy Commissioner since 2000.

Above Celebrating (with Ken Livingston and Lord Harris) the 30,000th police officer in the Metropolitan Police in January 2004 ; *Inset* With some of the new cadets.

Below As a result of my work with the Sikh community, the Sikh Association invited my wife, Cynthia, and me to visit their holy of holies, the Golden Temple at Amritsar. Earlier I had been made an honorary Sikh in a ceremony at the *gudwara* at Southall, and presented with a *siropa,* an honorific scarf.

Above In my last months as Commissioner I began the official inquiry into the deaths in Paris of Diana, Princess of Wales, and Dodi al-Fayed, an inquiry that I agreed to continue in my retirement.

Right My farewell photograph as Commissioner, appropriately in front of a portrait of Sir Robert Peel, who was responsible for founding the force.

Below My father ran an airline and I originally wanted to make flying a career. Now I am part-owner of my own plane, a twin-engine Cessna.

right next to the headquarters. Later, through a friend, we heard that a house was for sale out in the open country. We took one look, fell in love with it, bought it and did it up. It has been our home and haven ever since – an ideal retreat, in a sunny, secluded valley.

I was determined, during my first two months in Northumberland, to visit every police station in the force, to make myself highly visible, to meet as many people as possible, in groups large and small, to walk out on the beat with my police constables, and get a general idea of what was going on. The force was unique, in that it covered two counties, the urban sprawl of Tyne and Wear, and the rural expanses of Northumberland. The area I had to cover was enormous, and my self-set programme entailed a great deal of travel – so much so that I needed two drivers, working in shifts.

I was working eighteen or twenty hours a day, and some of the things that happened during my first weeks made legend. We went down to the Pennywell estate, for instance, in one of the white Lotus Elans that we had just taken on. I was wearing uniform, and as I went off walking round with the local beat officer, my driver took the car away, with instructions to return later.

I said to the PC with us, 'Let's go into that pub to see the landlord.'

'Ee-ai no!' he went, screwing up his face. 'Do you really think it would be a good idea?'

'Absolutely!' I told him. 'I'm going in, and you're coming with me.'

The publican was astonished, and so were the lads in the bar. They were not used to seeing any police in their pub, let alone a chief constable. But after a minute or two one quite notorious young villain, who knew my companion well, came up and said, 'You going to have a pint, Chief?'

'Aye,' I said. I turned round and said to the PC, 'Right – we'll make an exception and have a drink on duty for this particular half-hour. Let's have a pint.'

So we had a pint and a chat – and very interesting it was. When the Lotus came back to collect us, it provoked a storm of comment, and not a little envy. The car really captured the imagination of our new acquaintances – and this was what I wanted: to gauge the feel of the community. Dealing with the police organisation was easy for me, because of my own background and career. Much harder was to take the pulse of ordinary citizens, and to see how we could tackle their problems.

Another more complex priority was to create a new structure for the force, in conjunction with the Police Authority. The old structure had been in place for many years, and I felt sure that many aspects of it needed changing. In spite of all the good work that Stanley Bailey had done, things had gone sharply downhill in the past year.

Quite suddenly, Northumbria had more car crime than any other force in the country: it had become known as the car-crime capital of Europe, and the incidence of ram-raiding had reached nightmare proportions. Every night young men, most of them teenagers, were stealing cars, racing them about wildly, crashing them into shop windows, into each other or into police cars, and setting fire to them. They were totally out of control. Some boys would steal fifteen vehicles in a single night, or over a weekend. The Untouchables had become so brazen that they behaved like the Mafia: at football matches they spent money ostentatiously, taunting other spectators; in their inter-necine squabbles they thought nothing of torturing or kidnapping enemies, and their aggression sometimes broke out into street fights, during which they wielded guns.

I already knew that Northumbria had a tremendously strong feeling of community: north-easteners, and Geordies in particular, are very proud of who they are – but I found that there were great variations from one area to another: what was happening in Sunderland was very different from what was going on in Gateshead, and Gateshead, in my view, was nothing like Newcastle. The county as a whole was quite different from urban Tyne and Wear. I was struck by the fact that in several areas we had had three or four generations of unemployment, and my particular aim was to visit those places in which there was a feeling that the police had lost touch. On the Meadow Well estate, for instance, officers felt that they had not been as much involved as they should have been. In the west end of Newcastle there was suspicion that the Untouchables were involved in organised crime. The Pennywell estate in Sunderland was another difficult place, since it was home to a lot of aggressive youngsters. Our visit to the west end of Newcastle Community Centre was attended by 150 residents – mainly women. When they accused the police of doing nothing, I said, 'Give me the names of the criminals. We'll do the rest.' They did, and over the next six months, with their help, we delivered. They had simply had enough.

One result of the riots was a visit from Michael Heseltine, then the Minister for the Environment. I went to meet him at the Copthorne Hotel, down on the banks of the Tyne, with the aim of trying to secure new funds, because I knew there was money about. I found him quite impressive, with his tall figure, mane of sandy hair and steely blue eyes.

'Well, Chief Constable,' he said, 'how's it going?'

'We need more money,' I told him.

'Right,' he said. 'You've got ten minutes to convince me. Go ahead.'

So I talked fast, and luckily found the right answers when he asked questions. The result was that we got a grant of almost £4.5 million from the Urban Crime Fund – a very large sum for a force like ours, and a tremendous start. The money enabled us to lift the freeze that had been imposed on recruiting, and in a few weeks 4,000 people applied to join the force.

For the long term, I wanted to work out how to create a modern police service, and move the force on into the new world. Locked up in the bottom drawer of my desk I had a plan of what I wanted to do. But I was not going to present it as a plan that John Stevens had dreamt up, or something that was going to be imposed from above: it was going to be a plan evolved by the force itself, so that people could be proud of what they had created – and the Police Authority were going to be a major part of it.

My burning ambition was to reduce crime, reduce crime, reduce crime. After the riots the reputation of the north-east had sunk to an all-time low. Students were not applying to the universities at New-castle, Northumbria or Sunderland, because they or their parents thought the area was so dangerous – and this, to me, was intolerable. What struck me particularly, during press interviews, was the remarks of some people who said, 'You're the right man to come here, because you've worked in Northern Ireland.' In other words, they had the impression that Northumbria was as dangerous and criminal a place as Ulster.

At the beginning of 1992 we started discussions on how to develop a plan, and I looked around for the brightest and boldest super-intendents, who would be prepared to bring in changes. Before the search had progressed very far I was given a tremendous boost by Alan Brown, who, I heard, had certain ideas that he wished to communicate.

When I dropped in on him during my fourth day in office, he went straight to the point. 'Look, Chief,' he said, 'there are things we can do here. Number one, there should be a decanting of people from headquarters out into the divisions. I put this in front of the previous senior team, but they wouldn't do anything about it.'

His idea was ambitious, to say the least. He first suggested that we should move forty-odd officers out into the front line, but after I had taken his excellent draft plan to the Police Authority, the number rose rapidly. The clerk there, Les Elton (now Sir Les), was exceptionally bright, one of the youngest chief executives in the country. I took him and the Chairman, George Gill, a man of immense integrity and a tough, straight-talking Geordie, through the plan, and when they approved it, I went straight into action. The number of officers we decided we could move out rose rapidly – from forty to seventy, then to 100. We achieved the transformation by closing down some of the old specialist resources and transferring their functions to the new local commands. For instance, there had been a Clubs and Vice Squad, but under the new arrangement that was eliminated, and local com-manders were given the responsibility of managing the nightclubs and vice dens on their own patches. We asked hard questions of units like the School Liaison Teams: 'What do you do when the schools are shut during those long holidays?' 'Oh,' they groaned, 'we have to *prepare work* ... That's when we take our leave.' They went into the front line as well. So did nearly 300 people who regarded themselves as traffic specialists: they were told that their job was not to tackle motorists, but to take on criminals who drove. We took the white tops off their caps, told them they were no longer anything special, and briefed them along with detectives.

The aim of the reconstruction was not to save money: rather, it allowed us to employ more front-line officers at no extra cost, because we created them from other parts of the organisation. By the time we were finished, we had put nearly 400 more people into the front line – 12 per cent of the force. In the Marine Unit alone we achieved valuable streamlining: we were the national marine training school, and the only police diving training school in the country, but when we asked the senior officers there to take a hard look at their staffing levels, they decided they could do with twenty-six, rather than eighty. They also began patrolling the river in vans, rather than in their boat, which could take two or three hours to get anywhere.

In other words, the whole culture of the force changed. Our job, as we saw it, was to be out there on the streets, working with the public, gathering intelligence. In short, we aimed to become a target-driven, intelligence-driven organisation, with our focus on major criminals. Our whole thrust was to have one batch of people dealing with incidents on the ground, another tackling serious criminals, and a third providing the support mechanism, mainly the development of our IT system, which soon became the best in the country.

Inevitably, there was a good deal of resentment at first, and of course the specialists who lost their jobs were not pleased: after being office-bound for years, they were bounced out of a comfortable nine-to-five existence and asked to do things on the streets for which they needed further training. Nevertheless, the changes sent an incredibly positive message to the force as a whole.

The essence of the new arrangement was that we completely changed emphasis, from concentrating on headquarters to giving more support to our people in the front line. For instance, we put twelve officers into the centre of the Meadow Well area, working twenty-four hours a day, in a large building that also housed the local Social Services' bureau and officers from the council. I called it a one-stop shop, in which any kind of community problem could be resolved.

We also brought in a new shift pattern, known as 'Ottawa', after a Canadian model. I had already helped introduce it in Hampshire, and seen it working successfully there, and in the north it proved just as popular, as it made working hours far more sociable and allowed us to spread the use of police officers more efficiently. Other innovations included computer-generated warrant and identity cards, both designed to make people feel proud of being members of the Northumbria force.

When we decided we needed a more powerful computer, I dispatched Alan Brown and a representative of the Police Authority to

San Francisco to negotiate for a discount on the new model. He paid for the trip many times over by getting £250,000 knocked off the asking price, and into the bargain was given ten bolt-on boxes worth £40,000 apiece to enhance our system still further.

Another of our reforms was the launch of a PACT anti-car-crime initiative, which won the top Home Office award. We brought in criminals who specialised at breaking into cars, and got them to give us advice on how to harden up vehicles by fitting extra electronic devices, putting locks on steering-wheels or gear-levers, and so on, and we offered free advice to motorists who were worried.

When I asked the superintendents to find out what our troops wanted, I expected some ambitious requests – and what did we hear? A shower ... somewhere to park the bikes ... somewhere to hang coats. What the force as a whole wanted was woolly pullies, which were far more comfortable than cumbersome, traditional uniform jackets, especially for people sitting in cars. A trawl showed that 85 per cent were in favour of sweaters, so we issued them, and very popular they proved: it may sound a modest and minor innovation, but it helped show people that we were listening to what they were saying.

The same was true when we worked out our five-year Strategic Plan: rather than dictate from above, we energised people of all ranks and gave everybody the chance to put up ideas and develop them. Some senior officers, and chief superintendents in particular, found the process difficult to take, because they perceived that the new system, with constables contributing directly to the future of the force, was going to erode their authority; but I was determined to push it through. We also got the views of the community, and worked together with the Police Authority.

Always at the back of my mind was an incident that had taken place years earlier, when I went back to Kentish Town as a detective chief inspector: in an attempt to solve a murder, we brought a group of people together in a room, and when I asked for suggestions, one of the best came from a temporary detective constable. From that moment I had never forgotten how important it is to unleash people's ideas.

The plan, published in September 1992, had only two main aims: to reduce crime, and improve the quality of life by managing the increasing demand for police services. In it, we created the slogan, 'Making

Northumbria a Better Place to Live and Work', and once we had launched the initiative, I was determined to follow it through and complete our restructuring at one go: I felt, like a surgeon, that it was best to do the whole operation once, rather than keep going back into the body.

Our changes soon began to take effect. In May 1992, the IRA planted fire-bombs in the Metro Centre – the first time that Tyneside had been targeted by terrorists. In spite of that, in June 1992 our crime statistics started to show a small decrease. This was most encouraging, since the figures had gone up by 10 per cent in the year before I took over.

For the time being I was not concerned about detection rates, which had been running at the extraordinarily high figure of 50 per cent (in other forces anything between 25 and 30 per cent is considered good). The point was that the 50 per cent had been achieved only by including the results of visits to prisons, where many prisoners admitted crimes (and even crimes they had not committed) in the hope of securing an earlier release. I was determined to create a more realistic figure by excluding prison visits – a move that was queried by the Police Authority – and it certainly looked alarming when the detection rate plummeted from 50 to 7 or 8 per cent. I stopped all prison visits by police officers – a very difficult decision – partly because they were taking detectives off the streets, and I wanted my people out there, arresting criminals. (Today Northumbria is back to 25 per cent, and is second-best in the country.)

We also initiated a quality-of-service programme, designed to assess progress and see if we were setting the right standards. One excellent idea that we inherited from Stanley Bailey was the Coalition against Crime, an American scheme in which private industry joined the police to improve all-round security. By 1992 the scheme needed rejuvenation, so we injected more money and put it under the control of a well-known local figure, Tony Hill, the Group Managing Director of the *Journal* and the *Evening Chronicle*. He chaired the committee and encouraged local businesses to put up money and join in partnerships with the police, both to reduce crime and to ensure that we were giving value for money. The scheme proved a fantastic success, not least because it enabled us to hear the views of businessmen from all over

Northumbria. What did big enterprises like the Metro Centre, run by Sir John Hall, think about what we were doing? Under the new arrangement they could hold us to account, just as the Police Authority did.

In November 1992 we were visited by Sir Patrick Sheehy, head of the team reviewing police roles and responsibilities; and then, in December we got Newcastle Council to install the first-ever closed-circuit TV system in the city centre, round the nightclubs and in other trouble spots. The system was devised by a very energetic and charismatic superintendent, Peter Durham, and the moment it went live, crime dropped spectacularly, by as much as 50 per cent in some areas. At the end of the year, crime overall in Northumbria had dropped by 2.4 per cent – the first fall for five years – and arrests had gone up by 4.3 per cent.

As we made improvements, we sustained energetic media campaigns, to show people what we were trying to do, and to combat the negative image of police forces that the press sometimes presents. We knew we could never persuade the newspapers to drop the shock/ horror headlines with which they reported crimes and disasters, but we did our best to put over the level of our commitment to the community.

One of my most difficult days was 9 December, when Diana, Princess of Wales, came up to open a home for the elderly, and to visit a school in Gosforth. Through the Lord Lieutenant and her protection officers, I had prior warning that her trial separation from Prince Charles was going to be announced by John Major, the Prime Minister, that very day – hopefully, after she had left and returned to London. Things didn't work out that way. She came up in an aircraft of the Royal Flight, and we met her at the airport, together with her protection officer, Ken Wharfe, who drove with her to the first engagement.

All was well at the old people's home – although she looked pale and strained – but as we went from the home to the school, I received notification that the announcement had already been made, and that the press were on their way to get her reaction. As we went down the receiving line at the school, one reporter began shouting out, 'How d'you feel today, ma'am?' She was visibly upset, and Ken, who was extremely professional and sympathetic, took her aside into a small room to help her regain her composure. Meanwhile, I went up to the reporter and said, 'One more question like that, and you're out.' For a few minutes we thought we had better curtail the programme there and then, but she recovered amazingly well, and we carried on.

We began 1993 with an all-out war on bureaucracy, when I appointed a small team in North Shields to launch a ninety-day efficiency scrutiny, to examine the way the force handled paperwork and so on. Excessive paperwork was my own particular hate, and I was determined to eliminate as much of it as possible: if I had had my way, I would have got rid of *all* forms except those absolutely essential for the conduct of operations.

'Too much paperwork' was people's main gripe, and no wonder, for investigation revealed that the force used 184 tons of paper every year – enough for every officer to get through a stack of sheets 30 inches high. The team examined numerous processes such as those involved in collecting court fines, which we found cost more than the income generated, and we scrutinised a thousand different forms that were in use: one particular form was so complicated that it took up between thirty minutes and an hour of a PC's time every week, and when we tracked it down to the Home Office, we found that nobody there so much as looked at it, let alone made any use of the information it contained. When our scrutiny was completed in September, we withdrew seventy-five forms altogether, and our recommendations led to enormously valuable savings – more than £4 million in the first year, and a total of £23 million over five years. The achievement was hailed as Best Practice by the Government: people were sent up from Whitehall to learn how we had managed it, and to see if similar savings could be implemented elsewhere.

Everything was going well, until we had an unpleasant set-back. A brick thrown from a bridge smashed through the windscreen of a patrol car and inflicted a severe head injury on PC John Robinson, causing brain damage. We caught and arrested the young vandals responsible, but that was scant compensation.

March brought a still more distressing incident: the murder of Sergeant Bill Forth, who was stabbed to death after he had been called to a disturbance on an estate. What made it even worse was that he had volunteered to do extra duty that night: he had come from a wedding, gone on night shift, responded to an appeal for help, and driven out to the house where the fracas had taken place. Hearing that the youths responsible were still hanging about, he found one of them, chased him and caught him, only to be viciously stabbed. Later it turned out that the lads were high on a mixture of temazepam sleeping pills and alcohol.

Coming on top of the disablement of John Robinson, the murder disturbed me deeply. It shocked everyone in the force, because it was the first time a police officer had been murdered in Northumberland, and the thought went through everybody's mind, It could have been me. I was in Cambridge when it happened, but I drove north immediately I heard the news. Next morning I went to look at the body, and then met Jill, the widow, and her two children. With me I took one of my staff officers, Detective Inspector Sue Hall, a highly intelligent and exceptionally sympathetic person, who was the same age as Jill. At the house she sat next to her, and tried to give her some comfort, while I talked to Bill's father. Afterwards Sue said she found the experience the most emotional of her entire career: on that awful day it seemed almost impossible to say anything constructive, and she was forced to take refuge in talking about the practical details that needed to be tackled. She managed with such tact, however, that later she and Jill became good friends.

I came away determined to initiate drastic action against the city's young criminals, who had become altogether too cocky and confident. Apart from serious crimes, we were taking a lot of injuries in minor violence on the streets, and I decided that the situation had become intolerable. Why should ordinary people go about in fear? I told our officers it was time we put the fear into the other side.

Our response, in April, was to issue 22-inch plastic batons and rigid handcuffs – the first force in the country to do so, and the first to allow batons to be worn outside the uniform. We also stepped up our self-defence training. For these measures I took a fair bit of stick from the Association of Chief Police Officers, and at one meeting a senior chief constable accused me of acting irresponsibly, outside national guidelines. My retort was uncompromising. 'I'm sorry,' I said, 'but my responsibility is to my force – and I propose to go ahead.'

In June terrorists re-opened hostilities, setting off two explosions at

Dunston and North Shields within twenty-four hours of each other. The aim was to blow up tanks of North Sea oil, but fortunately both attempts failed. Through our link with MI5 we traced an active IRA unit, and arrested several of its members, one of whom had had the cheek to go into a hotel near the centre of Newcastle and book in under the name of John Stevens.

All the time we were bringing in more reforms. One minor but popular innovation was the introduction of anoraks, which could be worn in place of uniform overcoats and gave much greater freedom of movement. A little later we brought in new uniforms for the civilian staff. More important was the appointment of an Equal Opportunities Officer, to oversee the introduction of flexible working practices over the next twelve months, and also to revise our policies on racial and sexual harassment. At that time we had few officers from ethnic minorities, even though in Gateshead we had one of the largest orthodox Jewish communities in Britain, and in the west end of Newcastle there were considerable numbers of Muslims and Sikhs. We also had very few women detectives: visiting CID offices, I noticed that usually there was only one woman present, and when I asked why, the answer generally was, 'Oh, women don't want to be detectives.' I knew that was nonsense, and set about correcting the balance.

The most glamorous event of July was the start of the Cutty Sark Tall Ships' Race, for which thousands of people flocked to Tyneside. As an exercise in crowd-control, the event proved a triumph, and there were scarcely any arrests. I was lucky enough to witness the departure of the yachts from one of our Marine Division's vessels, out at sea, and a magnificent sight the sailing ships made as they hauled away towards Norway on a brilliant summer's day.

In August we again led the country, with the introduction of reinforced, bullet-proof windscreens made of hardened glass, able to withstand the impact of a dropped brick or concrete block, so that there could be no repetition of the incident that had disabled John Robinson. We also spent a lot of money on what I called technical-support equipment – small covert cameras that we could install in lamp-posts, and mobile cameras with which we could collect evidence of activity by criminal gangs. My view was that we could in effect seal a whole area with cameras, so that we knew who was going in and coming out.

In November, after a period of surveillance, we followed a man to London, where he wheeled a huge suitcase along the pavements to a hotel north of Oxford Street. The case turned out to contain a mass of forged £20 notes, with a face value of over £1 million, linked with the IRA and with drug barons in Newcastle, London and South America. In December 1993 we published the Northumbria Police Charter, outlining our commitment to customers, and our success was illustrated by the end-of-year statistics: crime down again, by 5.5 per cent, and over 1,000 more arrests than during 1992.

Life wasn't all work. One afternoon in the Wooden Doll four of us had had a couple of pints and fish and chips, and as we sat talking we could look down on to the entrance of another pub on the corner below us. On the lower level people were carrying out bulky black bin-bags, which we suspected were full of stolen goods, so the four of us went down to the other establishment.

To get in, we had to push some obstruction out of the way, and it turned out to be a fellow sitting on a stool against the door. The moment we were inside, the cry went up, 'Look out – it's the busies!' Someone else said, 'It not, man, it's the Chief.' Consternation! Then a big guy, a bit of a boozer, lurched across from the pool table and challenged me. 'Are you the Chief?'

'Yes,' I said, 'I'm John Stevens, and I'm pleased to meet you.'

'All right,' he went. 'When you've got a drink, I'm going to take your champion on.'

We didn't know whether he meant fighting or pool or what, so I pointed to Dave Mellish, my deputy chief constable, and said, 'He's my champion. He'll take you on.' So Dave was dispatched to play pool in the bar, while we had a chat with the others, who turned out to be fishermen and fabulous characters, full of stories. Their black bin-bags had been full of fish.

In January 1994 we carried out a complete review of the force. Fifteen area commands were replaced by six divisions and twenty-two sub-divisions. Our aim was to make each area coterminous with political wards, and to allow each superintendent or commander to work for the locality as he or she saw fit. We would hold him or her to account, but, having allocated the money that was needed, we left everyone to get on with the job. To evaluate individual performances, we would bring all the superintendents together from time to time and find out what was going right or wrong. 'Why *is* John, down at Byker, managing to reduce crime by thirty per cent, but you, next door, are nowhere near that?'

Another major feature of the review was that it reduced senior ranks by 30 per cent, thus saving huge amounts of money. We also created two new crime squads, one to work north of the Tyne and the other south, to be headed by senior detectives and to concentrate on fighting organised crime. Further, 360 officers were returned to operational duties, on top of the number we had moved out during my first two or three weeks.

In February I went to Teesside Crown Court to witness the trial of the two Gateshead youths who had killed Bill Forth. Partly because I had seen the horrendous stab wounds on his uniformed body, partly because I had visited his widow, Jill, just after the crime, I felt the murder deeply: that somebody trying to uphold the law had been attacked by louts out of control filled me with anger. The occasion was emotionally gruelling, because Jill insisted on attending, and it was the first time she had heard details of the murder. It was disappointing that only one was sent down, and not for very long at that.

Extensive community consultation, carried out in March 1994, resulted in the publication of local service plans for all our area com- mands – fore-runners of the crime and disorder surveys that are now standard practice. In April we became the first force in the country to wear knife- and bullet-proof vests outside our uniform – a direct result of all the violence to which our people had been subjected in previous years. To make sure that the new kit was not too uncomfortable, I several times wore it myself all day, and I made my staff officers, deputy and assistant chiefs do the same.

Crime had fallen yet again, and we had had considerable success in arresting some of the Untouchables: hardened criminals, they were sophisticated, tough operators, used to getting their hands on a lot of money, living what they regarded as a good life, and prepared to use whatever violence seemed necessary. They were too much for the average bobby on the beat, and criminality was growing. To tackle them, we set up intelligence systems and brought together a Serious Crime Group.

Following their movements round Newcastle with CCTV cameras, we would see a man go out dressed normally, and then walk back with his pockets bulging. When we stopped him, we would find he was carrying big rolls of banknotes – the money he'd been round collecting from the doormen at clubs. To put a stop to that, we brought in a scheme for registering doormen, so that nobody with a criminal conviction could get a job of that kind. That wiped out part of the Untouchables' market, without our having to make any arrests. From then on we made sure that all the doormen had radios, linked to the police net.

The best thing, from our point of view, was that the families tended to fight among themselves. After the Harrisons decided to have a go at the Conroys, in the west end of Newcastle, only one of the nine male Harrisons was able to walk without a limp: the rest were all knee-capped or shot in the legs. The dust-up also enabled us to arrest some of the Conroys for shooting their enemies.

Everything was going well, and because the covert cameras and various authorised bugging devices that we already had were doing a good job, we approached the Police Authority for more money, and secured an extra £200,000 for further surveillance and intelligence-gathering equipment, not just for use in the main cities, but for all the areas the force covered: a few organised criminals had been operating in Berwick-upon-Tweed, of all places. In general, there was a drive to gain more intelligence; but for me, the jewel in the crown was our new system of community-based policing.

In almost everything the Authority, ably led by George Gill, gave us strong support; but, understandably, they became nervous about the speed and number of our innovations, and at one point they approached the HMI, Colin Smith, to ask if he thought I was going too far. He came up to see for himself and gave us his unequivocal backing – a valuable professional ally.

In August 1994, together with George Gill, we launched a community-safety strategy, aimed at improving the quality of life for everyone. Our first priority was to tackle the ever-increasing drug problem. At that stage we had youngsters who were committing literally hundreds of offences and still being bailed; this, to me, was quite unacceptable. My view was that if persistent offenders continued to break the law, they should be taken off the streets and put in custody. We therefore led the campaign to get effective Government action, and because by then Whitehall had confidence in us, we were allocated an extra £1 million start-up money to create more secure accommodation for young offenders.

It was said that Northumbria was the favourite force of the Home Secretary, Michael Howard, who often came north to see what we were doing. He enjoyed walking the beats with me, and we frequently drove around in a car together, discussing the new ideas we were putting in. By that time I was Chairman of the Crime Prevention Committee sitting in London, so that I saw him in the south as well, and I formed a high opinion of his abilities. He was tough and uncompromising, and he supported our initiatives wholeheartedly.

Our CCTV cameras had proved an immense success in Newcastle: with the evidence they provided, we had arrested a total of 2,705 people for offences ranging from murder right the way down to indecent exposure and urinating in the street. Of that huge total, only three did not plead guilty, and the rest were convicted. In September 1994 we installed cameras in Sunderland and the result was equally impressive: crime went down by 25 per cent in the first six months. The cameras were sited so that each one could be seen by another, and this almost entirely precluded vandalism; those in rough residential areas were mounted high up on tall, ram-proof poles, so that they could not be knocked over or burnt down.

Our other equipment gradually became more sophisticated – for instance, we would stick a magnetic device under any car we wanted to follow, and the helicopter or plane could track it wherever it went. We also installed peephole cameras inside books in offices, or in lamp-posts, where they could be left on for days at a time, or monitored by someone sitting in a car nearby. Naturally the criminals didn't like this big-brother type of surveillance, but the ordinary people did: they were extremely grateful for the protection the cameras afforded. In all my five years as Chief Constable, I don't think we received more than half a dozen complaints about camera usage from members of the public.

In October 1994 we were awarded the Charter Mark for excellence in providing public service, and we formalised a new scheme, known as CAPE (Community and Police Engagement), devised by Superintendent Eric Mock, for the protection of witnesses, whereby we gave citizens in certain difficult areas of Tyne and Wear specific protection to go to court, and also promised them after-care if they needed it. Starting in the west end of Newcastle – one of our high-crime areas – we told people that if they were prepared to give evidence in court, we would drive them from their homes and back, and make sure they were not threatened or molested, either in court or for an indefinite period afterwards. We also promised to rehouse them if necessary. We gave them mobile phones, and got neighbours to stand up and say they would protect witnesses, so that people who gave evidence would be doing so on behalf of the community. We guaranteed witnesses that, if anyone tried to harass them, we would install cameras and make whatever arrests were necessary.

As a result of that one initiative crime in the west end dipped sharply, and conviction rates went through the roof; the annual figures, published in December, revealed that crime had fallen for the third year running, this time by 6 per cent – a cumulative total of more than 25 per cent since my arrival. Michael Howard hailed our investment in CCTV as 'leading the world', and the force won the regional Opportunity 2000 award, from the Home Office. Altogether, the year had been one of considerable achievement.

Community policing had proved most successful; but we had to back it up with the ability to have officers out knocking on doors at five or six in the morning, to arrest people for offences. We therefore kicked off 1995 with Operation Janus, a three-month offensive against organised criminals, named after the ancient Roman god who is always depicted with two faces, to show that he could look both ways at once. That was us – looking in all directions, whether electronically or with Mark One eyeballs.

I called for police officers to be issued with defensive weapons in the form of pepper sprays, and at the same time, we began to introduce a system of computerised custody recording, whereby an officer could bring a prisoner into a charge room and have his details entered in a computer, which would forward them straight to the Crown

Prosecution Service, thus avoiding a huge amount of bureaucracy and paperwork.

By March the Janus campaign had achieved another 7 per cent reduction in crime across the board. We were after criminals of all kinds, large and small, and they were feeling the heat.

In April a newly constituted Police Authority met for the first time, in the council headquarters in Gateshead, and a new funding formula increased our budget by 11 per cent. We used the money immediately, to put more officers on the streets and to buy extra equipment. A survey carried out by the Authority showed that 80 per cent of people in the north-east 'strongly trusted' their local police – a heartening endorsement of our activities.

In a joint venture with Durham and Cleveland, launched in June, we created the North-East Air Support Unit, and bought a fixed-wing aircraft, an Islander, to reinforce the helicopter we already had. Chasing stolen cars at high speed on the ground was too dangerous: far better to have someone overhead, and the spotter telling the driver of the police car, 'The junction you're coming up to is clear – you can go straight over,' or just following the stolen car till the thief became exhausted, and then telling our officers on the ground where he was. We also had heat-seeking equipment with which we could track runaway individuals. One day a dog-handler was chasing a fugitive, and when he caught him, he started laughing over the radio. 'I've got him!' he reported to the helicopter. 'I've arrested him – but he's bollock-naked!' When interviewed, the man gave an interesting explanation of his behaviour: 'I took my clothes off because then I'd be colder, and you wouldn't be able to heat-seek me so well.'

The Islander was much cheaper to fly than the helicopter, and could often function nearly as well. The direct impact of the airborne initiative was not easy to evaluate, but half-year crime figures showed yet another drop of 7 per cent.

It was during my time in Northumbria that I first owned a share in an aircraft – a single-engined Cessna Cardinal C 177, which I bought together with eleven other enthusiasts. The little plane was quite cheap – I put in only £2,500 at the start, and then paid £60 an hour to fly it. It was on the Cessna that I really cut my teeth: I passed my instrument meteorological conditions tests, which gave me the ability to fly in cloud, and I also got my night rating. With a cruising speed of 125 knots, the Cessna was a good touring aircraft: Cynthia and I had some very enjoyable trips, and we went to Annecy three or four times with friends, as well as to Nantes. I then moved up to a twin-engined Piper Seneca, which was a good deal more expensive. I put in £15,000 as my stake, along with four others. After a lot of study, examinations and assessment I gained an instrument rating, which allows me to fly in any of the world's airways, and into any airfield – even Heathrow.

Flying had always appealed to me, ever since I was only five or six. I love being in the air, and I enjoy the challenge of navigating with instruments – going from A to B and working out the optimum combination of fuel consumption and altitude. For me it is an intellectual exercise – to get all the mathematical calculations precisely correct. In general, I am not known for my attention to detail – or perhaps it would be more accurate to say that I am known for my inattention to detail. But when it comes to flying, I am entirely different. On the ground I work out my route and file my flight-plan with intense concentration, and then in the cockpit I go through my pre-flight checks most meticulously before starting up.

Some people have suggested that I am stimulated by the element of danger, but I don't agree. Flying, if you go about it properly, is *not* dangerous: you are more likely to be killed on the road than in an aircraft. On the other hand, in minimal conditions, coming out of cloud to land on an instrument approach, you have to get everything exactly right. For me, flying is simply the elation of being up in the sky, a wonderful relaxation: nothing is better than to be above the clouds and see the sun rising or setting below them. I find a great feeling of peace up there.

Although during the first months of 1995 we had unearthed little evidence of terrorist activity, a special operation led to the discovery of a dump of automatic weapons cached on Newcastle quayside. We also had a recurrent problem with arson. Unscrupulous criminals would burn people out so that they could buy the houses cheap, and in the rows of terrace houses we could see the buildings going down one after the other like a pack of dominoes. Criminals were buying up properties, installing alcoholics, people on the dole or on benefit, and making life hell for the neighbours – being noisy, setting fire to waste bins, dumping bin-bags on them – until they got out. The result was that in the west end you could buy a flat for £1,000. Landlords began to take over whole streets, until we launched Operation Rigsby (named after the landlord in the television series *Rising Damp*). We knew that the racketeers were claiming £300,000 of housing benefit from local authorities, for people who weren't actually living in the premises.

So far, we had successfully run a CCTV system in the centre of Newcastle, where it protected commercial property; now we became the first force in the country to set up cameras in a residential area – the Meadow Well estate. It was the local people who asked for them: they had seen what the cameras could do in the city centre, and we gave them our full support. When the cameras were switched on, the results were startling: over the next seven months we made 200 arrests. Part of this success was due to the measures we had taken to protect witnesses: because we had pledged to maintain people's safety, they were prepared to give evidence, and this resulted in more convictions. We also put cameras in the notorious west end, and the effect was to create a safe corridor for people going to places of worship: the Asian community soon took to walking the line of the cameras on their way to and from mosque or temple.

Not content with that, in September we launched Operation Scorpion, the biggest-ever coordinated targeting initiative, which led to 240 arrests and recovered £240,000 worth of stolen property *in a single day*. For some time we had known that local criminals were listening in to our radios, and in November we completed a two-year scheme to encrypt all our transmissions, which greatly increased the security and efficiency of our operations.

One day in November 1995, as I was inspecting the police station at Alnwick, a call came through from the Director General of the National Criminal Intelligence Service (NCIS), Albert Pacey. I went into a little office to speak to him, and he said he was having problems over alleged corruption in the use of intercept material, much of which was vanishing without trace. Would I come down, bringing some of my officers, to conduct an inquiry into the matter?

My immediate feeling was that I had already run more than enough inquiries, especially in Northern Ireland; and in any case, I was extremely busy where I was. Even so, Pacey managed to talk me into accepting, by saying that the matter was of national importance, and it would be extremely unfortunate if rumours of corruption were to put paid to covert surveillance and the gaining of invaluable evidence. I therefore collected a team of detectives from Northumbria and set up an inquiry, which ran for about eight months, with the team working from the NCIS headquarters in Vauxhall and myself travelling up and down between Vauxhall and Newcastle to direct matters.

The work was highly sensitive, and at first the team was viewed with some suspicion, coming as it did from an outside force; but by being open and straightforward its members soon established good relationships with their opposite numbers. The team interviewed hundreds of police officers, serving and retired, all over the country, and inquiries revealed that over 900 logs were missing or unaccounted for.

There were also occasional moments of light relief. One day a detective sergeant went round to Margaret Thatcher's private offices in Mayfair to interview a former detective who had become her protection officer. The sergeant telephoned in advance to confirm that he was coming, and was told to present himself at the front entrance of the house; yet when he rang the bell, the door was opened not by his contact, but by the Prime Minister herself, who greeted him with the words, 'Oh, *you're* not the Sultan of Brunei!' To which the detective replied, 'No, ma'am, but I'm better-looking than he is.'

Far from being annoyed, she invited him in, and just at that moment the Sultan and his entourage swept up. Then, as the sergeant was conducting his interview, Mrs Thatcher invited him to join her party, which he did. When he returned to the office, colleagues were sceptical about his account – until he produced a signed copy of her autobiography, *The Downing Street Years.*

On another occasion some members of the team had to make an inquiry in Orkney, so I flew them up in the twin-engined aircraft that I shared with three other enthusiasts. I made sure to keep two seats free, so that after our business had been concluded, we could load up with fish. On the way home the two people in the back shared the cabin with crates of frozen salmon and kippers done up in bin-liners.

The NCIS inquiry uncovered a great deal of sloppiness and lack of accountability and the report I wrote, with its 120 recommendations for refining procedures, called for much tighter control. This was the first major overhaul of the system since the Interception of Communications Act of 1985, and changed the way in which sensitive intelligence was analysed and disseminated.

In the north, the pace of change never slackened. Michael Howard came up to open a new custody suite at St James's Park, Newcastle's football ground – a room underneath the stands, with cells, where we could charge people without the bother of taking them to a police station. Until then we had had to deploy big vans, fill them with prisoners and drive them to a custody suite elsewhere. The, number of vans needed depended on the level of disorder – and there were always problems if rival fans were bundled into the same van, where they might start fighting again.

A further grant of £1.6 million for our community-safety strategy, and the one-day Christmas Cracker operation, carried out nationwide, brought us a real bonanza in the form of 198 arrests and £113,000 worth of stolen property on our patch alone. People who came up from the inspectorate to look at what we were doing found the whole place buzzing with enthusiasm.

A long-running operation, into which we put all our resources, including covert cameras and telephone tapping, at last bore fruit when we arrested two professional criminals, Paddy Conroy and David Glover, who were convicted of torture, kidnap and firearms offences, and went down for a total of twenty-one years. During the year crime again fell, this time by 5 per cent, and we seized drugs with a street value of £1.65 million – more than in all the previous six years combined. Arrests had continued to increase.

The launch of Operation Janus II gave us a flying start to 1996: in the first two weeks alone we made 459 arrests, and managed to get a second generation of protective vests for all our officers. These were lighter than the first issue, and had greater resistance to bullets; but stab-proof gloves, lined with metal, were a failure, being too clumsy and uncomfortable.

I again called for more secure accommodation, and for a fast-track system for dealing with young offenders – a request that Michael Howard once more supported. In February a comprehensive staff survey carried out by the Police Federation showed that the morale of the force was exceedingly high – the highest in the country. Satisfaction with working hours, and with supervision, had soared, as had confidence in Northumbria Police as an employer – all of which had contributed to the impressive results that the force had been achieving.

Almost every month brought some advance. In March we began a six-month trial of CS gas sprays, and opened two high-tech communications headquarters, north and south of the Tyne. Almost always new systems like that cause problems at start-up, but for once no hitches occurred. April saw the establishment of our own fingerprint bureau – we were determined to derive as much information from fingerprints and forensics as we possibly could. Until then our fingerprinting had been done in Durham, but we wanted to be able to process prints more quickly and interpret them in greater detail.

With the new equipment we started to take prints from every stolen car, and this saved time during interviews: if a man's prints had been found in or on a car, his scope for evasion was greatly reduced. We had some officers on every shift trained to take prints off cars, so that when they found a stolen vehicle they didn't just hang about waiting for a specialist to arrive, as they had in the old days, and the prints weren't lost in wet weather. The gain was human as well: ordinary constables felt empowered to take on more constructive tasks than just walking the beat, and the whole force benefited from the new flexibility.

Another excellent innovation, at Byker, was an identification suite equipped with a one-way screen, in which people could be observed and identified without being able to see the person looking at them, and confrontations were avoided.

At that stage the force had 3,600 police officers, and about 1,500 support staff, and in my view it was vital that we should take the best possible care of them. My motto has always been: look after your people, and your people will deliver. We therefore set up a working party to search out best practice on health and welfare issues.

Operation Caveat, launched in May 1996, recovered £1.5 million of 'ringed' cars – vehicles that had been stolen and had had their identity changed, to be sold on; and during the month-long national firearms amnesty 666 weapons were handed in. When violence broke out in central Newcastle after the last football match of the season at St

James's Park, our CCTV cameras proved invaluable in tracing the hooligans who went on the rampage.

In June we increased the number of our armed-response vehicles, and made big inroads into the Untouchables of South Tyneside when we arrested members of the BOSS gang, who were jailed for a total of 153 years. I was pleased, but hardly surprised, when a public survey in Newcastle West, one of the areas which previously had the highest crime rate and been subject to rioting, showed that nine out of ten people believed we were doing a good job, and that 70 per cent of crime was being reported. The final set of figures, for the six months to the end of June 1996, confirmed the longest decrease in crime in history, down 42 per cent since the peak of 1991, with house burglaries down 73 per cent, and total car crime down 66 per cent: the number of burglaries had fallen from 25,000 to 7,000, and the number of cars stolen from 25,000 to barely 8,000. Confidence about living and working in the north-east had been given an enormous boost: new businesses, as well as thousands of new people, were moving into the region and the Home Office, through the HMI, awarded Northumbria the Blue Ribbon in crime reduction.

We had shown what could be achieved by focusing operations precisely, by creating partnerships, and by using increased resources intelligently, all backed by strong local political support. Above all, we had proved that high morale produces high performance.

TWENTY

HMI

Within the police force Her Majesty's five Inspectors of Constabulary are known as HMIs. If the term sounds like the name of some strange animal, that is not inappropriate, for the inspectors, though usually policemen themselves, are lone operators during their term of office, looking into Britain's forces from outside.

On one of my periodic visits to the Home Office, I was approached by Sir Trefor Morris, the Chief HMI, who asked if I would like to take the place of David O'Dowd, who was about to move up and succeed him as Chief. My initial reaction was to decline; but Morris asked me several more times, and finally said, 'If you don't go for the job now, you may never get it.' I was held back by the thought that there was still a fair bit to do in Northumbria. My predecessor, Stanley Bailey, had kept the job of chief constable for fifteen years, until he was sixty-five; I had done only five years, and, as there was no set term on the appointment, I could have stayed on for quite some time. On the other hand, people were being very kind about what we had already achieved, and there was some suggestion that if I accepted the offer of promotion, I might in due course become the Chief HMI.

Another incentive was that I would be given national responsibility for crime, which meant that I would advise the Chief HMI and the Home Secretary on all criminal matters. The main role of the inspectors is to check up on management, performance, finances and so on, but they have no executive powers. This extra job would be to assess what was going on in the fight against crime, to examine the best practices in crime prevention and detection all over the country, and to produce a report that could be used as a template in future. For me, this was an added attraction, and so it was that I decided to move on.

In Newcastle I went to see the Chairman of the Police Authority, George Gill, and the Clerk to the Authority, Les Elton, both of whom had given me tremendous support. I think they were a bit disappointed when I told them I wanted to leave, because our working relationship had been so excellent. But they saw my point of view, and said goodbye with good grace when I left in October 1996.

There was no interview before I took up my new post. I simply went to see Sir Trefor Morris and had a discussion. Again, the appointment produced domestic difficulties. Cynthia and I loved living in North-umberland – 'the last unspoiled county in England', somebody called it. We got on exceptionally well with local people, and we had become so fond of our house that we had no intention of leaving it. So we decided that Cynthia would stay there, and I would travel up and down to work.

Thanks to the help of Jack King, the former bursar of Wolfson College, Cambridge, I found a flat in college, and made that my base for the time being. The journey home was long and tedious: by road or rail it took four or five hours, but sometimes I flew the Cessna, which I was then sharing with a syndicate. Taking off from Cambridge and landing at Newcastle, I could be home in under two hours.

Not that air journeys always went smoothly. Once, as I returned to Newcastle from Leicester, with three other people on board, I was flying at about 8,000 feet some forty miles south of Newcastle when the engine spluttered and cut out. I immediately called 'Mayday! Mayday! Mayday!' over the radio, and from behind me came an agonised yell from John Stoddart (then my staff officer, but now Deputy Chief Constable of Durham, and never a happy flyer). 'Did he say "Mayday"? God help us!' he shouted, so loud that I had to twist round and shut him up.

An air-controller came on the radio and told me that, with our height, we could either glide to Teesside Airport or make for a small field north-east of Durham. Before taking any decision, I switched on the electric fuel pump, and the engine coughed a couple of times, then came back to full power; so I flew around for a few minutes, deciding whether to try for Newcastle with an engine that might be dodgy. When everything seemed all right, I did head for Newcastle, and landed safely; but as soon as we reached the bar I had to buy all my passengers a couple of stiff brandies apiece, to settle their nerves. I, too, needed a strong drink.

Later, when I was Commissioner, I had another interesting experience on the twin-engined Seneca. The aircraft had just been serviced, and I was heading north from Newcastle with an accountant friend, to carry out an air-test, when I found that, on take-off and beyond the point we could stop on the runway, the air-speed indicator would not register above sixty knots. My companion, sitting in the right-hand seat, suggested I use the GPS (ground-positioning system) instead, and that worked well, giving us our speed over the ground. We then discovered that our nose-wheel would not go down. For an hour or so I flew around, burning off fuel; then, coming back in, we ended up landing without the nose-wheel, allowing the nose to stay up for as long as I could, and then gradually letting it down until at last it tipped forwards and scraped along the ground. By then the emergency services were lined up on the access tracks, and we jumped out pretty smartly; but the plane did not catch fire, and relatively little damage had been done. It turned out that the rubber on the tube of the air-speed indicator had frayed, and someone had inserted a bolt in the nose-wheel the wrong way round.

The HMIs are regionally based, each covering a number of forces, and my remit included Bedfordshire, West Midlands, Greater Manchester, the Metropolitan Police, Suffolk, Norfolk, Cambridgeshire and Lincolnshire. The job was a complete change from anything I had been used to – quite a culture shock – and it demanded a big mental readjustment. Instead of being in direct control of a force nearly 6,000 strong, I suddenly had no troops at all. Instead of initiating action and galvanising people every day, I became a monitor and a creator of standards. My back-up amounted only to a driver and two staff officers, and I had to write and type many of my own reports. It felt strange to go into a modern office block in the morning and realise that I had no responsibility for all the other people working there.

Nevertheless, an HMI is in quite a powerful position, because through his inspections and recommendations he can wield a more subtle influence than anyone in direct command, and he advises the Home Office and Police Authorities on the promotion of chief officers.

For candidates at assistant chief constable and deputy chief constable level, he takes part in the short-listing process, but at the selection of chief constables he sits on the interview boards as well.

As soon as I started, I found I was almost permanently on the road, moving from one force to another and living in hotels. I always tried to get home at weekends, but sometimes I didn't see my office for three or four weeks.

The first inspection I made was of the West Midlands Police, and I carried it out with another HMI, Tony Williams, who, curiously enough, had not been in the police service, but had worked as a director of the World Bank. A highly articulate person, but tough, he was an extremely effective operator, even if his direct style sometimes upset people.

For a former chief constable like myself, it was fascinating and daunting to judge colleagues and assess their performance – yet before my first assignment I felt quite nervous, since I was entering new territory and had had no training for the task I was about to undertake. After the Metropolitan Police, the West Midlands force was the largest in the country, with 6,000 officers – nearly double the total in Northumbria – and I had a lot of respect for Sir Ron Hadfield, the previous chief, as well as for Ted Crew, who succeeded him.

In the old days, he would have paraded his whole force for inspection, like an army unit, but such formality had long been abandoned. Instead, the ground had been prepared for me by a team who had previously spent three weeks in the force.

My task, spread over a fortnight, was to assess the force's performance in terms of crime reduction, detection rates, financial management, general efficiency, staff turnover and relations with the public. Armed with a set of criteria – a kind of template – which I could lay on the force to see if it was working well, I interviewed officers of many ranks, from junior to chief, as well as representatives of the Police Federation and members of the Police Authority. I also visited various police stations, to get a feel for how they were functioning. Every now and then I slipped away for a chat with people I knew, to pick up an idea of what officers and members of the public felt about the police, and I always made a point of going out on the beat with officers, in uniform, to give them a chance to talk. One of my aims was to gauge relationships between the various ethnic communities, and it seemed that things were working pretty well.

The HMI calls the shots: he can go anywhere and see anyone he wants. His primary aim is to form an accurate assessment of what is happening in each force; and sometimes his visit creates difficulties for the local chief, who knows that his organisation, and even he himself, is liable to be criticised. Inevitably every inspection is a sensitive process. To have outsiders on your patch, looking for deficiencies, and a former chief constable poking around, is clearly a recipe for aggravation, especially if the visiting chief considers himself more experienced than you.

It follows that the HMI must be fair and tactful. It is also important that he should strike up a good relationship with the Police Authority, for it is to the Authority, as well as to the Home Secretary and the Home Office, that he reports at the end of the day. (His report is first given to the Authority, and then put out for general publication.)

Further, he joins members of the Authority on the boards appointing chief officers, and if he does not hit it off with them, he is in trouble. At all times – not just during inspections – the HMI is the link between the Authority and Central Government, which produces most of the money for local forces, and the Authority can always approach him for advice. If tension develops between the Authority and Whitehall – perhaps because the Home Secretary is making comments that do not chime in with local strategy – it is up to the HMI to act as a diplomat and sort things out.

Far from being a sinecure, every inspection is a challenging assignment. In Birmingham, at the end of the day, Tony Williams and I would return to our hotel with our staff officers, to discuss our findings and start writing our report – a process that might easily go on until one or two the next morning. In my own mind I could not help making comparisons with what I had done as chief constable in the north, and I had to bear in mind that conditions in the West Midlands were in many ways quite different. My final task was to write a confidential report on the Chief Constable, which went straight to the Home Secretary, and was seen by no one else.

After the West Midlands came Cambridgeshire, which proved a good deal easier. For one thing, the force was much smaller, and for another I had started to get the feel of my new job. By then Ben Gunn had become Chief Constable, and as I already knew how the force worked from my own time in the county, everything seemed fairly simple.

Next I moved to Norfolk, where things again went well. I was familiar with some of the ground, I already knew the Chief Constable, Ken Williams, and I quickly formed a good relationship with the Chairman of the Police Authority. One innovation of particular interest was a new communications room, which had just been installed. Very few forces manage to bring in such a system without problems: linking 999 calls into a central unit very often seems to cause a vacuum, but in Norfolk they had overcome the difficulty by making a big increase in the number of people answering emergency phones.

Another issue that came up in Norfolk was the lack of women officers, particularly the lack of women who had been promoted and were in specialist organisations. There, as elsewhere, I made suggestions about how the situation could be improved.

A third vexed question was that of tenure – the system whereby personnel are arbitrarily moved from one job to another after a certain period, irrespective of their own wishes, or of their performance. In Northumbria it had been suggested that we should move people round on a circular track every three or four years, but I had refused to do that. Move people if the need really arises, by all means, I said, but to push people about willy-nilly, in a rigid, bureaucratic way, was something I could never agree with, because it struck me as counter-productive, and also unfair to the people concerned.

Unfortunately, it was HMIC policy at the time, and although I had had one or two quite robust conversations about it, tenure was coming in at many forces. The reasons for it were understandable, especially in forces where some units were thought to have become corrupt, and needed breaking up. In the Met, for instance, the Commissioner, Sir Paul Condon, had identified corruption as being one of the major problems. Later he went on record as saying that he thought 1 per cent of the Met was corrupt.

Most forces had not installed tenure across the board: probably quite rightly, they had introduced it into specialist squads, and into one or two of the anti-corruption squads, but they had not descended to the level of automatically moving an officer who had been doing a good job in one village, just because he had been there for seven years.

Until then, although I had heard tenure talked about, I had never seen it introduced. Northumbria had confirmed me in my belief that the policy simply would not work. The force area was large, and to shift people from one end to another would have caused chaos. It would make no sense to uproot those who had formed strong relationships and trust with local communities and dump them somewhere else. The same, I reckoned, was true in Norfolk.

Next on my list was Hertfordshire, where my old cricketing mate from Bramshill days, Peter Sharp, was Chief Constable. Fortunately, I found very little to criticise.

Tenure was very much the hot topic when I tackled the Metropolitan Police, starting on 17 February 1997. For the purposes of inspection, the Met was split into five areas, and I was allocated the central area, covering the middle of London. One of the weaknesses of the procedure then was that although the HMIs inspected their individual areas, they never penetrated the glass ceiling of Scotland Yard, to discover what was happening in the high-policy areas above.

What struck me most was the anger seething around the tenure policy, which was then being introduced. I've never seen people so furious. I met groups of officers, including members of the Police Federation and the Superintendents' Association, and all were incandescent at being moved around on an arbitrary basis. The other HMI working with me on that occasion was Colin Smith, a man for whom I have a lot of respect; but he and I had differed on the question of tenure when he came to inspect the force in Northumbria, and now we were at loggerheads again. I regret that when I came to write my report I was less forthright than I might have been: I simply recorded that the new policy was bedding in, and we would have to see how things settled down.

Personally, I knew that tenure was thoroughly unpopular, and I could not see that it was efficient to move people out of traffic patrol or dog-handling or the CID into new areas: it meant that all the expense of their specialised training would be wasted, as would much of the experience they had gained. Least of all did I think it right to move uniformed personnel out of posts in which they had been doing superb jobs, and for which they deserved praise rather than arbitrary disruption of their lives.

Let nobody think that an HMI is ever attached to any particular force, even on a temporary basis. He is an outsider, and is seen as one. He is viewed as a positive threat – an intruder who comes into each force for a short, intense period, and is to be kept at arm's length if possible. The result is that although he gleans information from statistics, and gains a reasonably good idea of the force's position on major issues, he cannot appreciate all the intricacies involved. So it was that although I knew the Met well, and had good friends there, it was difficult to get a completely accurate picture of the issues.

Outside the Met, some of the issues I came across were really difficult – so much so that I had to close the door and speak to the Chief Constable in private. Providing I was certain that he would tackle the problem, I would leave the matter to him, and avoid any public scene. From my own experience, I knew that the position of a chief is quite a lonely one, and I often found that a one-to-one talk gave both of us a welcome chance to unwind.

This was the case at Greater Manchester, where I found it necessary to have a private chat with the Chief Constable about crime recording: if I had attacked the force openly, it would have caused resentment, and it was obviously better to get things done by means of a quiet word, rather than by blazoning the problem round in the open. North Yorkshire also posed difficulties. The force was going through a rough patch, with allegations of sexual discrimination and bullying, and my report was necessarily hard-hitting.

After a few months on the road, I had begun to enjoy the job, which was quite challenging intellectually. But one aspect of it that I found difficult was its fragmentation: again and again I went into a force, talked to groups of people, started getting to know them, and then had to walk away, aware that I would probably never see them again. For someone of my gregarious nature, it was disheartening not to be able to get to know them better, continue the relationship and help them form strategies for the future.

I continued to operate from Cambridge for nearly a year, and then grabbed a chance of working nearer home. Although still covering much the same area, I shifted my base to Sheffield where, for a couple of months I had to share an office with another HMI, the highly experienced and shrewd Dan Crompton: 'hot-desking', he called it. Then we moved to Wakefield, where we found more comfortable working accommodation.

During that period I inspected the Metropolitan Police again, but I was also given the responsibility of carrying out a national survey of crime detection and prevention, reporting on the successes and failures of different forces. It was fascinating to go into a force like Gwent, which had a very high rate of crime detection, and excellent crime prevention, and then to visit urban forces that were doing far less well. At the same time I was acting as adviser to the Forensic Science Service, which gave me an insight into the latest techniques. The improvements being made in the field of DNA were unbelievable, and new opportunities for major investigations were constantly opening up. I was particularly interested in how DNA analysis could be applied to so-called 'volume' or minor crime.

One of the major issues in that sphere was the future of the Metropolitan Police's laboratory at Lambeth. The Forensic Science Service put forward a convincing argument that it should be amalgamated with their own establishments, on the grounds that all the work should come under one umbrella. My private concern was that the Met laboratory might lose its particular expertise in certain areas – but the amalgamation went ahead.

We HMIs all got on well together. We came together every month at the Home Office, at meetings chaired by the Chief HMI, David O'Dowd, a vigorous and energetic officer, whose job was to advise the Home Secretary, Jack Straw, on police matters. I had already seen a good deal of Straw when he was shadow Home Secretary, and had come to respect him immensely: his style was quiet, and he operated by consensus, but he was very persuasive, and got things done. When he became Home Secretary, he had an idea that the Audit Commission should take over the police's inspectorates; but he, being a lawyer and a skilled politician, soon realised that the way to wield influence and bring about change was to work through the HMIC. So he began to use us, and particularly David O'Dowd, as a sounding-board, and as an agency for securing change.

It was he who asked Sir William Macpherson to carry out an investigation into the murder of Stephen Lawrence, the black teenager who had been fatally stabbed as he waited for a bus in Eltham, South London, in 1993. Clearly, the inquiry would be a very difficult one, because a previous investigation by Kent Police had already been highly critical of the Met.

In general, my experience as an HMI convinced me that there are too many police forces. It seems to me that we should reduce the number from forty-one to twelve, probably on a regional basis. Such an arrangement would save money, eliminate bureaucracy, and mean that each local command unit continued to be in closer touch with the area it was serving. Norfolk, Suffolk and Cambridgeshire, for instance, could well be united as a single East Anglian force.

Over my two years as an HMI, I found many variations in the way chief officers received me at the start of a visit. Most of them met me at their front door, wearing uniform, but one, who shall be nameless, appeared in plain clothes, limping heavily. 'I'm very sorry, John,' he said, 'but I couldn't put on uniform, because I've hurt my leg.'

'No sweat,' I told him.

'I'll be with you in a moment,' he said. 'I've just got to nip into the toilet. You go on into my office and get started with my staff officer.'

With that he set off down a long corridor. I moved towards the office, but then stepped back and watched him. Sure enough, after three or four tortured paces, the limp suddenly disappeared. When he came back, I told him, 'What's the matter? I couldn't care less whether you wear uniform or not.'

TWENTY-ONE
Deputy Commissioner

During my time as an inspector, on several occasions it was hinted that I might become the Chief HMI, and I hoped that if I did well, I might get that job. I certainly didn't think I had any chance of becoming Commissioner of the Met. It was true that two HMIs, Sir John Smith and Sir Brian Hayes, had gone back to the Met as deputy commissioners, but no one had ever gone from being an HMI to being Commissioner, and the idea never entered my head.

Then in 1998 the Met made an unexpected announcement: Deputy Commissioner Sir Brian Hayes was going to leave. A former Chief Constable of Surrey (appointed at the age of forty-two, one of the youngest ever), he was, and is, a formidable operator, not only speaking several languages but also holding a black belt at karate. But after three years at the Met he thought it was time to move on, and accepted an offer to become Security Adviser to the Football Association.

Thus a vacancy was created in the top team, and David O'Dowd asked if I would like to apply for the post. At first I said 'No', because I knew that although I may not be a very good Number One, I am certainly not a very good Number Two. I am probably too forceful, probably too full of my own ideas.

For six weeks I stuck to my decision. Then David told me to go and see Sir Paul Condon, the Commissioner. I had known him as a staff officer, but in the intervening years he had moved on and become a national figure – a highly intelligent person, essentially private and reserved, but warm when you got to know him, and a man of excellent judgement, able to foresee future events with surprising accuracy. Meeting him again, I found him easy to get on with – and he was very persuasive. 'The Met needs you,' he said, 'specifically to tackle the anti-corruption programme, where there's a massive amount of work to be done.' His words were echoed by Sir Brian Hayes, who told me that anti-corruption was important, but emphasised that the deputy had many other responsibilities. But I was not reassured by the way he described the post to me. 'You're only the first among equals with the assistant commissioners,' he said. 'Under the present structure, you have no authority to tell them what to do.'

I remained unconvinced. Then, as a result of continuing encouragement, I prepared myself for an interview. This took place in the Home Secretary's own office, and the board was impressive, not to say intimidating: two ministers of state, the permanent under-secretary, the Commissioner, the Chief HMI, and Jack Straw himself in the chair. The questions were tough, and ranged from anti-corruption measures to financial problems that might assail the Met in future. Having inspected the force twice, I was quite well equipped with facts about it; but a more challenging question was, 'Why do you want the job?'

I said I would never apply for a job unless I intended to put my heart into it, or if I had any grave reservations about my ability to do the work involved. I also said that I believed I could get on with the Commissioner, and I hoped we would forge a good relationship. There came a few more questions about administration, management, my style of doing things, and my knowledge of what was happening in the Macpherson Inquiry, and, after fifty minutes of interview, I walked out.

A week of suspense followed, and then I heard I had got the job. Officially, I was supposed to join on 1 September 1998, but in fact Brian Hayes left a bit early, and I came in ahead of time, with the HMIC, agreeing to pay my salary from 5 May 1998, so that there was no break in the continuity of appointments.

Until then, in my twenty-three years with the Met, I had been on the eighth floor of New Scotland Yard only once, and I had never set foot in the Commissioner's office; but now I had an office of my own at that exalted level, across the corridor from the Commissioner. I found I had inherited an absolutely outstanding secretary in the person of Mavis McCann, who had worked for at least six other deputies, and understood every facet of her job so well that she would do a great many things without any instructions. To call her invaluable scarcely does her justice.

On my first day back at the Yard I got a briefing from Roy Clarke, the deputy assistant commissioner in charge of anti-corruption measures, and one on finances from Philip Fletcher, the Receiver – a rather anachronistic title for the man in charge of the Met's finances and buildings. Also, I was invited to sit in on the Macpherson Inquiry into the case of Stephen Lawrence, which was then in progress at the Elephant and Castle.

The first meeting of the Met's top team that I attended, at a hotel in south London, was absolutely driven by the implications of the Macpherson Inquiry. In the Met itself, there wasn't a gathering of any group, large or small, at which the subject was not discussed. Paul Condon told me that no day went past without him thinking long and hard about Lawrence and Macpherson. The case was already having the effect of a dripping tap, both on the reputation of the Met, and on the morale of its officers.

There were two less notorious but difficult cases that I had to deal with. One was that of Michael Menson, a young black musician who had been doused with petrol outside a telephone kiosk in north London in January 1997, and suffered such severe burns that he died sixteen days later. Because he was schizophrenic and a depressive, the police at first did not believe that he had been murdered, but thought he had set fire to himself. The family, quite rightly, were not happy, and demanded an outside investigation.

Having seen the Menson papers and talked to the officers involved, I decided that an inquiry must be set up, and arranged for an experienced detective superintendent from the murder team to examine the files. John Grieve, the deputy assistant commissioner, then reviewed the case, and decided it was murder. He and I therefore went to see the Menson family at their solicitors' in King's Cross, openly apologised, and promised that a murder inquiry would be held. We met the family in private, and then, with their consent, appeared in front of the television cameras with them. In due course three men went on trial, two at the Old Bailey and one in Cyprus. One was convicted of murder, the other two of manslaughter, and the case was taken as evidence of a new commitment by the Met to deal realistically with racial issues.

Subsequently an independent and hard-hitting inquiry was undertaken by Ben Gunn, the Chief Constable of Cambridgeshire.

The case of Picky Reel was in some ways similar. In October 1997
the black eighteen-year-old had disappeared after a row with a group
of young people in Kingston, and a week later his body had been found
in the Thames. His mother could not accept that his death had been
an accident, and although the incident had been investigated by the
Met, she called for an outside inquiry. The Surrey Police therefore
set up another investigation, supervised by the Police Complaints
Authority, but it proved inconclusive, and the matter went to an
inquest.

One of the most difficult decisions we had to take in such cases was
whether or not confidential papers should be made available to the
family. I set up a committee on which there were representatives
from the Home Office and from the solicitors acting on behalf of the
Mensons and of Mrs Reel, together with other interested parties, to
decide whether we could go further in allowing the family to see the
conclusions of the independent inquiries. My own view was that there
was nothing to stop us doing that; but the legal difficulty was that
disciplinary cases might be brought against the officers involved. As a
compromise, we concluded that we could allow certain parts of the
report to be made public, but that the officers involved had to be safe-
guarded.

As the deputy commissioner in charge of discipline, I also had to
tackle the difficult problem of deaths in custody. It had been calculated
that there were, proportionately, six times as many deaths in custody
in London as elsewhere. Here was another issue that urgently needed
examination. Was there another and more open way of dealing with
it? Should a new, independent Complaints Authority be created, to
oversee investigations?

Apart from the continued fight against corruption, and the various
miscarriages of justice that had to be cleared up, a third major undertaking faced me: the formation of a Police Authority for the metropolis.
Until then there had been no authority of the kind that governed
other forces, for the Met had reported directly to the Home Secretary.
Paul Condon and I were enthusiastic about the creation of the new
body, which we hoped would be constructive, and would hold us to

account if we did things wrong, but would champion us if we did things right.

It was my responsibility to assist in devising a structure and decide how the Authority would operate. The committee that formed it, and that I chaired, included Sir John Quinton, Chairman of the Metropolitan Police Committee, Lord Harris (who later became Chairman of the new Authority) and John Lyon, a senior official from the Home Office. One of our trickiest tasks was to delineate a suitable role for the new Mayor of London. Clearly, the Government would never hand over total control of the police to the Mayor, but at the same time, the Met would depend on him for much of its funding, and so he would have to have a say in policy and management. So many details had to be sorted out that the Authority did not come into being until the summer of 2000, six months after I had become Commissioner.

A further cause for concern was the structure of the Met itself. My inspections as an HMI had convinced me that the old structure had served its time. The Crime and Disorder Act was coming in, with its recommendations for partnerships between police and local boroughs, and its requirement for local councils to form a joint strategy with the police for tackling crime in their areas. I had done a lot of work on the preparation of the bill with Alun Michael, the Minister at the Home Office, and some of its clauses derived from the best practice in Northumbria – so much so that in the passage of the bill Michael referred to Northumbria twenty-two times. From my experience there I believed the borough commands should be coterminous with local authorities, and with their arrangements for health, education and so on. Our overall aim was to subdivide the Met into thirty-two borough commands, and I was very keen to bring the new arrangement into being, as it had worked so well in the north.

The boundaries of the Met were already changing. Jack Straw wanted to make sure that the policing of London did not spill over into other areas, such as those served by Hertfordshire, Essex and Surrey constabularies, and he ordered us to streamline ourselves. We thus had to reduce the Met's geographical size, and at the same time lose some of our officers to those counties, loan others and reorganise communications.

The force was already more than 350 officers under strength, with a total of 26,750 men and women, and the deficiency was increasing as recruitment failed to meet targets. From trends at the time we could see that the total would be even lower by the end of the year: we were recruiting officers at the rate of sixty a month, and losing thirty-three a week. The shortfall was nearly as bad among our civilian staff, who were equally hard to find. When I examined the state of workforce planning in July 1998, I found we could not fill fourteen vacancies for detective superintendents; we were short of 142 detective chief inspectors, and were having huge difficulty finding detective inspectors. We needed to devise some radical way of attracting candidates to these posts; for the truth was that, at that stage, people just didn't want to be detectives. One step forward was to coin a new slogan for the Met, quoting 'Mission, Vision and Values', our mission being to make London the safest capital city in the world. I kept using the phrase 'Looking to the new world' and saying that we must get ourselves fit for the new world that was coming.

On top of all our other difficulties, we were short of money. One day when I went to the Treasury in search of funds, I was appalled to find that a special policy adviser, who was briefing ministers, had no idea how the police worked, and had never been in a police station in his life. I invited him to come and see what was happening outside Whitehall. 'Right, Fluffs,' I said to my staff officer, Chris Allison, 'let's educate this individual. He needs to see our problems and our strengths.' So we showed him the reality, and asked him, if he had any sensible solutions, to come and share them with us.

There was also the continuing problem over tenure. Not only was the new system much disliked by the Met's officers, I had also inherited a backlog of 231 moves, and found that the scheme was not being fully implemented. As deputy, it was my job to back the Commissioner, and he supported tenure – so I had to go along with it.

While the Macpherson Inquiry was still in progress, many people were seeking to discipline Detective Inspector Ben Bullock over alleged failures in the Lawrence murder investigation. I had met Ben when I was an HMI, and he had told me that he feared he was going to be held up as a scapegoat. But, in an honourable way, he had said, 'I'm not going to run away from this. I'm going to stay and fight my corner.' As an HMI I had no direct responsibility for the case, and one or two people I talked to in the Met did not think Ben would be singled out.

When I became deputy commissioner, however, it was obvious that the only person likely to be disciplined was him: other more senior officers, who might or might not have done something wrong, had left the force. But I didn't see why one person at his level should take the entire responsibility, so I thought it was my job to argue his case with the Police Complaints Authority. The claim against him was that he had not run the office as well as he should have – but of course he had not been in overall charge of the murder inquiry. In the end he was cleared of almost all the charges of neglect of duty, and escaped any serious reprimand.

A quite different problem, which sprang briefly into prominence, was the behaviour of Ron Davies, the Minister of State for Wales, who ran into trouble in October 1988. As Paul Condon was on annual leave, I was Acting Commissioner, and I had hardly sat down at my desk to start work one morning at 8 a.m. when I got a call from Denis O'Connor, then an assistant commissioner, who rang to say that Davies had walked into the police station at Brixton the evening before and reported that he been robbed of some of his personal belongings. The worst feature of the incident was that he had lost his briefcase, which might have contained confidential Cabinet documents.

I immediately rang Chief Superintendent Simon Foy, the Divisional Commander at Brixton, and heard a curious story. Davies had told the police that he been robbed by two men in Battersea Park, who, he claimed, had driven him to Brixton and dumped him there, going off in his car. His story did not seem to add up, and during the night a young Glaswegian police constable had started asking awkward questions. Thus challenged, Davies dropped the bit about Battersea, and claimed simply to have been mugged in Brixton.

Hearing this, I rang the Cabinet Office to warn them that a minister had got into trouble, that confidential Cabinet papers might have gone astray, and that the press were pursuing the story avidly. What worried me most was the possible loss of vital documents. As it happened, I had an appointment that morning with Alun Michael at the Home Office, and I was with him when a phone call came asking me to go up to the Home Secretary's office as soon as I could. I hadn't told Michael about Davies, so I excused myself and went up.

By then more information had come through on my mobile phone. Davies had gone into No. 10 Downing Street to report his misfortune to the Prime Minister, and had changed his story again. The thing didn't hang together at all. I passed this on to Jack Straw, and then went back to resume my discussion with Alun Michael.

Back to Brixton. When detectives got Davies to describe his alleged assailants, they quickly identified one of the men as X – an unpleasant character with whom they had had dealings before. A party went out in search of him, and when Davies's car was found in Brixton, a watch was set on it. Presently, along came a fellow described by Simon Foy as a 'hooligan kid': when apprehended, the youth said he had been sent to get the car by X.

X was promptly arrested and held in custody on suspicion of robbery. Davies, meanwhile, had resigned from the Government and disappeared into Wiltshire, leaving a mobile telephone number. Simon rang him, arranged to meet him at Wiltshire Police headquarters, and brought him back to London in a police car. At an identity parade in Brixton Davies immediately picked out X as one of the men who had robbed him – whereupon X flew into a tantrum, shouting out that he hadn't stolen anything, and he was damned if he would go down and serve a sentence 'for a man like that'.

At this, Davies changed his story yet again, admitting that he had never been robbed, but that he had gone to Clapham Common for an assignation that had backfired on him. There was intense speculation in the media about what he had been up to – and even if no definitive answers emerged, the damage was done: he went back to Wales, his political career in ruins, having caused us a huge amount of trouble. His place was taken by Alun Michael, who was a loss to the Home Office.

Publication of the Macpherson report was incredibly traumatic for the whole of the Met. The official release date was set as 24 February 1999, but in the event the story broke prematurely. At about 11.30 on the night of Saturday 20 February I had just gone to sleep in my flat when I was woken by a phone call from Paul Condon, who said that the report had been leaked, and that parts of it were going appear in the *Sunday Telegraph* the following morning. The newspaper's aim, he thought, was to pull the rug from under his feet and force him to resign, by showing that he had been found guilty of negligence. Being an honourable man, he was deeply hurt by the suggestion, because he had already read the report privately, in the Home Secretary's office, and knew that although it dammed the Met with accusations of professional incompetence and 'institutional racism', it did not criticise him personally.

In the morning furious speculation raged about who had perpetrated the leak. Very few people had seen the document, and it looked as though one of the people involved in compiling it must have been responsible. Paul and I had discussed the report, but he had not revealed its contents to me: he merely gave me the impression that he himself was not blamed for the Met's failures, and I told him firmly that I did not believe he should resign.

The actual publication put the force into a state of shock. We all read copies of the report intensively – and a pretty tough experience it was, because we were the first organisation in history to have been found guilty of institutional racism. But Paul immediately made his own position clear at a meeting of senior officers, when he came out with the memorable catchphrase, 'I'm staying, and we're changing.' Having decided to shoulder responsibility, he told me he felt as if he was a lightning conductor, and that he was determined to put everything right before he retired, probably in February the next year.

In spite of his own determination, outside pressure could have forced him to leave the Met early; and the critical moment came when the Home Secretary presented the report to the House of Commons on 24 February. If Jack Straw had not supported Paul, his position might have been untenable. But Straw, far from calling for the Commissioner's resignation, spoke strongly in his favour. 'I have asked Sir Paul to continue to lead the Metropolitan Police, to deliver the programme of work which is now required,' he told MPs. 'He has agreed. He will use the remaining ten months of his office to take that work forward, including the agenda set by this report. I will be supporting him and his successor in the work which lies ahead.'

That was a powerful and welcome endorsement. Yet no one should underestimate the amount that publication of the report took out of Paul: in the run-up to Macpherson and during its aftermath, he had received a severe battering – and the stress he suffered was illustrated by an incident that took place later in the spring.

On 20 March I had to go to Hong Kong, to deliver a speech about the anti-corruption strategy that we had brought in, and the types of corruption we had found. I went out on a KLM flight, leaving Heathrow at 9.55 a.m., and landed in Hong Kong a day later. With me went my supporter, Sir David O'Dowd, the Chief HMI, and a member of the Met's anti-corruption team.

After a quick bath and change we drove to the residence of the High Commissioner, who gave us a warm welcome. We were standing on the balcony, enjoying a glass of wine as we looked down over the city, when a call came through on my mobile, to say that Paul Condon had fallen seriously ill: he had been found at home in a state of collapse, after a night of vomiting and diarrhoea, and he had been taken into the casualty department of a hospital.

The rule was that either the Commissioner or his deputy had to be present in Britain at all times, because by statute certain documents had to be signed by one or the other. So, after being in Hong Kong for no more and an hour and a half, I was faced with a tricky decision: should I stay on and give my speech or should I go straight back? I had a quick word with David O'Dowd, who said, 'There's only one thing to do: go back.'

Providentially, the High Commissioner's wife was flying to London that evening, so she gave me a lift to the airport, and we travelled together on a British Airways flight. On the way back one of the stewardesses, realising that I had only just flown out, arranged for me to have two seats in the Club Class section of the plane, so that I could really stretch out, and she and her colleagues treated me like a baby. Even so, I was pretty tired when I landed back in London after thirty-odd hours in the air.

The post-Macpherson weeks were an extremely difficult period for the Met. Every man and woman in the force felt that he or she had been personally accused of racism. As I went round, talking to different groups, I found that everybody felt contaminated by that phrase 'institutional racism': they all sensed that they, rather than the force, had been accused individually. As one officer said to me, 'If we'd been a boxer in a ring, we'd have been knocked out in round three, but here we are in round fifteen, still trying to stand on our feet.'

In terms of race-relations within the Met, Macpherson was a watershed. Some people say the report created a politically correct world, others that it went over the top. I have no wish to get into that argument. For me, it was enough that the report had come out, and that the Government had told me to press ahead with implementing its recommendations. So that is exactly what we did: we had no option. Quite apart from the racial element, the evidence given to the inquiry had exposed a lack of resources and inadequate training, and showed up deficiencies in the way we had conducted a murder inquiry – something for which the Yard has a worldwide reputation. In those areas we had been found wanting – so it was not just the institutional racism tag, damaging though that was, that had to be tackled.

In my view, there was only one way to carry on, and that was to treat the report as a springboard for taking the organisation forward into the new world, in terms of accountability and the way we dealt with things. Under the command of the Deputy Chief Constable of Derbyshire, Don Doverston, an outside inquiry was set up to examine how we conducted our murder investigations, and we benefited from the exercise: we pumped in more money and the latest technology, and made sure that the murder squads were properly staffed – for if they had too few officers, they obviously could not operate efficiently.

The accusation of gross negligence in criminal investigation, linked with the allegations of corruption that were already being investigated, had a further effect on CID morale and on recruiting. Very few people would apply for the Flying Squad or the other elite units like the Anti-Terrorist Squad. One advertisement that we ran in the early summer of 1999 attracted a single applicant for the Flying Squad. When I and other senior officers went round schools and universities, suggesting that youngsters should join the police, the reply was often, 'Who wants to work for a racist and corrupt organisation?' Furthermore, the number of officers from other ethnic backgrounds was extremely low – only 4 per cent of the total – and still falling.

All the time we were losing people, who were either moving to other forces or resigning from the police altogether. We countered this trend by increasing the differential between pay inside and outside London, and by introducing free travel for officers in the capital, within a seventy-mile radius. Both measures went through, supported by the Prime Minister, Jack Straw and Lord Harris, Chairman of the new Police Authority, and they encouraged people who could not afford a home in London to base themselves outside the capital and travel in to work.

Better pay certainly helped. But I never wanted anyone to join the police purely for the money. If good pay was the only incentive, new recruits might survive for a year or two; but to make worthwhile careers in the police, they had to enjoy the work and have pride in it.

During my last few months as deputy commissioner I spent much time and effort putting across my vision for the future. We approached consultants for advice on how to spread the message, and visited multinational companies, seeking ideas on how to enthuse people with our plans for the new organisation, and how to restore the image and pride of the Met. Members of our top team kept telling me, 'There's only one person to do it, and that's you. You personally have to put the message across.'

I was none too keen on playing such a prominent role – for three reasons. First, I found it daunting to stand up in front of 2,500 officers and support staff on the stage in Westminster Hall, and then in other parts of London. Second, I doubted if I had the ability to put the message across convincingly. Third, the leaders of major companies told me that if I didn't get it right on that very first occasion, I would fall flat on my face and have no future. Nevertheless, I did my best, spurred on by my memory of how the former Commissioner Sir Kenneth Newman had stated how much he regretted *not* going out and talking to the front line more often, because his attempts to put his message across had been blocked by middle management.

We also sought to engage the interest of the workforce by taking our ideas to them. Once a month the management team went to borough commands and talked about our plans in meetings that included officers of every rank, from commissioner and deputy commissioner right down to police constables and members of the support staff. Everyone was allowed to ask questions, and so became involved in the process of renovation.

We had hundreds upon hundreds of details to sort out. The new Police Authority was about to be created. We would no longer be run by the Home Office. The new Mayor, due to be elected in May 2000, would also have a say in our affairs.

Because the Met has national responsibility for countering terrorism and for protecting the Royal Family and members of the Cabinet, any government naturally wants to have a say in the direction of its affairs. The new legislation was obviously not going to give the Mayor unlimited power, for if it did, he or she would be able to control the Met in a political way, perhaps contrary to Government policies. Thus there had to be a sharing but also a separation of powers between the Home Office, the Metropolitan Police Authority, the Mayor and of course the Commissioner, and the allocation had to be enshrined in whatever legal arrangements we made.

One curious anomaly was that the Metropolitan Police had not had their accounts signed off for 175 years: the finance department had very few chartered accountants, and the auditors who came in had no confidence in the processes the Met had been using. It seemed to me essential that we should change this, and part of our restructuring was designed to ensure that in future we could manage our finances in the same way as local authorities, and show the various organisations supporting us that they were getting value for money.

We senior officers were working ridiculous hours, travelling round to make sure we kept a grip of the organisation, trying to restore pride and confidence. In spite of the loss of morale, I remained convinced that the only way to go was upwards.

Many of our senior officers stayed on, but others moved away. Denis O'Connor tried for the job of deputy, saw it go to Ian Blair, and went off to become Chief Constable of Surrey. Ian Johnson left to become Chief Constable of the British Transport Police. The Receiver's post was eliminated, so Philip Fletcher also disappeared. These were all substantial figures, and they were missed, but their departures gave us a chance to bring in fresh faces; one was the new Financial Director, Keith Luck, whose experience of local government and the private sector made him well equipped to drive our reforms through.

Yet another task was to open up the workings of the Met to the Police Authority. I was determined that things would work the same way as they had in Northumbria, where I had enjoyed a marvellous relationship with the Authority, based on an open-door policy, which allowed its members to come in and see whatever they needed to see, to get a feel for the force. Another essential element was that we treated them with respect – after all, we were accountable to them.

As the Met struggled with its reorganisation, the Home Secretary, backed by two of his senior officials, Charles Clarke and Kate Hoey, was moving towards a reform of the entire police service, and the Met clearly had to be included in the programme. As always, Jack Straw wanted to work with consensus, and I, along with the Chief HMI, would be on his committee.

As if there was not enough to occupy me on the mainland, I was also making visits to Belfast, where my team were running Stevens Three, my third inquiry into collusion. Over there, they were based in the RUC headquarters compound at Sea Park, from which we had run Stevens One, and at this end we had taken over the top floor of Teddington police station.

In London our problems were exacerbated by a series of three explosions, all within a few days of each other. The first was caused by a nail bomb, which went off at 5.30 p.m. on Saturday, 17 April 1999, outside a supermarket in Brixton; by a miracle, nobody was killed, but thirty-nine people were injured, several of them seriously. For the Met this was a critical moment, because it looked as if the attack, in the centre of a predominantly black community, was racially motivated, and might prove to be our first real test in the wake of Macpherson.

The local CID, led by Chief Superintendent Simon Foy, immediately went into action and discovered that the bomb had been deposited inside a black sports hold-all; someone had then taken a fancy to the bag, and removed its contents – a parcel done up in brown paper and Sellotape – but then, having second thoughts, had dropped the bag in case it implicated him in any incident that took place. By the time the device exploded, he was well out of the danger area.

While speculation raged about who the perpetrator might be – at least four right-wing groups claimed responsibility – a painstaking police investigation was under way. Scrutiny of CCTV footage revealed a man wearing a light-coloured cap and carrying the bag, but the images were blurred, and much computer enhancement was required.

On the following Saturday, 24 April, police staged a reconstruction of the scene, but just after 5 p.m. another blast went off, this time in

Brick Lane, Spitalfields, a predominantly Asian community. Once again, a nail bomb had been deposited in a hold-all, but this time a passer-by had picked it up and put it in the boot of his car. Because it was so heavy, he had left it there while he walked to Leman Street police station, intending to report it. While he was on his way, the device exploded, still in the back of the car: it destroyed the vehicle and caused a few minor casualties, but nothing like the havoc it would have wreaked if it had gone off in the open (it was found to have contained more than 300 nails).

Since the two attacks were almost certainly the work of the same person, we intensified our efforts to identify the man on the video tape. We went so far as to consult both the FBI and NASA in the United States, before deciding that the Met's own computer-enhancing equipment was the best. By the following Wednesday they had finalised their work, and they showed the results to a police audience, in the hope that someone would recognise the individual. When that failed, on Thursday we released the pictures to the media, which gave them huge exposure. Now, at last, a man did recognise the bomb-carrier, but unfortunately he did nothing about it until the Friday morning. Then he named David Copeland, a loner who hated homosexuals, Jews and black people, and police set out post-haste to arrest him at his home in the country; but by cruel timing Copeland had already left, to go and plant a third nail bomb at the Admiral Duncan pub in Soho. There, with the place packed out at six thirty in the evening, he created appalling havoc, killing three people and injuring more than a hundred.

Copeland had deliberately set out to murder or maim as many as possible, and although he was not part of any organised conspiracy, he showed all too clearly how a single person could send fear pulsing through a great city. It was exceptionally fortunate that we caught him before the Notting Hill Carnival: there were some indications that the annual jamboree would have been his next target – and if he had struck there, he could have caused fearful carnage.

Early in 1999, just after the Prime Minister had visited South Africa and shown a strong interest in African affairs, an urgent request came from the authorities in Johannesburg, asking me to go out and give a presentation on anti-corruption. Because we were leading the world in anti-corruption work, everyone wanted to know what our tactics were and how we had managed to persuade the Police Federation to accept ethical testing – the system of checking how police officers react when put into situations which tempt them to be dishonest.

The conference took place in Durban, and after I had given my speech the South African Attorney General, Bulelani Ngcuka, together with a couple of ministers, came up to me and said that President Thabo Mbeki wanted to create a new anti-corruption command, starting from nothing. The South African police, the prosecuting authorities and other agencies would provide the personnel, he told me, but they would need to have them trained. Having heard my speech (he went on), they would appreciate my help in starting up the new command and, further, if we had the capability, they would like us to undertake some of the training, in conjunction with the American FBI, because they thought that Scotland Yard and the FBI between them had the best instructors and investigators.

I quickly deferred to the Home Office, and they in turn referred the matter to the Foreign Office; after consultation with No. 10, the answer came that Her Majesty's Government was in favour of our involvement – and so it went ahead.

An official agreement led to a series of trips to South Africa, most of them very short – for, to the disappointment of people who travelled with me, I usually insisted on flying out one night, doing our business the next day, staying that night, and then flying back the following evening, so that we had one night on the ground and two in the air. It is a long stint – eleven hours or so – but I found that in Club Class I could get a good night's sleep on the aircraft, and because there is only a one- or two-hour time difference between Britain and South Africa, the jet-lag was minimal. At both ends, Chris Allison and I used to walk straight off the aircraft and into work. Coming back in to Terminal Four we would be met by my protection officers, and also by some uniformed police from Heathrow itself, and I made a point of marching off from the plane as fast as I could, partly to stretch my legs.

For our first meeting, I took along Chris Allison (one of my staff officers) and Roger Pierce, the head of our Intelligence Section. Our rendezvous was at Paarl, where we met the Attorney General, the

Director of Public Prosecutions (Percy Song), some people from the Secret Service, and the former secretary to the Truth Commission, Reuben Richards, a priest who had looked after us in Durban. For three days we worked together all-out, brain-storming to decide what we should create in the way of an ideal organisation – a mix of lawyers and investigators, linked to the Government, who would concentrate not just on anti-corruption but also on other major criminal problems. Our aim, in short, was to form an elite equivalent of the FBI – a national organisation that would work through the Attorney General.

I quickly realised what an extraordinary opportunity this was. I had never been involved in a creative process with such absolute freedom of choice. On our little panel we had some of the best brains in South Africa, chaired by the Attorney General and the DPP, both of whom were black. (The DPP also happened to be the President of South African cricket.)

So we laid the foundations for the force that became known as the Scorpions, and I got agreement from London that at first the Met would undertake most of the training of the investigators. These, it was intended, would be particularly intelligent people, since members of the elite group would qualify for higher pay than the regular police. I myself was to be one of the main advisers to the Attorney General and to the head of the new unit. When training started, the FBI did lend a hand, but later the Met took over the entire programme, and the Scorpions developed into a highly effective force.

In the course of our discussions I got very close to Bulelani Ngcuka and Percy Song, and on the final day of our first three-day session they said, 'John, we know you like red wine, and we want to take you to a place that sells the best, where we can get stuff at a discount.' So the three of us went into a wine-shop. Behind the counter were all white faces, and I was astonished to find that nobody would speak to my companions, both eminent lawyers and distinguished members of the Government (Bulelani had represented Nelson Mandela, and Percy was a specialist in civil rights). I was highly embarrassed, and angry, and as we came out of the door I said to Bulelani, 'How do you put *up* with that?' To which he replied, 'My dear John, if we showed the slightest irritation in the face of that kind of treatment, we'd descend to their level.' With that he just walked away, as if nothing had happened – and I thought, This is South Africa! (On other occasions we came across white South African police officers who had arrested both Bulelani and Percy, and they told us that neither man had shown any trace of resentment.) The wine they bought me was superb, and they have give me more on every return visit.

In the middle of June 1999 there appeared an advertisement announcing that the post of Commissioner would become vacant on 1 February 2000: for the first time, it said, applicants would be interviewed by a selection panel, and any serving police officer could apply. Before that, two or three chief constables had gone to discuss the appointment with the Home Secretary, and he had decided on the outcome. Paul Condon had already indicated that he wanted his successor, whoever he might be, to be in place early on; there was so much reconstruction work in progress that the new man or woman would need a good running-in period. (Paul had already done nearly seven years in the job – well over the normal five.)

I happened to be going on holiday at the beginning of July, so I took with me a mass of material about the Commissioner's role, efficiency savings, the restructuring of the Met's area commands, and so on, which I read sitting in the sun at the family's favourite holiday spot on the west coast of France, where we stayed half in tents and half in a house. The fact that I kept working was not altogether popular with Cynthia, but my studies led me to the conclusion that over five years the Met could make savings of £289 million, all of which we could transfer into the front line – and in the end we managed just that.

Back in London, I found that some newspapers had been saying that, at fifty-seven, I was too old to become Commissioner – a notion spread around (I suspected) by some of my competitors or their supporters. This struck me as a bit of a cheek, since I was still flying jet aircraft, playing squash and tennis, and walking a good deal. Even so, the criticism made me determined to sharpen up, and so did no harm.

What did irritate me enormously was an editorial in *The Times* saying that I was very conservative, and never changed things. The result was that the Editor, Peter Stothard, got a deluge of letters from Northumbria, all saying, more or less, 'What the *hell* are you talking about?' To be fair to him, he did publish some of them, and when I rang to remonstrate, he did apologise. 'You've really got this wrong,' I told him. 'It wouldn't do any harm if some of your staff occasionally ventured north of Hatfield, because clearly they've no idea what goes on in other parts of the country. You should really do some research before you print things like that.' I am glad to say that we ended the conversation on friendly terms.

In fact, I was determined to go all-out for the Commissioner's job, and my chances were obviously good: I had worked as deputy for more than eighteen months, and I'd put in so much time fashioning the Met's future that I had a clear idea of where the force was going. But there were other candidates in the running, the strongest being Ian Blair, who was then Chief Constable of Surrey and much younger than me.

When the time came, I went in front of a mixed board, chaired by Sir David Omand, the permanent under-secretary at the Home Office, and including Sir John Quinton, a former head of Barclays Bank, whom I already knew as a superb chairman of the Metropolitan Police Committee (an advisory body that reported to the Home Office), as well as two eminent independent members, with Sir David O'Dowd sitting on the sidelines as an observer. For over an hour I answered questions, and as a result of that first round the runners were reduced to two: myself and Ian Blair. Finally at the beginning of July I went in front of the Home Secretary, who chaired a further board.

Naturally I hoped for a quick reaction, but for week after week no news emerged. Not until 24 August, when I went to Chicksands, the Army intelligence base, to talk about what we were doing in Northern Ireland, did I hear anything. Then at last, at about lunchtime, a call came through, and Jack Straw himself told me I had got the job. He gave no explanation of the delay, but I believe the reason for it was that he had been away on holiday, and wanted to make the announcement himself, which was understandable.

My appointment seemed to attract immense media interest. On the morning of 26 August 1999 I met Straw outside the Home Office, and together we walked to New Scotland Yard, where he broke the news standing outside the front door, under the revolving sign. When he went across to ask a couple of officers what they thought of his decision, they coined the happy phrase, 'You've appointed a policemen's police-man,' and the reporters who overheard it took it up immediately.

I could not have been given a better launch, because my relationship with Straw had always been excellent. He had come to see my force in the north-east, and, along with Alun Michael, I had worked with him on the preparation of the Crime and Order Act, so that I had seen a good deal of him. Once I was appointed Commissioner, we began having regular lunchtime meetings at the Festival Hall so that we could discuss progress and policy. I found that a most congenial and effective way of doing business. I particularly liked his way of working, which was by consensus: he wanted to reform the police, but he wanted the police to sign up to his ideas, and did not try to force things on us. All the same, he was a tough negotiator and knew what he wanted – but he understood that we were eager to reform.

One long and difficult inquiry, which began when I was deputy but continued into my commissionership, was the hunt for the murderer of Jill Dando, the television presenter who had been shot dead on her doorstep in Fulham on 26 April 1999. The investigation was run by Detective Chief Inspector (now Detective Chief Superintendent) Hamish Campbell, and this was the first major murder inquiry in which the Met had to work to the standards recently demanded by the Lawrence report – decision logs, proper line control, management goals, and so on.

The crime was a 'stranger homicide' – no eye-witnesses, no finger-prints or DNA available to identify a suspect – so that it inevitably took the police some time to focus their inquiries. The only pieces of evidence found at the scene were an empty 9 mm short cartridge case and a spent bullet, which had passed through the victim's head from left to right, hit the door of the house quite gently, and fallen on to the mat. The unique feature of the bullet was that it had been discharged from a reactivated firearm: the fact that it bore no traces of rifling showed that it had been fired through the smooth barrel of a weapon converted from some earlier form. Forensic experts also recovered firearms residue – particles of lead, barium and antimony – both from the cartridge case, and from the hair and on the shoulder of the victim.

Because Jill Dando was so popular and well known, her death

received huge coverage in the media, and the inquiry team at the major incident room in Kensington was deluged with messages, reports and suggestions. On the day of the murder, the team was only twelve strong, but it rapidly built up to a total of nearly fifty. Even at that size it was temporarily overwhelmed by the torrent of letters, telephone calls and emails, which poured in at the rate of 3,000 a day. Members of the public were ringing not only the main incident room, but also other police stations all over the country, and every phone message had to be taken down by hand before being typed into a computer and collated into categories. Simultaneously, house-to-house inquiries and a search for eye-witnesses began. The victim's house was sealed, and remained shrouded in scaffolding for three weeks as a major forensic recovery was carried out.

On the very first day a woman rang in saying that there was an oddball character living in Crookham Road (where, it turned out, the murderer *did* live), but her message was at least number 1,200 that day: had it arrived in the first fifty or so, the hunt might have been a great deal shorter. On the Monday, two days after the murder, a man turned up at a local disability advisory centre, and then went to a taxi office. On the Wednesday he did the same, asking slightly odd questions: did people remember what time he had called in on Monday? And what had he been wearing? The messages came in to the inquiry team, and the advisory centre produced a name – Barry George – but unfortunately the conversations were not given immediate priority. In those early stages the team was following other lines of inquiry, which seemed to hold possibilities.

Two theories predominated: either Ms Dando had been shot by a contract killer in a planned assassination, and someone from the criminal world had paid for the job to be done; or she had been murdered by a lone stalker. In the first months, while the press put out fanciful stories about her contacts with Russian Mafia and East London gangsters, other people told us that she had been stalked by certain individuals for years.

Early in 2000, soon after I had become Commissioner, I asked Hamish Campbell to give me a personal briefing at Scotland Yard, and he came in with Detective Chief Superintendent Brian More. The briefing was extensive, and convinced me everything that could be done was being done. From my own experience I knew this was going to be a long and difficult inquiry – something of which I became even more convinced when I spent a day in the murder inquiry office.

In due course a detective visited Barry George and asked him if it was he who had gone to the taxi office and the advisory centre. He denied it, claiming to have been at home all morning, and said that he had never heard of Jill Dando. Hamish then decided to search his property, on a warrant, without arresting him. This time detectives took away his coat, a holster for a firearm, many gun magazines, and roll upon roll of undeveloped films, which contained pictures of all the girls he had followed over the years, some of them in Gowan Avenue, where Jill Dando had lived. One photograph of George himself showed him holding a blank-firing pistol – precisely the kind of gun that had been reactivated into the form of the murder weapon.

So George's background emerged: he had a criminal record of indecent assault and rape, and was a long-term stalker of women. After a second search of his property, he was placed under twenty-four-hour surveillance so that we could see where he was going and who he was meeting, and at the end of a month, when all the forensic tests had been completed, he was arrested on a charge of murder.

Although willing to talk about various aspects of his life, he never admitted the killing. But on identity parades he was picked out by two women, one who had seen him at 7 a.m. loitering in Gowan Avenue on the morning of the murder, and the other at 10 a.m. We also took statements from women whom he had stalked. It turned out that he had been unemployed for twenty-five years. For a short time he had been married to a Japanese woman: that was the only period during which he had stopped preying on women in the street, and when his wife divorced him, he immediately began again. When Hamish flew out to Japan and interviewed the former wife, he found that George had initiated their relationship by assaulting and raping her.

Although he was arrested in May 2000, the trial did not take place until April 2001, because an immense amount of work was needed to make the prosecution case absolutely watertight. With media interest so intense, the last thing we wanted was another Lawrence-type fiasco, in which the Met could be criticised as incompetent and unprofessional. Every thread in the skein of evidence had to be followed through with the utmost diligence.

The most crucial fragment came from the inside pocket of George's coat, where particles of discharged firearms residue were found that matched the constituent parts recovered from the victim's hair. Further, a fibre from his trousers was found on her coat. Other items included reports of Jill Dando's death, torn out of newspapers, which had been found in his flat, and written remarks about other women celebrities, but it was undoubtedly the forensic evidence that persuaded the jury to find him guilty.

His conviction came as an immense relief to us. When he was sent down, George still made no comment, but over the past five years various reports have come back from the prisons where he has been held, and where he has told other inmates, 'I did it.' I have no doubt that this is the case.

Perhaps I should mention the so-called loss of temper, for which I am notorious. I know that some of the people who have worked with me do not believe me, but the fact is that never in my life have I totally lost my rag. At times I have been angry, of course; but any apparent explosion has always been a controlled mechanism for getting things done. When I was applying for the job of Commissioner, the HMI, in an assessment, described it as one of my great skills. Early in my career in the police service I learnt that a little outburst of aggressive or robust behaviour can be extremely effective at precipitating action. There are occasions on which an eruption is needed to gain people's attention or wake them up: a bit of fear about the place does no harm, especially if someone is lazy. I have always been careful not to use the ploy too often – otherwise it would lose its effectiveness – and only to use it at the right moment, on the right person.

Most police officers need a roasting at some time or another – I've had a few in the course of my career – and if they can't take a dressing-down, they shouldn't be in the service at all. But one thing I have never done is to take somebody's respect away from him or her: I stick to the precept 'do as you would be done by'. Moreover, my view is that once someone has been told off, the business is finished, and you just get on with life. While I was Deputy Commissioner, one of my staff officers spelt my name wrong in a memorandum during his first week in the job. I pretended to be furious, and fined him a bottle of champagne. When he honourably paid up, I invited him into my office to have a chat and share the bottle. Sometimes when mistakes were made by me, I fined myself.

One colleague who rumbled my tactics was Ken Masterson, at the Staff College at Bramshill, who later became Deputy Chief Constable of the RUC. 'I've watched you, John,' he said one day. 'I know exactly why you pretend to blow up like this from time to time – it's to get things done.'

'Fair enough,' I replied, 'but for God's sake don't tell anyone!'

TWENTY-TWO
Good Works

I first got involved with charitable work while I was in Northumbria, through the advocacy of Sergeant Robbie Burn – a remarkable man who had seen television footage of orphans in Romania abandoned under the Ceauşescu regime and just left to die. Determined to do something about it, Robbie created Newcastle Police Aid to Romania, and persuaded Sir Richard Branson to lay on a jumbo jet, which flew to Bucharest with a load of essential medical and domestic supplies.

When I became Chief Constable, Robbie asked me to join his crusade, and I was glad to give up some of my annual leave to the cause. My personal method of raising funds was to publicise the convoys by flying small aircraft out and back, taking two or three VIP passengers or journalists each time. My first trip was in a Seneca, and I went with Keith Lister, the chief flying instructor of the Newcastle Flying Club. Having raised a good deal of money from sponsors, we flew out via Germany and Austria, aiming for Brasov, a sprawling industrial town set in a valley among the Carpathian Mountains about 150 miles east of Bucharest.

First, though, we landed at another airfield just inside the Romanian border, where we were instantly enmeshed in the sullen bureaucracy that gripped the entire country in the wake of the dictator Nicolae Ceauşescu. Even though I was carrying a letter from the President, and knew that a high-level reception committee was awaiting us in Brasov, officials did their best to stop us proceeding, claiming that we had no right to fly in Romanian airspace. So obdurate were they that I had to make a forceful scene before they let us go on.

We had been told that the airfield at Brasov, although only grass, was adequate for large planes, including Russian Antonov transports; but we knew that the undercarriages of those Soviet giants were far tougher than ours, so we circled warily for some time before going in to land. Only when we touched down did we realise how rough the ground was, and we got horribly bounced about as we rolled over recently levelled molehills.

We taxied across to a large waiting crowd, and received the most tremendous welcome. There were several senior army officers, all in full uniform, as was the head of the Romanian Customs and Excise, the head of Immigration, and the general in charge of policing. There were effusive speeches, and an immediate offer of free fuel for our return trip.

It was an auspicious beginning – yet the occasion was far from joyful. As we soon saw, Ceauşescu had reduced his country to a pathetic state. Many of the buildings in Brasov were still pock-marked with bullet-holes. People were bewildered, and help was needed everywhere. The Newcastle police aid team had already transformed an orphanage in the centre of Brasov, but the local police did not even know that it existed – and when they found out about it, they were so horrified that they supplied cots for the infants. We discovered that there was no concept of volunteering: the locals could not understand it when we told them that almost every single person on the convoy had given up part of his or her holidays to make the trip.

Meanwhile, another initiative had been launched by Chris, the Earl of Winchilsea, who was determined to help the displaced Western Moroccan people in the Sahara. In their struggle to liberate their country from Spanish colonialism and win independence, they had been pushed out of their homes and driven into refugee camps far out in the desert. They had received some help from the Algerians – water had been pumped in – but they had created their own oases, and made great efforts to become self-sufficient.

For Chris's first convoy, the Northumbria Police Authority donated a second-hand Land-Rover, and off went a column piloted by a strange assortment of enthusiasts – policemen, taxi-drivers and a couple of aristocrats in the form of Chris himself and Lord Redesdale, who brought a red fire engine given by the Tyne and Wear Fire Brigade. There was also a white taxi from Glasgow, piloted by an elderly man and his son, who leapt out and polished their paintwork furiously at every halt.

Cynthia and I flew as far as Alicante, expecting to take over the Land-Rover at that point; but the crew who had driven it out from England had taken a liking to the vehicle, and wanted to carry on the whole way into the Sahara. We therefore drove an ancient white van that had been presented by the people of Spain. Nursing that groggy old vehicle through Algeria and the desert was quite an experience, for its brakes and gear-box were no longer in their prime, and to get the engine started in the mornings, we had to ask helpers to push us.

One night, in transit between two Algerian villages, we couldn't find sanctuary in any kind of habitation, as the place for which we were bound had been attacked by terrorists, who had massacred, we were told, about fifty people. That meant we had to stop somewhere in the open. Had the van not been packed solid with supplies, we could have slept in it; as it was, Cynthia and I took refuge in the back of a minibus piloted by two police officers, and shared the space with them, each of us lying across a row of seats in our sleeping bag. 'If you ever get back to Northumbria,' I told them, 'and say you've slept with the Chief Constable's wife, you'll be in big trouble!' Another night, at the centre of a village, we did clear some space in the van and slept on the metal floor – and bitterly cold we were.

At our destination the whole village turned out to greet us. Most of the menfolk were away fighting the Moroccans in the long-running guerrilla war, but the women, in long blue gowns, their dark faces tinted indigo blue with the dye they use to protect their skin from the sun, wailed and screamed in traditional fashion, calling out 'Lordy Chris! Lordy Chris!' when they recognised their main benefactor, Lord Winchilsea.

They could not have been more hospitable; for five days we slept in their tents, which they had vacated on our behalf, and ate with their families, who were given extra rations – mainly tinned – to feed us, and we quickly came to respect them, admiring the way they had organised their lives in the most adverse circumstances. Many had lived in substantial houses in Morocco, and now they were in tents made of canvas and camel-skins; but with help from Spain and the

European Union they had built schools, educated their children from the age of three, and generally maintained their self-respect (if they had no other equipment, the children did their drawing in the sand). During the summer some of them were sent off to Spain, to escape the awful heat and further their education. Cuba took a few of the older children and trained them as doctors and dentists, some of whom stayed abroad, sending money home to keep their families going.

Almost every advance had been achieved by the women – most unusual in Muslim countries. One thing they had refused to do was to build a mosque: that would have been a sign of permanent occupation, and they were absolutely determined that one day they were going home. At the end of our stay, leaving the vehicles in situ, we were picked up and flown out by an aircraft that came into Tindouf.

On our second trip into the Sahara, when I was an HMI, we went with a different group, including a contingent from the Essex Police, organised by the Deputy Chief Constable, Jim Dickinson. This time Cynthia and I were driving an old Land-Rover that the Northumbrian Police wanted to donate to the refugees, and across France we proceeded in style, accompanied by the presidential escort. As we were taking on fuel at a filling station in Spain, Jim said, 'You know, John, this is really good. When the year 2000 comes along, why don't we get the police to think of a millennium convoy that could go anywhere in the world, and do what we're doing now on a big scale?'

I liked the idea at once, and we turned it over in our minds throughout the rest of the Sahara trip. Once again we were carrying a great variety of supplies – paper and pencils for the schools, clothes, blankets. Everything went well until we disembarked from the ferry in Oran, but there the police stopped us, claiming that there had been flooding on our route; terrorists were still a problem, and the Government was not prepared to give us a military escort, as they had before. The result was that we had to hand our loaded vehicles over to Polisario drivers and transfer to an Antonov transport aircraft produced by the Government, which flew us down to the encampment. That suited me fine, as I was allowed to go up on to the flight deck – but by the time our vehicles caught up with us, a good deal of their contents had gone missing.

By then the Polisario community had advanced a good deal. A Médecins sans Frontières hospital had been built, and telephones had been installed. But we were disturbed to find that the children had started begging, for sweets or money. We were accompanied by a group of Americans from Friendship Force, the organisation whose members believe that, if you meet someone face to face, you will never go to war with him. A coach-load had come out on behalf of Jimmy Carter and his son, to see what they could do to help the Polisario return to Morocco. When one of them died, the locals gave him a wonderful funeral ceremony. We ourselves again received a tremendous welcome, but local hygiene was primitive in the extreme, and almost all of us went down with severe food poisoning, either when we were there or when we got back.

In 1999, when I had been selected to be Commissioner of the Met, I took up Jim's idea for a millennium convoy, and mentioned it to John Harding, who was then Chief Probation Officer for London. We collected a group of eight people, from the Met, the London Probation Service and the Essex Police, to develop the idea and celebrate the police service in the year 2000. The group's unanimous decision was that we should go to Romania – and so Convoy 2000 was born.

Interest in the project was so great that we amassed a total of 160 people; those involved included the Special Constabulary, the Cadets, the London Probation Service, Rotary and Aid for Children, all of whom had their own projects, and found their own volunteers. Altogether the participants and their supplies filled thirteen articulated lorries, backed up by three white Renault Trafic vans as support vehicles, one of which was driven by Cynthia, acting as the convoy nurse.

For the three nights of the journey the personnel stayed in police barracks, and always found meals awaiting them, as well as bed and breakfast next morning. Leaving at 5 a.m. or so each day, the convoy proceeded at the rate of the slowest, but the camaraderie was fantastic.

Once inside Romania, one police car led the column, and another brought up the rear, forcing all other vehicles off the road, and accelerating through villages, as if to prevent any contact with locals. If a native driver misbehaved in any way, the police would casually knock off a wing-mirror or even smash a windscreen with their steel batons, known as wands. We suggested that this was not the way policing should be done, but they were not impressed. The end of the road was Constanta, on the coast of the Black Sea, where Aid for Children was creating a hospice for about a thousand children dying of AIDS.

To attract attention and lend the operation a bit of glamour, I flew out, taking two of the sponsors, David Ashe (the husband of Margaret Barbour, head of the clothing firm) and Barbara Coates, who gave a lot of money. (Another time, I took a reporter and photographer from the *Sun* newspaper, and unfortunately the air-controller at Vienna vectored us straight into the worst thunderstorm I have ever experienced. The aircraft was thrown all over the place, and the people in the back were terrified – but at least it yielded a great newspaper story, and brought in more money for the cause.) My own reward – which I felt really belonged to all the people who had made our idea a reality – was to be invested with the Star of Romania by the President, Emil Constantinescu, at a ceremony in the colossal palace built by Ceauşescu in the centre of Bucharest. Dreadful though it is in some ways – the creation of a megalomaniac – that building is a phenomenon, descending six or seven storeys into the ground, its main rooms sumptuously decorated with marble.

Over the next few years we took out three more convoys, delivering drugs (especially for AIDS victims), clothes, blankets and so on. Many firms contributed, not least Procter & Gamble, the producer of household and pharmaceutical goods, who gave a large sum of money for urgently needed drugs, which I flew out late one autumn. To be able to go straight to the institution that needed the supplies, and hand them over in person, was extremely satisfying. In general Cynthia found it easier to amass goods than to collect money: on the whole, firms were extraordinarily generous. All the vehicles were donated, and in the last two years BP sponsored all the fuel. Building supplies, paving slabs, paint – almost everything needed to extend the Constanta hospice was given.

As a result of successive visits we opened several homes for physically and mentally handicapped children; we started a soup-kitchen for poor and disabled people in the centre of Brasov, and set up a mobile dentistry. Yet the worst legacy of the Ceauşescu years was not physical, but mental: the lethargy, lack of initiative, dishonesty and universal corruption.

On our first journeys our vehicles were simply swept through the border into Romania, but then, each year, more and more obstacles were put up. It took ten months to organise each convoy, and all that time we were in touch with the Romanians, checking the rules and regulations, which the authorities were liable to change on a whim. Yet, when the drivers reached the border after three days on the road, they were told, 'Oh, you can't import so-and-so. A new law came into force yesterday.'

The customs demanded bribes, and when Cynthia and her colleague Christine Kirk tussled with them, there were pointless, inexcusable delays, lasting up to eight hours. Once when the two women – the only two on the convoy – repaired to a local hotel for the night, they realised too late that the place was a brothel: as Cynthia collapsed exhausted on the bed, she thought the room seemed unnaturally light, and when she looked up, she realised that the ceiling was covered with mirrors.

Every time they returned to Romania, equipment had gone missing, probably sold on the black market. One year Christine asked for a store room to be opened, and the locals refused to do so until she forced them. Imagine her chagrin when she found that it was full of the food she had taken out the previous year, by then rotten. She threatened never to come again, whereupon the Ministry of Health offered her a derelict two-storey building and a piece of land, and she signed a contract agreeing that within two years she would build a hospice, to be run and financed by Romanian nurses. Now it is up and running, with twenty-three beds – but many contractual difficulties remain.

All this was a poor reward for the participants, who were required not only to give up two weeks' holiday to go on each convoy, but also to find sponsorship of £250 apiece, though the volunteers felt it was all worthwhile when they saw the children's faces light up.

TWENTY-THREE
Commissioner

When I became Commissioner on 1 February 2000, I inherited a spacious office on the eighth floor of the Yard, dominated by a life-size portrait of Sir Robert Peel, founder of the Met. Behind the main office was a bedroom, with a shower cubicle and toilet attached – altogether a covetable private domain. That end of the corridor, opening out into a wide reception area, tended to be rather quiet, not getting the volume of traffic that pulsed through other parts of the building.

Because I was determined to reduce antiquated formalities and make things more democratic, I started chatting to all and sundry in the lift as I went up and down. If I had time to spare, I would invite people into the office for a cup of tea or coffee and a chat – an excellent way of picking up information. Soon a rumour got about that people had begun hanging around on the landing outside the lift, in the hope of catching me as I started down – or, alternatively, that they cleared off when they heard I was coming, so as to avoid being interrogated about what they were doing. Either way, I did not mind, as I felt that a bit of modernisation was definitely needed: I tried to make myself available whenever I could, to show people that I was aware of their problems.

Right at the outset I decided I was going to work absolutely flat out, fourteen or even eighteen hours a day if necessary, and put every ounce of my energy and experience into the job. My aim was to change the Met for the better – no less. When I took over, I told a reporter from the *Daily Telegraph* that the force was in crisis, and I meant it. There was a very great deal to be done. If at the end of five years I had succeeded, all well and good. If I had failed, at least I would know that I had done my best.

The Met was, and is, a formidably large organisation. It had 26,500 officers when I took over, 30,300 when I left – a quarter of all the police in England and Wales. Along with MI5 it is responsible for coordinating the drive against terrorism, and it has the task of protecting the Royal Family, the Prime Minister and members of the Cabinet not just in the United Kingdom, but anywhere in the world.

The agenda that I faced was much the same as the one I had been tackling as deputy: the implementation of the Macpherson report's recommendations; the bringing in of boundary changes as the Met contracted; the re-formation of the force into boroughs that matched local authorities; the beefing-up of the CID (on which I was particularly keen), and follow-through with anti-corruption measures.

Among my early initiatives was a war on bureaucracy, similar to the one we had waged in Northumbria. The review was headed by Tarique Ghaffur, then a deputy assistant commissioner, who very soon identified £10 million of savings – whereupon I asked him to go back and look for more.

At the end of February and the beginning of March we held a series of meetings at which we discussed how to improve our methods of dealing with bulk or volume crime, which may be low-level, but is nevertheless very important to members of the public. Our aim was to apply some of the techniques used in investigating major crimes, such as fingerprinting and DNA, to lesser crimes as well.

One special interest of mine was the launch of the Scientific Support College at Hendon, where the Detective Training School had closed down some five years earlier. Spurred on by some of the criticisms levelled at the Met in the wake of the Lawrence and other inquiries, and fired by the example of the training school we had had in Hampshire, I was very keen that the premises should again be used for detective training, and as an academy for scientific development, and major investigations. I was delighted when we reopened it in March 2002.

On 7 and 8 March 2000 the Met's top team held all-day policy meetings, to work out a way forward. High on the list of issues, inevitably, were corruption, and the anti-corruption initiative launched by Paul Condon and myself a year earlier, which now needed revamping. We also planned yet another attack on bureaucracy, and discussed

methods of consulting the Police Authority and our other new partners, to ensure that they had their say about how the Met should be
managed and financed.

Crime featured largely in our deliberations. I was determined to
launch a major attack on crime and drive it down, while at the same
time pushing up our detection rates. Having enjoyed considerable
success in this field while in Northumbria, and having written a report
on national crime reduction, I felt confident that we could make
significant improvements in London. My instinct, once again, was to
get as many officers as possible into the front line.

There were many loose ends to be tied up. Some criminal cases
that were still running had to be brought to a conclusion, and the
recommendations of the Macpherson report had to be implemented.
There could be no argument about that. The previous Commissioner
had signed up to the report, and I as his deputy had done the same; so
had the Prime Minister. Everyone concerned had agreed that we
should go through with the reforms, and once they had said so, I was
absolutely determined that we would give nobody any grounds for
complaint.

We also had to arrange financial compensation for the Lawrence
family, and along with the Chairman of the Police Authority, Lord
Harris, I was given the task of sorting the matter out. The legal position
was complicated, because the family themselves had not been the
victims of police negligence. I met Neville Lawrence several times, and
formed a good relationship with him; I also had several meetings with
Doreen Lawrence, the first being organised by a distinguished church
leader, who brought her to see me in my office at Scotland Yard.

I knew that she had been reluctant to come into the headquarters
of the Met, but in the event we had a rewarding conversation, which
lasted an hour and a quarter. It certainly did me good, as it enabled
me to understand her point of view more clearly, and I believe it was
a cathartic experience for her – a turning point in her long ordeal. I
think she saw that I was genuinely anxious to help her, and thereafter,
whenever we ran into each other, we got on very well. Several of our
meetings took place at the award ceremonies of the Anne Frank Trust,
which recognises members of the community who have shown outstanding moral courage.

My encounters with the Lawrences confirmed me in my belief that, busy though I was, I should meet individuals as often as possible, so that I could see difficult matters in personal terms, even if it sometimes meant listening to things I did not like to hear. I recognised that people had the right to tell me that we, the Met, were doing things in the wrong way.

Another crime that raised awkward problems was the murder of ten-year-old Damilola Taylor, who was stabbed in the thigh by another boy, or boys, with a broken bottle, on his way back from school in Peckham, and left to bleed to death. Our inquiries showed that in the area where he had lived there were several groups of disadvantaged youngsters who had more or less run wild. Many of them had been abused from the age of five onwards, often while they were in care, and when they got back into the community, they dropped out of school. Many were on drugs, and had no one to look to other than their gang leaders. The word 'feral' was applied to them, and it was no more than the truth: they really had turned wild.

We had to build up our evidence stage by stage, and during the trial it looked weaker and weaker, as one of the witnesses' accounts was found to contain inconsistencies about the youths we had arrested. It came as no surprise to us when the case was thrown out by the court. I was at a meeting of the Police Authority when the news came that all the defendants had been found not guilty, and I realised with a heavy heart that we were going to have to start again. A great rush of media people assembled outside the building, demanding to know what we were going to do about it; but because I had nothing to say at that stage, I slipped out the back. I felt our failure personally, because I had got to know the Taylor family well, and now we had let them down. My reaction was to set up an inquiry under Bishop John Sentamu, the Bishop of Birmingham, and now Archbishop of York, who had served on the Lawrence investigation, and give him carte blanche to re-examine every aspect of the case. Many within and without the Met had grave reservations about his appointment; but his conclusions, although critical in some areas, stated that the Met had moved on considerably since Macpherson. It was a huge relief when different youths were arrested later – but, as I write, they have yet to come to trial.

One very important initiative was Strongbox, an operation designed to show that proactive policing, led by intelligence, could be effective in reducing crime. A small team of about twenty officers went into one borough at a time, intelligence officers first, and then detectives. The outcome was a significant reduction in offences in most of the boroughs visited, and the drop was sustained, because local commanders reorganised their methods and worked on the lines the Strongbox team had pioneered.

The early days of my commissionership seemed to be punctuated by terrorist explosions – eighteen of them, as splinter groups of the IRA detonated bombs in efforts to unsettle us. There was one outside the BBC, another at Ealing, and in September a rocket was launched at MI6's headquarters building on the south bank of the Thames. We were lucky not to lose many lives, particularly in Ealing.

During September we moved 300 more officers from central posts into the front line, but the reality still was that we didn't have enough men and women to police London properly. Although, that year, we managed to secure the biggest budget in the Met's history, with provision for 1,000 extra officers to go on the streets, I wanted still more.

In the autumn of 2000 I launched a new policy for relations with the media. Over the years the Met had become more and more secretive and cautious: officers had not been allowed to talk to the press without the authority of an inspector or someone of more senior rank, and this attitude had tended to attract suspicion and contempt. The Stephen Lawrence case had put our reputation on the floor, and it seemed to me that we needed to make strenuous efforts to rehabilitate ourselves and restore our own confidence. Perhaps because we ourselves had gone into our shell, the press, for their part, had withdrawn and distanced themselves.

After consultation with the top team, I decided that we should become far more open: it seemed obvious that we should make ourselves more accessible and answer any sensible questions that were put to us; also that we should spread good news whenever we had some to give out, as well as coming clean when things went wrong. Apart from anything else, greater accessibility suited the Met's new structure. Addressing the Society of Editors' national conference in October

2000, I explored the relationship between police and press, and declared that I was committed to 'improving our mutual relationship. All I ask is that you fairly report on the ninety-nine per cent of work we do well – and not major on the one per cent we do badly.'

I am glad to say that the initiative was well received all round, and I am sure it increased public confidence in us.

I myself worked hard to foster good relations with national newspapers, mainly by being open and making myself available to the editors – Piers Morgan at the *Daily Mirror*, Rebekah Wade on the *Sun*, Andy Coulson on the *News of the World*, Dominic Lawson on the *Sunday Telegraph* Alan Rusbridger on the *Guardian* and Paul Dacre at the *Daily Mail.* I also struck up friendships with several broadcasters, in particular Nick Ferrari, which prospered on mutual respect and straight talking. Sometimes this policy alarmed my own public relations staff – in response to requests for interviews they were saying 'No' while I was saying 'Yes' – but on the whole it paid off handsomely. I owed much to the skill and diligence of my press team, headed by Dick Fedorcio and Joy Bentley: we were in touch almost every day, and I relied on them to contact me immediately whenever important news broke.

Hardly ever was there a misunderstanding, but a ridiculous one occurred early in my commissionership, in July 2000, when Dick rang me in my flat, late at night, to say that Euan Blair had been found lying drunk in Leicester Square and had been arrested. Because I thought Dick had said '*Ian* Blair' – my deputy commissioner – I was naturally somewhat alarmed. When I realised that he was talking about the Prime Minister's sixteen-year-old son, I relaxed. Oddly enough, although the media had the story, it was not included in the *Today* programme at six o'clock the next morning, and it did not break until later in the day.

One major cause of concern at the time was the level of violence against women, particularly in their homes. In October we held a conference on the problem, during which we went through all the incidents of domestic violence recorded in the United Kingdom during one twenty-four-hour period. The meeting attracted widespread publicity and helped bring the subject into the open, even if it increased apprehension by making some women more fearful of being attacked.

By the end of the year our innovations were starting to show results. Crime was already on the way down. The annual total of offences had fallen by 23,000, and in the same twelve months the intake of police recruits had risen to double that of the previous year.

My instinct, always, was to launch what I called 'thousand-bomber raids' – to do things in a big way. In February 2001 we started Operation Crack Down, a major offensive against drug-dealers. Targeting some 700 addresses, our officers seized heroin, crack, cocaine, cannabis and ecstasy with a street value estimated at £2.3 million, and arrested over 1,000 suspects. But although the raids themselves were successful, they did not have the knock-on effect we hoped for. We thought that if we could drive drugs off the streets, the number of street robberies would fall dramatically – for many minor crimes are committed by addicts desperate for money to feed their habit. In the event, the impact of Crack Down were disappointing, and it seemed to have no effect on street crime.

To the police, 'street crime' is robbery – theft, and the use of force to commit the theft, mostly in public, but also sometimes in private. For five years from 1995 until 2000 there had been a steady climb in the volume of street crime, which could be directly correlated with the increased opportunities created when ATM cash machines were first brought in. A person who had just taken out a handful of bank notes, and had a card with a pin number, was an obvious target; but the phenomenon that really hit the Met, and indeed the whole of the United Kingdom, was the proliferation of mobile phones.

As the number of subscribers rocketed, rising from 500,000 to nearly 50 million in five years (almost one per head of the population), mobile phones quite suddenly became the new visible opportunity on the street: they were immediately saleable, as there was a good second-hand market for them, especially overseas, and they were worth quite a bit of money. The manufacturers were not particularly interested in making their equipment secure, because of the expense, and went on pouring out ever-greater numbers.

In the United Kingdom mobile phones are subsidised, so that a handset is relatively cheap, but with it a subscriber buys a package of calls, so that the price paid depends on the amount of time for which the phone is used. If it is stolen, the service-providers start losing money, because they need the subscriber to be making calls. The handset is less important. The service companies therefore made arrangements with their insurers, which meant that someone who had a handset stolen needed only to report it over the phone, whereupon he or she would be immediately authorised to get a new one free, because the company wanted the person back on line as soon as possible.

As a result, many people began to report robberies falsely, and this caused us a great deal of work. Early in 2001 I called for the mobile phone companies to make it more difficult to swap SIM cards between sets. Already more than 30 per cent of all muggings and robberies in the Metropolitan area involved handsets, and because three-quarters of the offenders were under seventeen, I considered phone mugging an extension of school bullying. Then, after the terrorist attacks of 11 September 2001 in America, Operation Calm drew more than 1,000 officers out of London boroughs, for redeployment in the central Government Security Zone (see page 273). This greatly reduced the presence of uniformed police in the outer boroughs, and so increased opportunity and led to another sharp increase in thefts.

In February 2002 the rise in street crime induced the Home Secretary, David Blunkett, to tell the *Evening Standard* that I had until next August to get the matter in hand, or else I would be replaced (more of that later). In fact we had already launched a major initiative for recovering control of the streets, and at Christmas 2001 we had begun Operation Safer Streets.

For this we took 50 per cent of the traffic officers off traffic duty and posted them into boroughs with a high incidence of robberies. We moved their lockers and vehicles there, and although a few of them objected to the change, the vast majority set about their new task with a vengeance. We also brought back the Q-cars, and put dogs in them, so that trackers and handlers could reach the scene of a robbery within minutes, and pick up the trail of the thief from the spot.

The outcome was a massive reduction in street crime during the first month. Our team was then interviewed by the Prime Minister's Delivery Unit, to elucidate the main causes of robbery, and we more or less repeated the mantra of 'tough on crime, tough on the causes of crime', which Tony Blair had used years earlier. We pointed out how unhelpful it was that all young offenders got bail, because if they thought they were going to be gaoled, they would commit as many robberies as they could before they went down. Lenient sentences were another problem, because offenders were back on the streets so soon.

We also made some fairly robust remarks to newspapers about the failure of the mobile phone service-providers, and this publicity led the companies to revise their arrangements with insurance companies. When we suggested that they should devise a means of turning a stolen handset into a useless lump of plastic, they created a CEIR database, which meant that if a phone was stolen, and the user reported the theft, that handset could be immediately blocked across all the networks. The response of users was to find, on the Internet, a system whereby they could re-programme their phones – whereupon we negotiated new legislation to make that a crime, and we set up a Mobile Phone Crime Unit to identify people who were re-programming and stealing handsets.

Our other main focus was on schools and youth communities. Many robberies were taking place not only on the way to and from school, but also inside buildings, and a great deal of victimisation was going on. Especially in central London, teachers were having a hard time. We therefore created the Safer Schools Partnership, whereby we put police officers into the schools, not to teach, but to help run the establishments and support the staff. The officers concerned could intervene immediately in cases of bullying, and were trained in 'restorative justice' – the system of bringing together offender and victim, together with their friends and families, to discuss what had happened in each incident. The school police naturally had their full range of powers, including that of arrest.

Our innovations created widespread interest all over the country, and I was summoned by Tony Blair to discuss them. Our meeting was one of the most successful I have ever had, and afterwards I said in public how much we, the police, welcomed support from the highest level. In due course it gave rise to the Prime Minister's Initiative on Street Crime, and the net outcome was that some London boroughs received significant contributions towards programmes of behavioural improvement. The Department for Education and Science negotiated for us to station police officers in schools full-time, and we now have 160 officers working in that role.

Throughout this period our general performance was constantly being compared unfavourably with that of the New York Police Department. But the fact was that we had 26,500 officers against their 42,000, and both cities were much the same size, with the same population mix, and a similar distribution of wealth and deprivation. Another advantage for the NYPD was that it had no national responsibilities. I kept saying, 'Give us 42,000 police officers, and we could do as well as them.' A superficial look at the figures suggested that the police budgets in both places were much the same, but when the costs were analysed, it became clear that in New York buildings, pensions, information technology and so on – many of the major expenses – were funded by the Mayor, and the NYPD only paid salaries. We, in contrast, had to pay for everything, and the real difference in revenue between them and us was identified as £1 billion a year. Besides, the chances of getting murdered were far higher in New York than in London: the NYPD might have reduced the number of homicides, but their rate was still three times worse than ours. Furthermore, we worked for the most part unarmed, whereas all their officers carried guns.

Until 2001–2, the Met had never achieved all of its targets, but since then we have hit all our targets bar one. Improvements have been continuous. In the Safer Vehicles campaign we started taking fingerprints and DNA samples off cars and trucks – something we had never done before. We increased the field-force of SOCOs (Scene of Crime Officers), and after I had initiated a review of our fingerprinting process, we speeded it up so much that the time taken to get an identification was reduced from two and a half weeks to twenty-four hours. DNA testing came down to six days. These improvements were so startling that one judge refused to believe that we had taken a fingerprint from a crime scene, identified the offender within three hours, and found the stolen property on him. Smelling a rat, the judge insisted that everyone who had been involved in the case must come to court to give evidence – but when they did, he admitted that he had been wrong, and the burglar was convicted.

By 2003 we were wanting to widen our mission beyond the area of small crime and get away from the fixation on robbery. Certain sections of the Home Office by no means welcomed the idea: they wanted to keep the Street Crime Initiative going, because they felt comfortable with it. In our view it was out of date. At first it had seemed exciting and original, but a couple of years later it had become no more than a yardstick for measuring police performance. I became very keen to change things, and I decided to have a go during a meeting with the Prime Minister. Maybe I got a bit carried away, but at a critical moment there came a lull in the discussion, and I seized the chance to stand up and say to Tony Blair: 'Do you know what you ought to do, Prime Minister?' You want to widen this from purely street crime. You ought to look at volume crime, and I think probably you ought to split it . . . You need to consider a wholly different way of doing things.'

Blair smiled and said, 'Oh – yes – well. OK, John.' When he glanced at the other Cabinet ministers and asked 'What do you think?', they all agreed and the policy was changed. Then and at other times I found that the Prime Minister was perfectly willing to listen to what professionals had to say, and act on their recommendations – a sign of strength rather than of weakness.

The Met's relations with the Home Office were often edgy, especially when David Blunkett became Home Secretary. We knew that the citizens of London wanted us to tackle the problems that were making their lives miserable, and we wanted to work to a citizens' agenda, rather than being driven by the Home Office. Tim Godwin set up a project called Reassurance Policing, the forerunner of what are now known as Safer Neighbourhoods, under which we worked to the priorities of people living in particular areas. There are now 265 teams at work, and the level of public confidence in the Met is the highest for a decade, and the highest in the country.

At the same time we were looking to enhance the effect of Trident, the operation run by a special squad of officers against black-on-black shootings linked with drugs, which had been launched by Paul Condon in 1998 and had proved very successful, this was assisted and driven by the courageous Lee Jasper, now advisor to the Mayor of London. In some parts of London, Brent and Lambeth particularly, the level of violence had become appalling: a new culture had grown up in which young black thugs known as 'Yardies' ostentatiously drank champagne, drove high-powered cars and casually shot anybody who annoyed them. Even the most trivial offence – accidentally treading on someone's foot, or looking at him in a way he did not like – could amount to a death sentence. Among the fraternity, every killing enhanced the status of the murderer, and almost all shootings were carried out with handguns that had started life as toys or blank-firing pistols, but had been turned into lethal weapons by some back-street armourer.

There was no secret about the fact that this violence was being fuelled by the importation of drugs from Jamaica. Carriers known as 'mules' were bringing drugs into this country, usually cocaine packed inside condoms, which they then swallowed. These criminals were completely unscrupulous, prepared to prey on young and vulnerable people in the course of their trafficking. The Jamaicans had asked for help in their attempts to stop the traffic, and through Trident we established a crime liaison post in Kingston, funded by the Met. Then in July 2002 we brought over some police officers from Jamaica, to work with us in identifying gang members.

It was important to understand what Trident was trying to confront, and to refute the popular conception of Jamaica as a tropical holiday island. In fact it is a desperately poor society, conveniently positioned halfway between the suppliers of drugs in Colombia and the ever-voracious markets in America and Britain. Once you have seen the poverty, and realised how few chances people have of earning good money in a legitimate way, you can immediately understand why so many of them go into drug-trafficking.

In London the black murders were hard to investigate, because fear of reprisals made witnesses extremely reluctant to come forward. But gradually, as the Operation Trident team built up to a strength of nearly 300 officers, we began to glean more intelligence from members of the afflicted communities, and the number of murders started to fall.

Working with the Jamaican authorities, we installed new detection equipment at both ends of the drug couriers' line – in Kingston and at Heathrow – to pick up any form of narcotic or explosive substance, and this effectively stopped imports of cocaine by the ingestion method. The kit is extremely sensitive, and needs to be set at precisely the right level: if it is on too fine a scale, it will pick up tiny traces of drugs on anyone who has done no more than handle Jamaican money.

One day a telegram came from Kingston to say that there had been a shooting by the Jamaican police in a remote area called Crawle. The suggestion was that a senior policeman called Reneto Adams – a senior policeman, and a very charismatic character, voted Jamaica's Man of the Year in 2002 – had gone out with six others to a place in the backwoods ostensibly to arrest a man, but in fact had shot two men and two women in cold blood.

Within two days another telegram arrived at the Yard. Would the Commissioner consider sending a team to investigate? We felt that if we failed to help, it would seriously damage our other efforts at cooperating with the Jamaican authorities; so, at two days' notice, I dispatched Alan Brown to do the reconnaissance, telling him I would join him at the end of the week.

Alan flew out a couple of days later, and, because of its political implications, the investigation turned out to be one of the most important he had ever conducted. As I write, in June 2005, its outcome remains undecided, but it could bring the Jamaican Government down.

Adams had been put in place by the Prime Minister over the head of the Police Commissioner, Francis Forbes, and it seemed that he had carried out political murders under the guise of crime prevention. When I went out to Kingston, I became very good friends with Francis and he used me as a confidante. While in Kingston I continued to develop the excellent working relationship with the Minister for National Security, Peter Phillips, and he involved me in some of the difficult decisions which faced Jamaica.

I returned to England after only three days, but Alan and his team spent six months in Jamaica, investigating the circumstances of the shooting. As I write, in June 2005, the outcome of the case remains undecided: Adams's trial is set to take place in the spring of 2006.

At home in the Met, we carried out surveys of staff morale, spread the message of what we were trying to achieve, and listened to what all ranks had to say. We were also bringing in a new system of command and control, known as C 3I, and replacing out-of-date equipment with the latest technology, including issuing all officers with Ground

Positioning System sets, which told them their whereabouts to within a few metres, so that we could tell where they were at any given moment. My deputy, Ian Blair, was extremely successful in recruiting funds for the new system: he raised £180 million, and we certainly needed it, for we were sometimes lacking in even the most basic forms of communication. I myself used to test a police station every now and then by trying to ring in on the ordinary telephone line, and if my call went unanswered for twenty minutes, as it sometimes did, I would become quite cross.

Above all, I was anxious that the force should become proactive, rather than reactive: I wanted us to be thinking ahead like chess players, devising possible moves to counter problems that might crop up in the future. Shortage of money was a serious problem: over the past ten years the Met had suffered a fall in income, in real terms, and I was determined to go before the Police Authority and the London Assembly to argue our case, forcefully if need be, for a substantial increase in funds – as much as 30 per cent over the next three years.

During my eighteen months as deputy I had given talks in the House of Lords and other centres of government, explaining the initiatives that we proposed the Met should take. As a result, one or two eminent people came up to me and offered to serve on an advisory committee, rather on the lines of the one I had convened in Northern Ireland. I suggested that we should meet at the Yard, over dinner, once every three or four months, to give everyone a chance to air their views about what we were doing right or wrong.

In the end I had a group of ten or twelve people, all at the zenith of their professions – businessmen, church leaders, captains of industry. The range of talent was astonishing, and as conversation flowed, I would make notes of what was being said. So excellent were the meetings at producing ideas that I kept them going throughout my five years as Commissioner. None of the participants was paid a penny: all came along purely out of a desire to see the Metropolitan Police succeed, because they realised that effective policing was vital to the well-being of the city, and of the country as a whole. The advice they contributed was invaluable: we could not have afforded to retain even one of them on a professional basis, let alone the whole group – yet they gave their services free. One lesson I learnt from them was the value of collecting people from a variety of backgrounds and professions.

Among the most intractable problems, which persisted right through my time as deputy and as Commissioner, was that of trying to eradicate corruption from the Met. My predecessor Paul Condon had made the first major attempt to tackle it with the launch of Operation Othona in 1994, when a number of episodes had given concern to senior officers at Scotland Yard: police surveillance logs had mysteriously gone missing at Hainault; and in 1993 a drugs trial had collapsed in such suspicious circumstances that the judge declared that the drug dealers' criminal activity paled into insignificance compared with what the police appeared to have done.

A number of Met detectives were confidentially telling senior officers whom they trusted that there were corrupt elements in both the Met and the National Crime Squad. These people, it was suggested, were destroying covert police investigations and subverting them, by selling intelligence to criminal enterprises.

All this led senior officers at the Yard to set up Operation Othona, which turned out to be the longest-running and most secret investigation in the history of the Met, and continued right up to the creation of the anti-corruption squad in 1998. The unit that ran it was covert in every detail: it was set up on a site outside London, and was staffed only by hand-picked detectives whose integrity was beyond question. The first few were chosen by the Commissioner himself, and the remainder by those whom he had selected. They were led by two formidable detectives, Deputy Assistant Commissioner Roy Clarke and the then Detective Chief Inspector David Wood.

Detectives appointed to work on Othona were shocked by the scale of the corruption that their inquiries began to reveal. It seemed that there were probably 200 'nominal' offenders, in various categories: some were actively corrupt, some were thought but not proved to be corrupt, and others had been corrupt in the past, but now were dormant.

Over a number of years the operation built up an intelligence database of names of suspect officers. Information and ideas were gleaned from studying suspicious incidents, especially trials that had broken down, or covert investigations that had been compromised. Othona officers networked into the criminal fraternity and spoke to informants who came forward to allege corruption. They also used intrusive surveillance methods, bugging police stations, police telephones, and on occasions officers' cars and even homes, to elicit evidence of corrupt activities.

For the time being no action was taken against suspects, because the evidence against them was not conclusive. But towards the end of the 1990s the Commissioner decided that the problem of corruption was serious enough for him to go public on the matter. On 4 December 1997 he appeared before the Home Affairs Select Committee and caused a sensation by declaring that maybe 1 per cent of his force – which meant (though he did not say so) some 250 officers – might be suspect.

Until then the campaign had been covert. Now it went overt, and the anti-corruption squad was created. At first it was called CIB3, but later it was renamed the Internal Investigations Command. In January 1999 Detective Superintendent Bob Quick (later Chief Constable of Surrey) was placed in charge of its operations, and had three teams, each headed by a detective chief inspector, reporting to him – about sixty officers in all. The other superintendent was Brian More, later Deputy Chief Constable of Surrey.

Bob was new to the world of police complaints and corruption, and confessed that when he heard what was going on, 'it came as a shocking revelation'. The new unit went into action at once, its first case being that of three men who had been frequenting a flat in east London. Intelligence came in that two former members of the Flying Squad, and one serving member who had been posted to Limehouse police station, had corrupt relationships with informants and were seeking through their underworld contacts to identify a criminal who had a stash of drugs. Their plan was to execute a warrant under the guise of being police officers, search the premises, seize the drugs and sell them. They might then give some of the drugs back to the informant, as a reward, and siphon off the rest of the proceeds.

Armed with a forged warrant, all three men went along to the flat one evening. The place had been fitted up with video and audio coverage inside as well as out, so that they were caught absolutely red-handed. Covertly taken video footage showed them turning up at the address. When no one answered the bell, they jemmied the door and broke in. When they came to trial, extraordinary as it seems, one of them was acquitted by the jury on the grounds that during the raid he had been suffering anxiety and panic attacks, and did not really know what was going on. For anyone who saw the video tape of him keeping a watch outside the building as his colleagues jemmied the door, and then loading drugs into a carrier bag before leaving the premises at speed, this seemed a strange decision. But at least the other two were convicted.

Other initiatives soon followed. One was Operation Ethiopia, an inquiry into the Flying Squad. Two of the squad's officers turned supergrass, and that led to more arrests and the discovery of more corruption throughout the London area. Operation Russia was an investigation into the Regional Crime Squads in south London: again, it emerged that detectives had been dealing in drugs and falsely claiming rewards. If they got hold of some information, they would attribute it to one of their friendly informants, and put him up for an award, which could be of several thousand pounds. They would then split the money with him. Also revealed were instances of detectives fabricating or destroying evidence in return for backhanders.

At the end of the 1990s an independent detective agency called Southern Investigations, based in Sydenham, was frequently coming up on the anti-corruption squad's radar; so it was decided to conduct intrusive surveillance and bug the firm's offices. The task proved extremely challenging, because the premises were built like a bunker, and it took six months to drill – very slowly – through walls of steel-reinforced concrete. Eventually it became possible to monitor conversations, and the hidden microphones picked up much intelligence about the activities going on inside: via the agency, corrupt officers were selling stories about their investigations to newspapers, and being paid quite handsome amounts of money – an unsavoury business all round.

That surveillance exercise triggered Operation Two Bridges, which illustrated the extraordinary complications to which corruption can lead. A criminal called David James, living in Forest Hill, was married to a young model, Kim, who had appeared in television advertisements; but their relationship was failing, and James wanted to ensure that when they separated he would win custody of their one-year-old son. In the agency's office he hatched a plan whereby the firm would arrange for drugs to be planted on Kim, so that he could get her convicted and destroy her chances of keeping the child.

The agency then contracted another criminal from south London to plant the drugs, which he duly did, placing them in Kim's car in the middle of the night. Unknown to him, the man had been under surveillance by our anti-corruption officers, who took the car away at 2.15 a.m., searched it, found the drugs, replaced them with a placebo pack and drove the vehicle swiftly back to the place where it had been parked.

Kim had no inkling of what had happened, and for the time being our officers took no further action, because they did not yet know who the corrupt policeman or policemen were. But then, on the Met intelligence system, up came the name of a detective constable stationed at Bexleyheath – I will call him DC 'A' – who revealed himself by putting an entry on the database which said, 'There's a woman called Kim James who lives in Forest Hill. She's a drug-dealer, and often carries drugs in her car.'

We already knew that DC 'A' had connections with an ex-police officer, here called 'B', who frequented Southern Investigations' office, and was often on the telephone to them. Obviously, 'A' was being paid to get Kim James arrested, and he began to put pressure on an officer at Mitcham police station to make the arrest.

Then, under 'participation authority', with the agreement of the Crown Prosecution Service, I personally authorised the drastic step of feeding the false intelligence about Kim to a team of local officers, who believed it was genuine, and allowing them to act on it. Having searched Kim's home and car, and found what they believed to be drugs, they arrested her. The shock caused her to faint – which did worry us – but we took the conscious decision that although it was extremely regrettable to upset her so badly, on balance the public interest demanded that we should follow through and expose the corrupt officers, who would have been in a position to cause enormous damage if they had been left alone. At the police station Kim would normally have been charged and detained, but we managed to orchestrate things so that she was released on bail, without arousing the suspicion of the arresting officers.

Eventually, after several months, everything was sorted out. By roundabout means we forced 'A' into a compromising position, so that he was caught lying, and trying to force an informant to lie on his behalf. 'A' and a number of others were arrested: he and David James were convicted. Kim, in the end, though distressed by the whole episode, was able to keep custody of her child. From the Met's point of view, the operation carried high risks, but I have no doubt that we were right to go through with it, because corrupt officers are so dangerous, not only to the public, but to honest police officers and to undercover officers, whom they can betray.

Another case had an even more bizarre conclusion. Three corrupt detectives, consorting with some criminals, were led by our people to believe that their intended victim would be at a certain hotel on a certain day. To lure them in, we hired a hotel room in the name of the man they were after, bugged the room, left his car in the car park, and deposited his car keys and passport in the room.

Along came one of the corrupt detectives, who used his warrant card to gain access, pretending that he was going to arrest the man who had reserved the room. Instead, by the back door he let in a posse consisting of three other corrupt officers and a couple of criminals, who, having seen the decoy car, had punctured its tyres. The whole lot then lay in wait, discussing what they intended to do to their victim. Through the equipment we had planted, we heard them planning to bash him over the head, roll him in a carpet, carry him off in a car and throw him in the sea. Instead of any of that, they were all arrested.

Roy Clarke and Bob Quick could scarcely believe that police officers would go to such lengths, and act in such purely criminal fashion, simply to line their pockets. As they said, it was a public outrage. With so much dishonesty coming to light, it might sound as if corruption was universal in the Met. Yet this was by no means the case. Only a very few officers broke the rules. No doubt some of their colleagues who suspected them lacked the moral courage to expose them, but that did not make them criminals as well.

The main difficulty in trying to combat corruption is that you cannot fight it from outside: you can only tackle it from within. Corruption is like a virus, mutating and adapting to new circumstances, and its forms have changed over the years. In the 1960s it was mostly low-level bribe-taking – officers accepting backhanders from pubs, clubs and betting shops, in return for turning a blind eye when they broke the licensing regulations. Then, as the law changed, and there was more legislative scrutiny of the police, corruption became much more a business of selling intelligence: crime had grown more sophisticated, and had often become a business in its own right, albeit illegal, and huge sums of money were involved. Criminals were therefore prepared deliberately to corrupt officers as a business strategy, and to cultivate people who would alert them if the police were showing an interest in their activities. Hence sights like that of a police constable driving round in a £90,000 Mercedes.

In earlier days officers who had been caught out were dismissed from the force without prosecution; but we believed it was essential to convict offenders, because if they were allowed to retire, it only moved the rotten apple somewhere else. We described the problem as 'the revolving door of corruption', whereby officers who left the force under suspicion maintained their contacts with former colleagues and set up new alliances. Ours was a difficult war, because the officers we took to court were almost always very able: we recognised that no one can be lazy and corrupt. The bad egg was often somebody well respected on the surface, and seen by his peers as industrious, highly motivated and successful.

It used to be said that there were three types of police force – those who had lifted a stone, seen the creepy-crawlies underneath and stamped on them; those who had lifted the stone, seen what was lurking there and hastily put it back; and those who said, 'What stone?' But now, in response to this campaign, many forces outside the Met have taken a much more robust line with the problem.

The strategy and methods developed by the Met have won acclaim around the globe, and our force is now regarded as one of the world's leading anti-corruption agencies. Its status is confirmed by the number of delegations that come from other countries to study our operations, and the Met works with agencies in the United States, Holland, Australia, Hong Kong, Malaysia and South Africa.

It should be emphasised that our principal task in this field is to ensure that the Met is the most honest and ethical police service in the world, and that it does not actively investigate corruption in other organisations, except to target people suspected of corrupting police staff. Nevertheless, undercurrents of dishonesty run in numerous other spheres – in the Customs, the prison service, the law and business; and, human nature being what it is, corruption will never be eradicated.

TWENTY-FOUR
9/11 and After

In the autumn of 2001 I made several trips to the United States, to visit Mayor Rudolf Giuliani and Howard Shaeffer, the Commissioner of the New York Police Department, who had been a fellow graduate on the same senior FBI course. I had the great privilege of spending five days with both of them, going around to see how they worked, and getting to know them well. At one meeting, which Shaeffer chaired, there was a lot of aggravation about his force's shooting dead a drug-dealer: senior religious figures gave him a hostile reception, complaining about the alleged aggression of his men towards the public. As Shaeffer patiently and skilfully explained what he was trying to do, in walked Giuliani. At once the religious leaders got up, stating they were not prepared to be in the same room as him. They then marched out, and took up position outside police headquarters at Number One Plaza, where they declared that more public demonstrations should take place to get their message over. Giuliani turned to me and said, 'I bet that was the shortest meeting you've ever been to,' and I replied, 'It was – when you arrived!'

In the Met we had started up the Racial and Violent Crime task force, and I discussed its success with the two Americans. Giuliani said to the Commissioner, 'You should have one.' Half a million dollars was given then and there for a similar task force to be set up. I was impressed by the speed of it all. My main question to both men was, 'What are the main reasons for your success?' and they both gave the same answer: one was the huge recent increase in the force's manpower, from 27,000 to 40,000, and the second, strong political support. Whatever else may have been said about Giuliani, he backed the NYPD to the hilt.

At about 1 p.m. (GMT) on 11 September 2001 I was on board a British Airways 747 heading for New York yet again, this time with Chief Superintendent Simon Foy, by then my staff officer, to see Bob Muller, the new head of the FBI. About two hours into the journey we were sitting in Club Class, having just finished lunch and enjoying a glass of champagne, when I heard the captain call for the purser, asking her to come to the flight deck immediately. The announcement struck me as odd, and I said to Simon, 'There's something wrong here – something strange is going on.'

A minute or two later the purser appeared and said, 'The captain would like to see you on the flight deck.' I thought it was just a social summons – an invitation to have a look round the cockpit – and that the captain had made it because he knew that I had multi-engine and jet licences, and would be interested.

'Can I finish my drink?' I asked

'I'm sorry, sir,' the purser replied. 'He wants you right away.'

I went up the stairs to the top deck, and forward to the cockpit. There in the left-hand seat was the captain, who (I later discovered) was only four weeks from retirement, and in the right-hand seat his first officer, who had been a member of the Red Arrows, the RAF's acrobatic team. At once I could see that things were not normal. The crew members were listening intently to news transmissions on the radio, and getting confused reports of a terrorist attack on buildings in downtown New York.

Quickly it became clear that some huge atrocity was being per-petrated. The captain told me that an aircraft had flown into one of the twin towers of the World Trade Center, that three or four other suspect planes were airborne over the United States, and that American airspace and all airports had been closed, so that we would not be able to land at JFK. In fact he was already heading for home, having made such a gentle about-turn that we had not noticed it. What should he do, he asked, to secure our own aircraft?

'Lock the door of the flight deck and give me the key,' I told him. I had scarcely done that when still worse news came through: another aircraft had hit the second tower of the World Trade Center, and a third plane had impacted on the Pentagon in Washington.

My most immediate worry was that something similar might

happen in London – or that our own aircraft might have a hijacker on board. Everyone on the flight deck was in a state of shock, because it was obvious even then that a large number of people must have been killed and injured. In the first-class cabin were a number of eminent American Jewish leaders, and the captain had to decide whether or not to tell them what had happened. My advice was that he should, so he made a brief announcement, explaining why we had had to turn back; but also, as a further security measure, he switched off the equipment that transmitted mobile-phone messages.

I stayed on the flight deck for the remainder of the journey, sitting on the jump seat behind the captain. The purser, knocking on the door every time she wanted to come through from the first-class cabin, told us that some of the passengers were becoming distressed, either because their journey was being aborted or because they feared they might have lost loved ones. The British Airways crew acted with their usual professionalism, and did their best to keep everyone calm. Two hours later, around Heathrow, the sky was full of returning aircraft, circling in holding patterns. But because we had sent messages ahead, our 747 went straight in through the swarm, landed and taxied to a ramp.

My protection officers met me, and we drove to the Yard, where I was briefed by Ian Blair and David Veness (Assistant Commissioner, Specialist Operations). Within two hours I was in the Cabinet Office Briefing Room (known as COBRA), at a meeting chaired by the Prime Minister and attended by most of the Cabinet. Tony Blair ran the meeting superbly, and his leadership in that fraught situation had to be admired. When the Home Secretary, David Blunkett, raised doubts as to whether the Association of Chief Police Officers could deal with terrorism, I became quite vigorous in saying that it could: the anti-terrorist branch was one part of the organisation that really did work. Immediately after I had spoken I wondered whether I should have given such a forthright reply, but at the end of the meeting two members of the Cabinet came up and said, 'Well done!'

The events of that day entirely changed the scale and nature of the terrorist threat to the United Kingdom. So far, in my time as Deputy Commissioner and Commissioner, the main threat had been from the IRA, which in recent years had carried out several attacks on the mainland. From September 1994 to February 1996 the organisation had observed a ceasefire; but on 9 February 1996 an explosion on South Quay, in London's dockland, had injured fifty people and caused widespread damage. Nine days later a bomb went off in a double-decker bus in the Aldwych, central London, killing one person and injuring eight. Then on 15 June an enormous explosion in the Arndale Shopping Centre in Manchester left 200 people injured and caused millions of pounds' worth of damage.

From the spring of 1997 the chances of peace in Northern Ireland increased, and the likelihood of terrorist activity declined. Although dissident republicans rejected the peace process, and remained determined to cause trouble, the threat from the Provisional IRA was less acute. Then, however, there was a rejection of the peace process, led by the dissidents of the IRA – the Real IRA and the Continuity IRA – who brought about a series of tragic events within the United Kingdom.

In other words, terrorism was a continuous threat, like a storm rumbling on the horizon, with occasional outbreaks of thunder and lightning. In countering it, my main agent was David Veness, a man of enormous experience and resource, whose good humour and gentlemanly manner belied a hidden toughness.

On 9/11 the threat assumed a dramatically different dimension. With suicide bombing suddenly in vogue, and any number of young Muslim extremists ready to believe that martyrdom would bring them a thousand virgins in heaven, we were faced with the possibility that attacks would be launched in the United Kingdom without warning, and with the intention of causing mass casualties among innocent victims. The scale of the new threat was not easy to grasp – but it meant not just the horror of broken bodies and wrecked buildings: what might occur could change people's very way of life.

One innovation that I brought in at Scotland Yard was the compulsory wearing of passes. Especially after 9/11, I made sure that everyone wore them, and if I found anybody without one, even in the lift, I would take him or her to task. Quite quickly everyone else followed suit, challenging people who wore no overt identification. Until then, there had been a real danger of unauthorised entry.

I myself took to keeping a full set of uniform in my flat in west

London, so that if anything happened to New Scotland Yard – a nerve centre that was and remains an obvious target – I would still be able to function fully, and would be able to appear at the scene of an outrage, or for an interview, properly dressed.

Three weeks after the attacks in the United States, I flew to New York. I went on my own initiative, and I would have gone sooner, had not the Americans asked me to wait until things had settled down. That brief visit was an extraordinary experience. At the scene of the attacks, the remains of the Twin Towers were still smouldering, and round the outside of the site people had put up posters lamenting the loss of loved ones – a tragic, pitiful sight. I spent some time with the New York Commissioner, Bernard Kerik, and with other officers who had had to deal with the appalling consequences. I spent more than an hour in Bernard's office as he took me through the events of that dreadful day, and during the course of our conversation I asked him, 'What was your biggest frustration?'

Without hesitation he replied, 'That I didn't have a phone number for the US Air Force' – for, like many of his colleagues, he had thought the country was under air attack by a foreign power – which, in a way, it was. From Bernard I went on to see the chief of the detectives, a typical NYPD cop, tough as old boots. He had been sitting in his office when the first aircraft went in, and he had witnessed the impact. *His* immediate reaction had been to rush to the armoury for a sub-machine gun, to repel the attack that he was sure was coming.

I also visited a mixed team of officers who were dealing with the relatives of British victims who had vanished in the attacks, trying to find out what had happened to individuals – a terribly difficult business. With our consular authorities, I went to see the team and thank them for what they were doing.

Down on the piers by the harbour, a headquarters had been established to give help and comfort to the bereaved – and most impressive it was. There were lawyers to sort out wills, people to identify bodies, city authorities to deal with financial problems – everything had been thought of. A boat was making regular runs from the harbour to the World Trade Center itself, so that anybody who wanted to could go and see the place where a relative had died.

I found that my three-day visit was immensely moving, but also immensely instructive. I made detailed notes of everything I saw and heard, and when I returned to England, one of my first actions was to send over a team, to see what lessons could be applied to our own planning for some similar event, if – God forbid – one should ever happen here.

On that one day we had lost more lives than in all other terrorist outrages committed in this country. Thirty-odd bodies were brought back, and later a memorial service for the victims was held in Westminster Abbey, attended by the Queen. When the service was over, I and my companion, David Veness, watched as the relatives came out, grief-stricken, and I whispered that I was going to count the number of people involved. When I reached 900, I stopped, and I said to David, '*That's* how important it is: look what a devastating effect one attack can have. One mistake in our fight against terrorism, and we could have a catastrophe on our hands.' Neither of us will ever forget that moment.

Once a month I had to present a Commissioner's update on events to the Police Authority, and any of its twenty-seven members, from all political parties, had a chance to ask me questions. When I returned from New York, I was asked what the level of threat was to this country. Not intending to tell lies, but at the same time not wanting to alarm people, I said that, along with America, we were obviously a target.

Our immediate response to the events of 9/11 was to launch Operation Calm, for which we deployed about 1,500 extra police officers in the Government Security Zone of central London, at Canary Wharf, the City Airport, Heathrow Airport and other key sites, to increase our own vigilance and to reassure ordinary citizens. In order to collect as many officers as we needed for the city centre, we had to leave some of the boroughs short of staff, and this caused distress to their management teams, who found it difficult to carry out their day-to-day duties. Much leave had to be postponed, and local politicians accused us of overreacting, so that once again I, together with David Veness, had to explain the necessity for our action.

At the Met we had to upgrade our resources and increase the anti-terrorist squad from not much over 100 to nearly three times that number. Men and women were drafted in from other parts of the police service, and specialised training was stepped up. The direction of counter-terrorism became, unequivocally, a more political matter – for the obvious reason that if the potential public harm was on an enormous scale, this was no longer an internal security issue, but a national or even international one.

Special Branch and Anti-Terrorist Branch activities increased significantly. Discussion with central government produced a clear appreciation of the changed nature of the threat, and at the same time, international cooperation and partnership was stepped up. Faced by such a complexity of threat, no single nation could hope to maintain its security by acting alone; in contrast, the collective activity fostered by 9/11 prevented several potentially disastrous events that would have affected the United Kingdom, or even occurred inside it. On an international scale the number of partners engaged in surveillance and terrorist-hunting is now surprisingly high, and it extends far beyond the United Kingdom's traditional allies.

In this country the events of 9/11 gave senior politicians a clear understanding of the threat. The Prime Minister, in particular, quickly grasped the scale of the harm that might be caused by an attack, and ever since he has displayed enormous vigour and leadership in addressing the problem.

Public awareness was sharpened by what one might call a series of wake-up events around the world – 9/11 itself, then the horror of the explosion in Bali, a classically innocent venue, where 202 people, many of them tourists, were killed by a bomb on the night of 12 October 2002. Next came the attacks in Turkey on two synagogues, on the HSBC Bank and on the British Consulate in Istanbul, all in November 2003. Still nearer home were the bombs on three suburban trains in Madrid in March 2004, when nineteen people died and 1,500 were wounded. The attacks in Spain were seen as particular successes for the terrorists: large numbers of casualties were inflicted, the Government was removed within two days, and within months Spanish troops were pulled out of Iraq.

All these attacks were clearly intended to have an impact on the morale of Western communities. Some people in Britain were still inclined to think that nothing untoward had happened. Dire events *had* happened: it was true that the attacks had not been made in the United Kingdom, but I took every opportunity of saying how dangerous it would be to assume that we ourselves were not under threat. During my time as Commissioner the combined efforts of the Anti-Terrorist Branch, the Special Branch, MI5 and security agencies abroad foiled no fewer than eight attempts by terrorists to launch attacks in this country. We believed that up to 3,000 British-born or British-based people had passed through Osama Bin Laden's training camps, and we suspected that some of them had returned home to become Islamic terrorists. A large number of suspects had been kept under surveillance, and occasionally we had lost track of one, who simply vanished from the scene – always a deeply worrying event.

My warnings were not fully vindicated until after I had retired; but then, tragically, with the London bombings of 7 July 2005, which left over fifty people dead and 700 injured, the full horror of the threat exploded on the capital. When I suggested, in a newspaper column three days after the attack, that the bombers would turn out to have been British citizens, living openly in this country, there were cries of protest. Yet brilliant detective and forensic work by police all over England quickly proved that this had indeed been the case, and that the enemy were in our midst.

Today counter-terrorist activity is centred primarily in the Middle East, in Western Europe and the United States, and its success depends on mutual analysis of intelligence, as well as on a considerable degree of personal contact and trust between security staff working in different countries.

When it comes to protecting individual public figures – members of the Royal Family and leading politicians – one key necessity is to strike a balance between providing too little cover and creating a hermetically sealed operation that cuts the individual off from his or her surroundings. Official processions are always a security nightmare, and, again, there must be a balance. You can always eliminate risk entirely by cancelling the event, or by keeping people so far away that it is hardly a public event any longer – but what does that achieve? If you restrict freedom of movement so severely that life becomes unnatural, you are in many ways handing victory to the terrorists.

The Queen Mother's funeral in April 2002 was the biggest royal event since the death of Princess Diana. Because it took place after 9/11, the potential security problems were phenomenal. Everyone knew that all the great and the good were going to be in the open – you could even buy a plan to show where they would be sitting – and also that events would take place with split-second timing, at precisely the moment predicted. Our challenge was to maintain security, but at the same time to let the procession take place in a dignified manner, as the coffin was carried from Westminster Hall to the Abbey. The crowds were immense – it was estimated that more than a million people turned out in London and Windsor – but their mood was serious and patriotic, and no ugly incidents occurred.

Barely two months later, in June 2002, the Queen's Golden Jubilee set the Met a whole series of challenges, combining the demand for the control of very large crowds with the need for the highest level of security. It should have been – and in the end was – an occasion for national rejoicing, in which the mood was one of celebration. Yet it was preceded by a significant threat directed against the Prime Minister, Tony Blair, and his wife Cherie.

As soon as David Veness's intelligence contacts became aware of this. I went to see the Prime Minister at 10 Downing Street, and warned him that we had come across something potentially dangerous. To his credit, he immediately said that he put duty before his personal safety, and that he intended to take part in the ceremonies, as planned. Cherie was equally resolute.

The result was that when they took their places on one of the temporary raked stands that flanked the Queen Victoria Memorial in front of Buckingham Palace, to watch the carnival pageant come down the Mall on the afternoon of 4 June, a considerable number of covertly armed officers were deployed all round them. I myself was not armed, but my own protection officers were, and they too were on hand. Even so, I felt acutely nervous as the procession approached, and I was constantly scanning faces in the crowd for signs of trouble and thinking, I hope to God nothing comes from somewhere. The fact that nothing untoward did happen was again a tribute to our intelligence gathering and to the precautions we took.

Another nightmare for the police is that of individuals gaining entry to royal premises. It makes no difference if an intruder turns out to be eccentric or harmless: the fact that he has penetrated security defences is always a grave concern, and completely unacceptable, for it exposes deficiencies or weaknesses in the system. Another cause for alarm is that it may encourage other people, possibly with more sinister intent, who see that security can be breached.

The most notorious case that I had to deal with was that of Aaron Barschak, who dressed up as Osama bin Laden and infiltrated Prince William's twenty-first birthday party in Windsor Castle in June 2003. The theme of the evening was Africa, and many of the guests' costumes were so exotic that Barschak managed to reach the stage and grab a microphone before he was apprehended; his father afterwards described him as a 'comedy terrorist', and said he had been seeking publicity in advance of an appearance at the Edinburgh Festival. But if he had been a suicidal extremist, with a bomb strapped to his abdomen, an unthinkable disaster might have ensued.

The fact that he was able to get in at all meant that we had to carry out a rigorous re-examination: our defences and procedures, our professional skills, our command-and-control systems had all been put in question. I happened to be in Northumberland that weekend, but David Veness made contact with me in the early hours of the following day, and he himself went down to Windsor that morning. It was clear that there must be an external inquiry, not just into the circumstances of this one incident, but into its implications for the future. I myself also visited the control room at Windsor to make a personal assessment of what had gone wrong. Imagine my anger when I found that a police officer, who had intercepted Barschak after he had climbed into the castle grounds over a wall, had accepted his explanation that he was a stray guest, and taken him along to the party. The combination of faults I found inexcusable.

One difficulty over protecting the Royal Family is that the task is not the Commissioner's alone: rather, the responsibility is tripartite, shared by the Commissioner, the Home Secretary and the Palace Authority. The political accountability is unequivocally the Home Secretary's, who bears responsibility for the security not only of the Royal Family but also of leading political figures. The Palace Authority has its own role as guardian of the Royal Family. But the operational responsibility rests with the Commissioner, not least because the

United Kingdom has never had a federal or national police service. This responsibility, moreover, extends not only to the UK, but all over the world, wherever a protected person happens to be. In this country it is obviously essential that the three different bodies involved are properly coordinated, and regular meetings are held to ensure that this is so.

Nevertheless, after the incident at Windsor, I was fully prepared to take responsibility on my own shoulders, because it was the police who had been on duty, and I went in front of the television cameras to say so. The incident led to further refinement of procedures and equipment – a process that had been going on steadily for the past twenty-five years.

After any incident involving public security, or if any major threat has been detected, the police have the difficult task of deciding how much detail to release. A certain amount of disclosure is often beneficial, in that it encourages people to come forward with information which leads to criminals being pursued and arrested; in this way, the public play a valuable role in counter-terrorism. If you take people with you, they often amaze you by the alertness and intelligence of their responses. 'Communities defeat terrorism' was at one stage the buzz phrase, and there is a great deal of truth in it.

Too much disclosure, on the other hand, can jeopardise subsequent investigations. The determining factor is always public safety. If there is a risk to health – as there clearly was when the lethal poison ricin was found in a London flat in January 2003 – it is essential to give out some basic information immediately.

To keep potentially dangerous people guessing, defensive measures should never follow any given pattern; nor should they be any more visible than is absolutely necessary. Yet, inevitably there are some occasions on which security precautions cannot be concealed. When armoured vehicles and troops appeared at Heathrow Airport in March 2003, the Home Secretary, David Blunkett, issued a statement saying that this was a response to a series of terrorist threats. Because it was nine years since the military had last been deployed at the airport, and people were not used to such a show of force, there were protests, and criticism of myself for overreacting to threats whose nature we could not, for obvious reasons, disclose in any detail.

Suffice it to say that we had clear indications that terrorists were hoping to shoot down an airliner soon after take-off or on approach with a surface-to-air missile, and we, the police, simply did not have the resources to cover the large expanses of open land to the west of the airport, from which any attack would almost certainly be launched. Hence the need for support from the Army. The irony, for me, was that the warnings had been picked up by the security services and David Veness's counter-terrorist organisation, through their international network, but there were allegations that the whole thing was a political stunt.

As for my own habit of going out on the beat even when I had become Commissioner – I felt it was necessary to demonstrate that every policeman, of whatever rank, was a constable, and committed to protecting the public, and that the safety of the public as a whole must be seen to come before the safety of any particular officer.

British measures to protect politicians are relatively low-key, compared with those used in other countries; but for them to work, the police must have the complete confidence of those whom they are protecting. This in turn means that persons being protected must undergo training with their minders, so that they come to trust them implicitly, and, if suddenly told to do something, do it immediately, no matter how inconvenient it may seem. Without such trust, the operation will fall apart. Every now and then somebody lodges a complaint to the effect that he or she has been exposed to danger at a particular time; almost always, it turns out that protection was in place, but so discreet that it went unnoticed.

TWENTY-FIVE
Law and Order

One of the major challenges, right through my time as Commissioner, was to maintain public order and prevent mass demonstrations getting out of hand. Protests taking place elsewhere while I was still deputy gave all too clear an idea of what we might expect. On 18 June 1999 (known thereafter as 'J 18') riots in the City of London had caused damage estimated at £3 million, and in Seattle on 30 November that year, even though the police had worn gas-masks and used tear-gas and pepper sprays in attempts to control the crowds, some 50,000 people had thrown the city into chaos, causing widespread damage and preventing delegates from reaching the third ministerial meeting of the World Trade Organisation.

In London my first major test came with the parade on May Day 2000, during which – we knew in advance from our intelligence sources – a hard core of anarchists, anti-capitalists and anti-globalisation militants were planning to stir up trouble. It was clear that the theme of the day, 'Guerrilla Gardening', would be a cover for all kinds of violent lawlessness.

The officer in immediate charge of our containment tactics was Commander Mike Messenger, designated the Gold Commander, who directed operations from GT, the control room on the third floor of Scotland Yard. There he sat at a console, in front of a battery of television monitors, at the hub of the most up-to-date and effective command-and-control system in the world, with officers from the Special Branch, British Transport Police, City of London Police, fire and ambulance services all at hand. A tall, slender man of vast experience, never afraid to take a quick decision, Mike had handled many a demonstration before this one, and was recognised up and down the country as 'Mr Public Order', the Met's leading expert in crowd control. Out on the ground, acting as his principal lieutenant, was another seasoned campaigner, the Silver Commander, Chief Superintendent Chris Allison.

The organisers of the May Day event had negotiated in advance for permission to hold a rally in Parliament Square: because the European Convention on Human Rights had recently come into full operation, they had the right to demonstrate, and we had to be careful that we did not infringe that right, provided it was exercised reasonably. All the same, I was worried that if a mass of anarchistic demonstrators collected in the square, they might start to daub or otherwise damage the statues, and I was in favour of boarding up the monuments. But when I suggested this to English Heritage, they declined to have anything done.

The marchers foregathered in Hyde Park, about 6,000 strong, and at first they were relatively peaceful as they moved down Constitution Hill and along Birdcage Walk to Parliament Square; but when the police corralled them in the square, they began to dig up the turf and lay it on the road in an attempt (as they put it) to turn the square into a garden. We had already decided that if they did that, such low-level criminality would not much matter, as the turf could simply be put back in place afterwards. Yet things rapidly went downhill. Naked anarchists started rolling around in puddles, and others desecrated the statue of Winston Churchill by scribbling and spraying slogans on it and laying a strip of turf over the statesman's bald bronze head, so that it looked as though they had given him a Mohican haircut.

Worse occurred when a group of about 2,000 people were allowed to move on into Whitehall, but then broke through the police cordon round the Cenotaph and vandalised it by urinating on it and spraying it with paint. Until then I had been following events from my office, but I was aghast at what I considered an unforgivable outrage, and went down to the control room, so as to be in direct touch with Mike. From that moment I was absolutely determined that nothing like this must ever be allowed to happen again.

Next the marchers rampaged up Whitehall, and a small band of about thirty masked raiders trashed the McDonald's premises at the top. In Trafalgar Square the atmosphere became seriously unpleasant, as fights broke out, bottles were thrown and cars were smashed. Then, as our officers moved the rioters on, criminal damage was done to shop windows and cars in the Strand, particularly at the Aldwych end, before the mob went off along the Embankment and over Lambeth Bridge, where Chris Allison met them, and, in Mike Messenger's words, 'took them for a walk to Kennington Park', where more fighting erupted. Meanwhile, our officers had managed to corral a large group in Parliament Square, and these gradually dispersed.

By evening there had been quite a lot of disorder, and we had made ninety-five arrests. As always in situations of that kind, our difficulty had been to decide how hard to retaliate to violence. If you start making large numbers of arrests, you lose the officers who take the detainees away, and your lines are weakened. Hence the importance of targeted intervention – of going for the people whom you know from your intelligence-gathering to be top-level agitators.

For myself, the real challenge of May Day 2000 came the following morning, when the media were full of the previous day's events. Together with the Prime Minister and the Home Secretary I went out into Whitehall to review the damage, and in front of the television cameras I stood up for the action my people had taken. I reminded the public that it was not the police, but the marchers, who had caused the trouble, damage, disruption and injuries by deliberately setting out to break the law. I pointed out that there had been a significant degree of organised criminality, and that, but for robust police action, the damage and looting would have been very much worse. I praised my officers for having acted with considerable courage, and for having been very patient and controlled in some extremely demanding circumstances.

I believe my words helped maintain the morale of the force, many of whom had had a pretty tough day. Things went less well, however, at another big public event later in 2000 – the Notting Hill Carnival, which ran from 26 to 28 August. At the carnivals of the past few years the level of violence had been steadily decreasing, and we all expected that the downward spiral would continue, without any forceful policing. We had a good relationship with the event's organisers, and we naturally hoped this would persist.

It was therefore an unpleasant surprise when the carnival turned out to be an exceptionally violent one. Two men were murdered, and the number of robberies rocketed from thirteen to 132. After the event there was some suggestion that we had allowed cannabis to be smoked openly, and allegations that our handling of the crowds had been altogether too soft.

I believe that our slightly tentative approach reflected the lack of confidence that had sapped the force's morale in the wake of the Macpherson report; but, whatever the cause, the level of violence had been totally unacceptable, and I was not surprised when Jack Straw asked to see me. We agreed that a crack-down was needed, and that we must step up our intelligence-gathering ahead of such events, so that we could take out known trouble-makers before they had a chance to make mischief.

The lessons learnt from May Day 2000 gave us plenty of time to prepare for the same date in 2001. As spring came round again, I realised that, a year before, we had placed too much faith in the organisers' promise to cooperate with us, and I was determined not to repeat that mistake.

Once again our pre-event intelligence showed that in London the hard core was hoping to cause widespread havoc. They were clever enough not to have any single organiser with whom we could negotiate coherently: instead there was a collection of elusive ring-leaders, who appealed to a large cross-section of people. Many of the crowd, we knew, would be law-abiding, and genuinely concerned about poverty and debt in the Third World; but to ensure that they created the maximum disruption, the organisers encouraged them to lay on numerous little events, based on the game of Monopoly. 'Go to the Strand and find such-and-such a firm' was a typical order. This was to be 'Monopoly May Day', and the culminating event was to be 'The Sale of the Century', which would take place at four o'clock in Oxford Circus.

Some of this information had come through the Special Branch, which always passes on useful tips, and helps Gold and Silver build up the best possible picture of what forces they may need on the day. But since the early 1990s we had been developing our own intelligence service, principally by training Public Order Intelligence Officers, and setting up Forward Intelligence Teams, known as FITs, who go to all big rallies and marches, so that they can recognise the leading trouble-makers. This had proved so successful that from 2000 onwards, before big events, we put in place significant intelligence-gathering operations, with the aim of collecting incriminating evidence about ring-leaders in advance, so that we could arrest them early on the morning of the event, or even a day ahead, before they could cause any more problems during the march itself. Most of the intelligence-gatherers were not covert – they went out in uniform, and looked like ordinary officers – but their specific role was to look for the trouble-makers.

In April 2001 the Special Branch assessed the risks of major disorder as 'serious', and we knew in advance that a vast number of people would be coming into London with the sole intent of committing theft, criminal damage and arson. They had been urged on by leaflets inciting them to 'repossess property for society', and similar slogans, and their ultimate aim was to blitz the big stores in Oxford Street. 'Oxford Street has always been the scene of riots,' said the pamphlets, quoting examples from history to prove it. Our fear was that if two or three thousand people did manage to break into Oxford Street and run amok, we would have great difficulty dealing with them.

On 30 April 2001 the Home Secretary (Jack Straw), the Mayor (Ken Livingstone) and I all went public asking people to stay away. We were not trying to stifle protests, I said; but the fact was that the marchers' behaviour last time had been completely unacceptable, and I was not going to tolerate anything of that kind again. I had not expected that I would get on so well with Livingstone, but I did, then and later, and he proved one of our strongest supporters. What he promised, he always delivered. He, too, liked red wine!

At the Yard we prepared elaborate plans, and for these, since my own expertise was in detection and investigation, I relied on the Met's public-order specialists. With the help of Michael Todd, an assistant commissioner (now Chief Constable of Greater Manchester), Mike Messenger was again in charge of crowd control: he had devised a scheme that he described as 'fluid and flexible', with a special emphasis on reserve groups of officers, who could be rapidly deployed to reinforce the main lines as and when necessary. He had already asked for a large number of extra police, but I insisted that he be given even more. At the same time we were trying to establish a good relationship with the demonstrators – not easy, in view of what had happened the previous year – and I asked David Veness to step up our intelligence-gathering, using CID spotters and covert cameras to discover the hard core's intentions. Not entirely in jest, I said to Mike, 'I want the Cenotaph guarded, and if necessary I'll stand by it with my own truncheon in my hand to make sure no one gets to it.'

All this made the build-up to May Day 2001 very tense. A couple of days beforehand, Mike Messenger and I went across to the Home Office to brief Jack Straw. 'John,' he said, 'I reckon your head and mine are on the chopping block this time!' I was confident that he, being an honourable fellow, would take some of the blame if anything went wrong; but at the same time I knew that the overwhelming respon-sibility for making sure that things went right was specifically mine, and I was utterly determined that we were not going to lose the streets of London to a riotous, unlawful mob.

For me, May Day began at 3.30 a.m., when I got up, shaved and dressed, and went down to the big breakfast laid on in the East End by the Met's Catering Department. Together with the men and women, I sat down to bacon and eggs in a vast marquee, and found the atmos-phere very optimistic. I was determined to give personal leadership on what promised to be a critical day for the Met.

For the marchers proceedings started with a demonstration at the Elephant and Castle, south of the river, and another outside Coutts Bank in the Strand. There were also mass movements of about 500 cyclists, one along from King's Cross towards Regent's Park, and another that came over the river from the Elephant and Castle, pro-testing against traffic congestion (and of course causing it), but they gave no serious trouble. After a while the main crowd moved to the World Bank, in the bottom of New Zealand House in the Haymarket. At first everything was rather like the start of 2000: the atmosphere was reasonably light-hearted and gentle.

By midday the group outside the World Bank had swollen to about 2,000, and suddenly they surged in one huge body up Regent Street to Oxford Circus, where they arrived at 2 p.m. There were still two hours to go before the official meeting time, and it did not look as though the crowd was likely to wait that long before starting its rampage down Oxford Street. At that moment – as at other critical times – I went down to the control room and slipped in to sit beside Mike at his command console, not to take decisions myself, but simply to be there, and give my moral support to the decision-takers, endorsing what they did. As always, I took care to appear calm and relaxed, because I knew that everyone was watching me, and that if I showed any sign of nervousness, it would infect others. Inwardly, I *was* extremely nervous.

Silver, the tactical commander on the day, Chief Superintendent Steve French, in the control room at Scotland Yard, recommended to Mike that he should put in a containment there and then. Mike agreed, and the order went out. On the ground Chris Allison, working with a colleague, Alan Webb, was given the task of putting in the containment – which he did by swiftly bringing in substantial reserves from other parts of the West End and moving them up to seal all four streets leading from the circus.

When a crowd realises that it is about to be contained, it almost always tries to break out; and if people do succeed in breaking through police lines, the adrenalin released by the excitement is liable to make them extremely violent. Once they cross the mental barrier of being prepared to commit crime, they become willing to do almost anything: the mass of the crowd suddenly goes critical and explodes.

Knowing this, we put the containment in place partly by stealth, and at first the crowd did not realise what was happening. When they did see that they were trapped, tempers rose rapidly. Because some tourists had been caught up among the demonstrators, we let a few people go; but then we had to harden the lines up, because our officers were getting aggravation from behind as well as in front, as scattered elements tried to join the main throng.

As the afternoon wore on, the crowd became more and more abusive and violent, and even in their riot gear, with shields and helmets, the police had a tough time, standing face to face with screaming agitators for hours on end, being insulted, spat on, shoved and jostled. Once again, their restraint was exemplary. Our aim all through was to let the crowd filter away in dribs and drabs, but every time we allowed a few to go, they started fighting us and each other again.

When people *were* let out, we made them head north, along Upper Regent Street, because everywhere else was a target-rich environment. One vociferous posse, about 100 strong, stormed off towards

Tottenham Court Road, and on the way did serious damage in Great Titchfield Street, where they smashed shop windows, stole electrical goods and set fire to cars – ironically enough, on my old stamping ground, where I had been on the beat.

There is no doubt that the day was a great victory for the Met. In contrast with 30 November in Seattle, we had held the crowd and kept the situation more or less under control. May Day 2001 was the day when the Metropolitan Police demonstrated that they were in control of the streets. We showed that people would *not* be allowed to go trashing shops and cars, attacking members of the public and frightening citizens to death. Next morning we got newspaper headlines like ONE NIL TO THE BILL, and we received many plaudits from more responsible sources, not least the Home Secretary, so that I was able to send out messages of thanks and congratulation to everyone concerned.

I grant that seven hours – from 2.30 to 9.30 – was an exceedingly long time for people to be corralled, especially as they had no toilet facilities; but had we not held them, there is no doubt that many millions of pounds' worth of damage would have been done in Oxford Street, and numerous people would have suffered physical injuries. As it was, the shopkeepers there were terrified, and spent a most unpleasant afternoon, expecting the worst.

After the event we held a number of public meetings at the Police Authority, at which people came along to claim that their human rights had been infringed. Two in particular pointed at me, and spat out, 'You'll never be forgiven for this. We'll take you to cleaners.' I said very little, but I remained confident that the greater good had been done.

In January 2005 two test cases, representing 150 others, were brought to the High Court, making out that we had infringed people's rights by unlawfully imprisoning the complainants in the circus. We were nervous of the outcome, in that we thought we might be vindicated over having penned the crowd up, but censured for having held them so long. To our great relief, in April 2005 Judge Michael Tugendhat found that, considering all the circumstances, our action had been necessary and appropriate, and that what we had done was entirely correct – a notable victory for public-order policing.

In retrospect, it is clear that Oxford Circus was a turning-point: since then May Day marches in London have been very muted, and other major events have passed off without any serious disturbance. Possibly the biggest of all was the Stop the War march, on Saturday, 15 February 2003, when a million people walked noisily but harmlessly through London. Afterwards I praised the sterling efforts of the Catering Branch, remarking that 'an army marches on its stomach, and the same can surely be said of the Met'.

It was unfortunate that violence did break out during the pro-hunting demonstration, which took place outside the Houses of Parliament in September 2004. We had no prior intelligence to say that there was going to be trouble – and at first there was none. Two-thirds of Parliament Square were full of people standing around, fairly boisterous and noisy, but law-abiding. Then, in a little roadway down past St Margaret's, Westminster, a punch-up started between the police and a relatively small group of about 300 people, who seemed to be fuelled by alcohol, and were determined to join the main crowd. We were equally determined that they should not gain access to the House of Commons.

My impression was that the mainstream of the Countryside Alliance were horrified by what had happened, and did their best to distance themselves from the fighting. Afterwards I stood up for the way the police had handled the affray – sixty of our officers were injured – and said that nobody had got cracked over the head without good reason. I could have added that, since we ourselves now video every dem-onstration, we had the evidence to prove what I was saying, and also to investigate the behaviour of our own men, if any claims were made against them. If anyone *had* overstepped the mark, he would face the legal consequences.

In the past five years counter-terrorism and the maintenance of public order have overlapped more and more, as uniformed police have taken on many counter-terrorist functions. In the past, security at public events was directed mainly at safeguarding against possible attacks by the IRA or its offshoots. Today, with the dimension of international terrorism, arrangements have to be much more comprehensive.

The visit of President George Bush to London in November 2003 was a prime example: a massive security operation had to be put in place to ensure the President's safety, but at the same time an enormous public order operation was needed to control the many thousands of people who wanted to demonstrate against the war. We had to allow them to assemble and march, because they had the right to do so, but we also had to keep the principal secure.

I myself had the privilege of meeting the President at a reception in Buckingham Palace. As the Queen brought him along the line of guests, introducing each one, the Duke of Edinburgh followed her, escorting Laura Bush, and when he came to me, he was momentarily (and understandably, in view of the numbers present) lost for my surname. 'This is Sir John ...' he began – and before he could add 'Stevens, the Commissioner of the Metropolitan Police', Mrs Bush said, 'Oh – I know him. He's the head of Scotland Yard!'

The longer I served as Commissioner, the more clearly I saw that an international centre as big as London cannot be effectively policed from the United Kingdom alone. People from all over the world are constantly pouring in and out, some to stay for a while, others to pass quickly through. Immense amounts of money circulate legally through the City, one of the largest financial centres in the world. If the Commissioner sits in Scotland Yard and thinks, parochially, that he can police the metropolis from there, he has got it wrong. What he must do is form relationships and forge partnerships in other countries, visiting them to discuss their problems and to establish close relationships.

That was what I did – in Eastern bloc countries, in Paris, America, South Africa, India and Jamaica. In September 2002, for instance, I went to Paris to see Nicolas Sarkozy, the French Home Secretary and Prefect of Paris, to exchange views about ways of combating terrorism and organised crime, and to arrange an exchange of officers, which proved highly fruitful, especially when I was asked to take charge of the inquiry into the death of Princess Diana.

As I have said, I did quite a lot of work in Romania, and became an adviser to the Prime Minister on anti-corruption measures. When things went well in Bucharest, where we advised the police on anti-corruption strategy, we set up a similar exercise in Sofia: I flew to

Bulgaria several times, and became friendly with the head of the police, whom a public survey had revealed as the most popular man in the country – a status I cannot see being achieved by any Commissioner of the Met. Among his other accomplishments he was the national karate champion, who sometimes took out his gun and laid it on the table during a meal. Our relationship, based on mutual respect, became very warm, and he was eager for Scotland Yard to be involved in his force's affairs. I was pleased when the John Jay College, at which I had taught law in New York, took up my suggestion and organised a conference in Bucharest, sending a team over to exchange views on a variety of legal and political subjects.

We also established useful contacts in Qatar, after an official from the Ministry of the Interior came over to study British methods of policing. Late in 2003 Hamish Campbell (by then my staff officer) flew out to make a quick assessment of local police needs, and in February 2004 he and I went out to meet the minister and build bridges – a trip that led to a Memorandum of Understanding between our two countries.

These overseas trips often paid such dividends. From Romania, for example, we got information about a solicitor in England who was smuggling illegal immigrants into this country; and numerous tips from South Africa helped us with operations in London. Another valuable relationship was with India. I have many Indian friends in England, and see a lot of Ranjit Singh, the head of the Sikh Association, both socially and professionally. Through the auspices of Richard Barnes, one of the Conservative representatives on the Police Authority, I was made an honorary Sikh in a ceremony at the *gudwara* at Southall, and presented with a *siropa*, an honorific scarf.

Then in November 2004 came a far greater honour: as a result of my work with the Sikh community, the association invited me and Cynthia to visit their holy of holies, the Golden Temple at Amritsar. In Delhi I established contact with our High Commission and met the police chief, who showed a keen interest not only in combating terrorism, but also in methods of traffic control. Then, after a visit to Agra and the Taj Mahal, we went on to Amritsar, where we were greeted by the Police Commissioner, a brass band, and banners proclaiming 'Welcome Sir John Stevens!' Cynthia and Richard Barnes went for a ride on an elephant, and at the invitation of a general we witnessed the evening ceremony at the frontier with Pakistan, when soldiers of each side parade in immaculate full dress and haul down their national flags, to the accompaniment of bugle calls.

Best of all, I was given the extraordinary privilege of helping to carry the *Granth sahib*, or Holy Book, a wonderfully ornate tome, which is brought out every day at 4 a.m. into the Golden Temple, and then, in the evening, borne back in a litter into its inner sanctum. To shoulder one of the litter's poles was an astonishing and humbling experience. During our tour of the precincts all our party were struck by two ancient trees growing in the temple compound: one had stories of miracles connected with it, and it was occupied by hundreds of small birds roosting – so many that it looked as though the branches were covered with snow.

Throughout my commissionership I was troubled by the weaknesses, contradictions and sheer inefficiency of our criminal justice system, and when I was asked to give a speech as part of the eightieth anniversary celebrations of my Alma Mater, Leicester University, in February 2002, I seized on the occasion to air some of my views. My particular subject was the way in which witnesses are intimidated in court, with the result that criminals often get off scot-free.

I quoted a survey in Manchester, which found that 83 per cent of witnesses who had appeared in court wanted nothing more to do with the criminal justice system. Forty per cent of witnesses felt intimidated by the defendant or lawyer. A gun gang walked free because the judge would not allow a witness to give evidence from behind a screen. The mother of a murdered child was forced to sit within inches of the man who admitted killing him. 'We know all this, and thousands of other cases like it,' I said:

> And yet we tacitly condone it and allow it to continue. Is this how we should treat people? Is this what we call support and assistance? Research tells us that fewer and fewer people are coming forward to help police, to risk going through the trauma of a court appearance. The public are becoming more and more disengaged from the criminal justice system that is meant to be there to protect them.

I went on to say that the development of our legal system in recent times had tended to be to the advantage of the defendant, 'and the guilty are walking out almost as if through a revolving door':

> So we see robbers with strings of previous convictions strutting across the estates of Inner London, having won their most recent game in court – arrogant, untouchable, fearless and ready for anything. The process actually encourages criminals in the belief that crime is merely a game of no consequence to society, local communities or their victims, so that they are not held to account.

In conclusion, I called for the implementation of reforms proposed by earlier reviews, especially the one carried out in 2001 by Lord Justice Auld. Otherwise, I warned, the country would be heading for anarchy. Afterwards, I was afraid I might have been a bit extreme, so it was a relief when I found I was being given full support by the newspapers, not least the *Sun*, which splashed my speech across its front page. Everyone seemed glad that I had rattled the lawyers' cages – except, of course, the lawyers themselves. Later, we held meetings with the Lord Chief Justice and the head of the Bar Council among others, and I stuck to my guns, emphasising the need to change the system to favour the victim. I believe that a considerable improvement in joint activity can be traced back to that time.

TWENTY-SIX
Taken to Court

On 24 October 1999, towards the end of Paul Condon's commissioner-ship, an Asian police officer, twenty-four-year-old PC Kulwant Sidhu, fell fifteen feet through the glass skylight of a factory in Twickenham while chasing two suspects, He landed on machinery and died of his injuries. The Health and Safety Executive investigated the case, and there was some suggestion that they might prosecute the Com-missioner for not issuing more comprehensive safety equipment and providing more training; but then, just after I had succeeded Paul, we got a message to say that no prosecution would take place, because the HSE recognised that the constable had been doing his duty, and that Paul had provided the Met with more safety equipment than any predecessor.

That seemed to be the end of the matter. Then on 5 May 2000 the HSE notified the Met that they would, after all, be initiating legal proceedings against Paul for alleged breaches of the Health and Safety at Work Act of 1974. Three weeks later there was another accident, remarkably similar, when PC Mark Berwick fell through the flat roof of a garage only 2.2 metres (7 feet 3 inches) high, in North London. Together with a colleague, he had been chasing three suspects: his partner crossed the roof successfully, but Mark, being heavier, crashed through and injured his back seriously enough for him to require prolonged treatment.

The reaction of the HSE was to bring charges against me as well as against Paul. From the start we agreed that a prosecution would be patently ridiculous, in that both accidents had occurred when the constables were doing their best to carry out their duty. Nevertheless, the prospect of being taken to court was highly alarming for me, because the charge of negligence, and of failing to meet the HSE's standards, was a criminal one, and could have dire consequences for my career.

In June 2001 the HSE served us with six Improvement Notices, which covered the training of officers in recognising risks, the management of incidents, and so on. We tried to settle things out of court by offering to make the safety improvements they suggested, and for a while we believed that was the end of the matter. No matter how much training is given, the fact remains that police officers often have to make snap decisions under extreme pressure, and we hoped the HSE had belatedly recognised this. Not at all. The next thing we heard was that the prosecution was going ahead.

When I had the first meeting with solicitors in my office, they warned me that the charges would be difficult to defend, because I would have to prove my innocence, rather than requiring the prosecution to prove their case against me. During the past five or six years most defendants, similarly charged, had pleaded guilty and paid fines of £15,000 or £20,000, rather than go through the aggravation of court proceedings.

For Paul and myself, it was quite different, because the cases against us were personal. If we were convicted, Paul would not only be fined: he would also lose all his directorships and business interests, and would never get any more. As for me – in Northumbria, I had introduced new safety equipment before anyone else, and had always held the safety of my officers to be of prime importance. In the Met, I had put safety at the very heart of everything I had done as a supervising officer.

I decided that if I was found guilty of neglecting the welfare of my officers, I would resign. I was in no doubt about that. Within a week of knowing I was going to be prosecuted, I wrote a letter of resignation which I put in my safe, directing that it be handed to the Police Authority if the worse came to the worst. Whether or not they accepted my resignation, I would have gone, because my position would have been untenable.

The implications for the police in general were potentially devastating. If Paul and I were convicted, I would have to issue, that same day, an instruction to all officers telling them not to climb anywhere above a height of 2.2 metres, and not to chase people for any crime –

not even for rape or murder – unless they believed that the person they were chasing was in danger of *their* life – not the police's. The whole nature of policing would be changed, and we would not be able to do our job in any shape or form. A negative ruling would destroy every officer's chance of exercising individual judgement or initiative, and would be extremely debilitating to the service as a whole.

In any event, we were served with summonses, and held consultations with Ronnie Thwaites, the QC who was to represent us. At first he was reluctant to take on the brief, as he thought there was little chance of conducting a successful defence; but when the papers came in from the HSE, and we all saw the weakness of their position and the extraordinary way in which they were pursuing the matter, he decided to defend us, becoming as determined as we were that we should be found not guilty.

After various preliminary hearings, we were committed to the Old Bailey, and each pleaded not guilty to five counts of failing to discharge our duty or contravening requirements under the Act. The trial was held in No. 2 Court, where, ironically enough, on my last appearance thirty-two years earlier, I had received my first commendation as a result of the fight and pursuit in Tottenham Court Road.

So important did we deem the trial that within the Met we formed a special group to monitor proceedings and marshal our own arguments for the media. Operation Rose was led by Assistant Commissioner Bernard Hogan-Howe (now Chief Constable of Merseyside), who held a briefing for members of the Crime Reporters' Association at Scotland Yard on 28 April, the day before kick-off, and in the course of it remarked, 'The service has always sought to work with the HSE, and this prosecution is unnecessary and unhelpful. Prohibiting officers from using their own judgement about going on roofs will be a victory for criminals, and could encourage more suspects to use this as a means of escape: a veritable "burglars' charter".' One of the key messages the group put over was that officers should be praised, rather than prosecuted, for their willingness to face dangerous situations when protecting the public and catching criminals.

The trial started on 29 April 2003, and I went to court in full uniform, because I was being charged as Commissioner. Press interest was intense, and everyone was discussing the question of whether or not we would be bailed, or whether we would have to appear every day. It was said that the prosecution would take two weeks to put their case, and that the defence would need the same amount of time.

Proceedings were opened by Mr William Norris, QC, the prosecuting counsel, who pointed out that this was a very serious matter, and suggested that the Metropolitan Police did not enforce adequate safety regulations. It was not easy to warm to Mr Norris, who had a sneering, condescending manner, and gave the impression that he was expecting an easy victory. He concentrated on the death of PC Sidhu, but said it was impossible to dissociate the two cases. He then made a serious mistake by remarking, 'Of course, Mr Stevens was the Deputy Commissioner at the time [of Sidhu's death].' Ronnie Thwaites was quickly on his feet to point out that it was the Commissioner who was personally responsible for the safety of his officers, and that the deputy had nothing to do with it.

I began giving my evidence on 15 May – from the witness box. Ronnie Thwaites and I agreed that it would be a good idea if he referred back to my first commendation, and that between us we should give the court an account of the fracas in Tottenham Court Road. After I had described how the gangsters broke into the club and carved up the proprietors, before trying to get away in a milk float, I went on:

So I was there, blowing my whistle. Another colleague came up, and there was one hell of a fight then, with me and my truncheon and them and their hatchets, and so on and so forth. And that fight spilled round the way into Tottenham Court Road. It was then actually I realised the truncheon wasn't much use. I broke it. By that time the early-morning relief was coming on duty, and they came, and as a result of that we arrested all four. It was a bloody business, and I was given a good hiding.

Q. Was the truncheon the only piece of protective equipment you had in those days?

A. Absolutely, other than fists.

Q. Well, we all come with a fist.

A. And some of us can use it better than others.

At that point I swung a right through the air, just to emphasise my point – and I think the story had some effect, as it demonstrated that I had no illusions about the reality of police work.

When Norris asked 'Was there any professional operational need for PC Sidhu to climb on to the roof?' I let fly. 'You don't *know* why officers make decisions,' I told him. 'It's a split-second decision. No one will ever know why he went on to that roof.' After I'd told of the incident that led to my commendation, I added sharply, 'Don't second-guess me about when I was on that roof in 1965. I was there, and you weren't. I feel the same about PC Sidhu.'

His Honour Judge Crane, presiding, told us we need not appear in court every day; but in fact I did go every day, except for one, when a critical anti-terrorist operation was in progress. Often I was in court from 10 a.m. until 4 p.m., after which I had to return to the Yard and start a day's work at teatime: I was back to eighteen- or twenty-hour days.

In court the case ground on and on and on, through the two accidents, and all the safety training we gave. The main prosecution evidence was given by the HSE inspector who had been in office when both accidents occurred; but in my view the witnesses called by the prosecution gave evidence very favourable to *us*. PC Sidhu's former colleagues from Twickenham praised his courage, and said he had died a hero's death doing his duty. In my own case, PC Berwick, who came to court to testify on our behalf, said the same in a typically honest and forthright way: he had been trying to apprehend criminals, which it was his duty to do. When asked if he would do the same thing again, he replied, 'In similar circumstances, of course.'

Emotion ran high when another constable, PC Steve Carlow, described how he had once wanted to climb some scaffolding in an attempt to save a builder who had suffered a heart attack. His aim was to give mouth-to-mouth resuscitation, but he was ordered by his sergeant in the control room not to go up, because there was a high wind and conditions were too dangerous. The builder had later died, and PC Carlow said, 'I felt I had let him down. I felt I had let the service down as well.'

We went through every step we had taken to provide the Met with safety equipment and training. I described how in Northumbria we had led the country investing in new equipment, and spent more money on it than any other force. We considered calling Jack Straw and David Blunkett as witnesses, because one of the Home Secretary's responsibilities is to provide the Commissioner with adequate resources, so that he can do his job. Neither was keen to appear, although both did say that, if we were convicted, they would give mitigating evidence on our behalf.

The trial was a long and debilitating experience – one of the worst and most humiliating I have ever known. (Paul Condon told me he felt exactly the same.) Although I kept up a cheerful front throughout, I did not enjoy standing outside the court in full uniform, waiting to be called. Inside, progress was snail-like, but I listened to every word and took notes all the time, to ensure that I had my own record of what was said.

Up in the public gallery one woman appeared every day. Most people didn't know her – but in fact she was an official of the Home Office, sent along to keep a detailed check on how the trial was going. My wife also was there every day, and at one stage she got into conversation with a visiting European judge, who was bewildered by the court's proceedings. He described the trial as 'an outrage', and stood it for only half a day. After that, he could take no more of such nonsense. 'Has your country gone mad?' he demanded, and away he stormed, angered beyond endurance by the futility of what he had witnessed.

One evening I went back to the Yard sickened by the idiocy of the whole performance, and my staff were getting the rough end of my tongue when suddenly in came Susannah Becks, who had worked closely with me as my chief of staff. At the time I did not know that someone had summoned her in desperation, hoping she would talk me out of my foul mood – but when she walked into my office and greeted me with the words, 'Bloody hell! I thought you'd be inside on remand by now. You mean they've let you out on bail?' my spirits rose like a rocket.

I think it helped that Paul and I got on so well together, and were manifestly at ease with each other, so that the Met past and present put up a united front. But it was not until 23 June that the jury came out with verdicts of not guilty on all the charges bar three, about which they could not agree. The judge then told the HSE to go away and consider carefully whether it was worth pursuing the matter still further.

They could, in theory, have reopened proceedings on the three outstanding charges, but fortunately they saw sense and decided to capitulate. The judge then made some scathing remarks about the HSE. That body, he said, should 'look carefully at whether the decision to prosecute in the first place was a wise and sensible decision'. In awarding £300,000 costs against the prosecution, he estimated that the trial had cost 'something over £1 million', and questioned whether 'this vast sum of public money might have been better spent on safety'. He pointed out that the case had also cost the Metropolitan Police a great deal of time and money, which 'could have been much better spent, particularly in the dangerous times we now live in'. (Other people reckoned that the total cost was closer to £2 million than to one.)

I felt hugely relieved, and glad that we could get on with our job of policing London. In a statement for the media I described the result as 'a victory for good sense', and said that the 'ill-considered pros-ecution' had demonstrated 'a fundamental misunderstanding of the unique nature of policing'. I added that if the verdict had gone against us, it would have done 'irreparable damage to the way we police Britain'. In an article for the *News of the World* I pointed out that 'officers on horses would be above the two metres from the ground rule', and asked, 'Do they want us to ride around on Shetland ponies?'

The Home Secretary (David Blunkett) also welcomed the verdict, and declared that 'the present law, which attaches personal liability to chief officers for organisational breaches of health and safety legis-lation, is unacceptable'. Our vindication attracted an enormous volume of support from the media, and the HSE was bombarded with abuse, much of it sarcastic. As Alasdair Palmer remarked in the *Sunday Telegraph*, 'The best way to protect people's health and safety is usually to find a way round the rules which the Health and Safety Executive wishes to impose.'

I am still mystified by the fact that the charges were brought at all. After the definite assurances that no prosecutions would be forth-coming, the attack came completely out of the blue. What seemed to me most extraordinary was that no one in the HSE appeared to have thought through the consequences. They were prepared to put two commissioners into the dock at the Old Bailey, for a trial that lasted six weeks, for two incidents that had nothing to do with either of us. As the judge said, the prosecution should never have taken place. It was a scandal. Some research that we put in suggested that the HSE wanted two high-level scalps, because they had been put onto a target regime, in which they had to issue more prosecutions to justify their existence. Many of our team sensed an almost personal antagonism coming from the other side: it was as if they wanted to take the Met on and teach us a lesson. The case became a battle between two giant public-sector organisations, with the taxpayer footing the bill. Whatever the truth, the HSE came seriously unstuck.

TWENTY-SEVEN
Poisonous People

The end of 2002 brought the Hackney siege, which dragged on for sixteen days – the longest that a police operation of this kind had ever lasted in Britain – and ruined the New Year for a considerable number of people who were inadvertently caught up in its ramifications.

It began on Boxing Day morning, when officers tried to tow away a car which they suspected had been used in a shooting in the West End. The vehicle, parked in Marvin Street, Hackney, was wanted for forensic examination; but when police started to remove it, a coloured man yelled at them from the window of a nearby first-floor flat. They then set up a cordon round the building and the car, and called in the Met's SO19 unit – but when armed officers tried to enter the flat, shots were fired at them, so they fired back and withdrew, uncertain whether or not they had injured anyone.

Our response was to put in a containment – an inner cordon of armed officers, and an outer cordon, unarmed. We knew the identity of the gunman: he was Eli Hall, a thirty-two-year-old Jamaican who had worked as a nightclub bouncer and had served half a dozen prison sentences for offences that included violence, drugs and the possession of weapons. He had already twice fired at police, once in Soho in August, and again more recently in Hackney. In other words, he was a desperate individual, and we knew that he was holding another man hostage. It was clear that he was highly dangerous, and would not hesitate to shoot if we tried to storm his flat: he was in an advantageous position, and if he opened fire, our officers would have no option but to shoot back, so there would be a high risk of someone getting wounded or killed. We therefore decided to settle down for a period of attrition.

301

Delay did not go down well with the sixteen residents who had to be evacuated from the block of flats. Another forty-three, who lived in neighbouring houses, were told to stay inside – much to their annoyance – and had to wait for armed police escorts if they wanted to leave the buildings. Traffic congestion inevitably built up around the area. Several people began to agitate for quick action, but were told firmly that any sudden move would be too dangerous. Considerable pressure came on us from the media, and from other members of the public who thought we were being too soft, and should take the man out regardless. In fact we were not being soft – only sensible – and we got a lot of support from local politicians and community leaders whom we took to the scene so that they could see the problem for themselves. Once we had decided to play long, I had no doubt that we should stick to our strategy.

The operation demanded a high degree of patience and stamina from the men on the ground. The weather was intensely cold, and the officers in the inner cordon, whether they were on the ground or on rooftops, had to keep still for long stretches. Arrangements were made for a service vehicle to deliver food and water to the flat: the supplies were tied to the end of a rope which Hall lowered from the first floor, so that he could pull consignments up.

At Scotland Yard the operation was directed by a Gold Commander, and the Silver Commander operated from a control van on the scene, in the outer cordon. As the siege went on and on, day after day and night after night, the senior officers worked in relays: in all, four Golds and four Silvers took part, putting in twelve-hour shifts. The operation put a heavy strain on resources, for in the middle of it large numbers of officers were needed to police the New Year celebrations which brought over 100,000 revellers onto the streets of Central London.

From the start it was obvious that Hall's state of mind was volatile, to say the least. He told police that he was on a mission from the Rastafarian deity Rah, to kill as many police officers as possible, and that he had enough ammunition 'to fill a bath'. Even when we brought other members of his family to the scene in the hope that they could coax him to come out, he made no sense.

Ever more frequent attempts to communicate with him were made by telephone and loudspeaker. But not until the eleventh day –

Sunday – was there any significant change in the deadlock. Then the hostage managed to slip out of the flat, bringing the news that Hall was indeed armed with a handgun and ammunition, and confirming that we had been right in not trying to end the siege by force.

I myself took no direct part in the operation, since I had every confidence in the officers running it. My role, rather, was to provide what might be termed high-level political leadership, keeping the Home Office, the Mayor and the Police Authority informed of what we were doing, and justifying the prolonged delay. As the days and nights passed, we kept making comparisons with other notable sieges, principally the one in Balcombe Street, which had lasted for six days in 1975, and ended when four IRA gunmen freed their two hostages and gave themselves up. Much more violent was the siege of the Iranian Embassy in April and May 1980, which left five terrorists and one hostage dead after the SAS had stormed the building in a brilliantly planned attack.

In Hackney, after Hall had lost his hostage, he went quiet for twenty-four hours. Then he began talking to the police negotiators again, but he became increasingly erratic. Cold (because his electricity had been cut off), hungry (because his food was running out) and exhausted by lack of sleep, he announced that he was not going to be captured alive. Eventually, on the sixteenth day, armed officers saw smoke coming out of his windows. What he had done was set light to his own furniture, to create some warmth, but from the outside it looked as though the whole flat was on fire, so hoses were trained on the windows until the smoke was extinguished.

Everything then went quiet. When Hall made no reply to further overtures broadcast at high volume through loud-hailers, the Silver Commander assumed that he must be incapacitated or dead, and so took the decision to put in an entry team. Officers found Hall sitting dead on the floor near the stair-well at the back of the premises, facing one of the doors: it was not immediately clear what had happened to him, but he appeared to have died of smoke inhalation.

So a marathon operation ended in partial tragedy – for we had been guided throughout by our belief that in such situations the right to life is the most important consideration, and everyone had hoped that the siege could be concluded without any casualties.

*

My warnings about terrorist activity in the United Kingdom were amply justified by the ricin poison affair. This came to public notice only in 2005, but by then officers of our anti-terrorist branch had been working on the case for more than two years.

Investigations began in September 2002 when intelligence contacts warned us that a network of Algerians in this country were raising funds for terrorism. They were going into shops, buying goods, paying for them with stolen or forged credit cards, and then selling them back, either to the same shop or to other branches of the same store. Some of the money was going to good causes – for cover – but most of it was being passed to Algeria and other places and finding its way into terrorist hands. For the time being we could not discover its ultimate destination: it is extremely difficult to collect precise information about where terrorist funds are going.

In England our people identified three or four separate groups – about eighty people in all – working in different parts of the country, but when we launched Operation Springbourne, we concentrated on one group in London, raiding all their addresses simultaneously and arresting fifteen of them. One of the men we wanted – David Khalef – was missing, but the trail led us to Norfolk, where we picked him up, and it was there that we found recipes for making ricin, cyanide and other lethal poisons. He had been working in food factories, and it seemed that he had been hoping to put poison into some of the products that were passing through his hands. Another worry was that he was close to American bases: he had befriended some service people, as well as women who were going out with servicemen.

Of the first fifteen suspects, one escaped and managed to leave the country, but we traced him to Algeria and re-arrested him there. It was he who told the authorities that people had been manufacturing ricin in London, and this led us to the flat in Wood Green, the North London suburb, which we raided on 5 January 2003. In the scruffy apartment we found ingredients for the poison – castor oil beans, cherry stones and so on – and remnants of the poison in a bowl, along with other recipes. Our intelligence – though we could not prove it – was that the occupants of the flat were planning to mix ricin into jars of face-cream and smear it on the doors of tube trains and restaurants, in the hope of causing deaths and spreading panic. Although the remaining traces of poison were very small, there is no doubt that it could have been lethal, and in spite of intensive searches by the police, two jars of cream remain unaccounted for.

Until then we had not heard of a man called Kamel Bourgass, also known as Nadir Habra. Now it emerged that he had entered Britain illegally in 2000, had been refused asylum, and later had disappeared. After his fingerprints had been identified in the flat at Wood Green, all Special Branches were alerted, with a warning that he was dangerous; but it was pure chance that on 14 January he was accidentally cornered in a flat in Manchester during a hunt for another suspect. Just after the officers had confirmed by radio that he was the man we were looking for, he tried to escape, stabbing Detective Constable Stephen Oake to death with a kitchen knife.

That was a stroke of appalling bad luck. It was the poison recipes that led directly to the raid on the mosque in Finsbury Park later in January, and it was a moment of carelessness by one of the terrorists that gave them away. In Wood Green the documents were found in a re-used envelope, on which someone had obliterated an earlier address by inking heavily over it. Forensic examination revealed that under the top layer of writing was the address of the mosque, and it emerged that the recipes had been photocopied in the mosque before they were taken to Norfolk. The terrorists had also left hundreds of fingerprints all over the documents: either they knew little about forensic detection or they simply didn't care.

Operation Mermant, the raid on the mosque, carried very high risks, and was authorised by Assistant Commissioner David Veness for the night of 19–20 January 2003, after repeated representations from members of the anti-terrorist branch who had been pursuing the ricin investigation. The operation was directed from GT, the control room on the third floor of Scotland Yard, by Mike Messenger, the Gold Commander. Silver for the night was Detective Superintendent Colette Paul, a specialist in anti-terrorist operations and the chief investigating officer on the case. It so happened that she led the raid on her birthday.

Our officers did all they could to keep the operation secret and make sure that as few people as possible knew in advance what was planned.

Those who did hear about it thought we were going in to arrest Sheikh Abu Hamza, the mosque's hook-handed Imam, who had already been detained once (in 1999) under the Prevention of Terrorism Act, and we encouraged this belief. In fact, we were out to clinch the evidence in the ricin case.

Every precaution was taken to avoid hurting Muslim sensibilities. Beforehand, we arranged for anyone coming to prayer early in the morning to be diverted to another mosque nearby. All police officers who were to enter the mosque wore overshoes and headgear, and the raiding party included Muslim officers to handle copies of the Koran. After the raid, we took the trustees of the mosque into the building to explain how we had managed everything.

Elaborate assessment of the risks was carried out, for we knew that there were terrorists inside, and that they had weapons. The most drastic possibility was that they might have set explosives around the building so that they could blow it up at a moment's notice. More probable was that one of them might blow himself up in a suicide blast if he found himself under attack. Speed and surprise were therefore prerequisites.

Around 2 a.m. more than 1,000 officers were briefed at Scotland Yard, ferried up to the site in a convoy of cars, vans, trucks and buses, and deployed round the mosque, sealing it off in a complete ring. Firearms officers were on stand-by. The timing was critical: the raid had to go in after the last people had left late at night, and be finished before the first worshippers arrived for morning prayers.

When everyone was in position, Colette gave the signal by radio. All ground-floor doors and windows were smashed simultaneously, and she was first in through the main door. In the fetid basement eleven men were asleep on the floor, lying on scraps of carpet – not even on mattresses or palliasses. Some were taken by surprise so completely that they were handcuffed where they lay. Others jumped up and tried to run but were brought down in the hall. All were arrested, including the two most wanted men, and taken straight to various police stations.

The initial raid was over within minutes, but the search of the premises took the rest of the week, and the mosque remained sealed for that time. The search revealed that although the main prayer rooms were obviously a genuine religious centre, the office, basement, kitchen and washroom had been used for terrorist activities. In the loft at the top of the building our people found a stun gun, a CS gas canister, hunting knives and combat gear, including two suits of nuclear, biological and chemical overalls. Hundreds of false documents were hidden above the tiles in the ceiling, along with evidence of the multiple identities used for fundraising.

After the raid, we took photographs of the damage caused by our forced entry, so that we could make good the doors and windows, and restore the building to a better state than it had been in before. When news of the operation became public, many people were sceptical, and questioned whether such a violent assault had been necessary. In fact the information gained from it sparked off a huge investigation into terrorist activities, extending to twenty-six countries.

We were naturally amazed and dismayed when, in April 2005, a jury at the Old Bailey cleared eight of the men charged with involvement in the ricin plot – but questioning such decisions, other than to learn lessons from them, is not productive. Such setbacks are something that every police officer has to learn to live with.

In spite of my efforts to maintain good relations with the ethnic communities, relationships were not always easy. In July 2004 the veteran and controversial Sheikh al-Qaradawi was invited by the Mayor to speak at a conference at Wembley, and the Met put up some of the funds. The sheikh is revered by Muslims as an important senior cleric, but seen by Jewish leaders as a terrorist, and rumoured to have associated with gay men and indulged in domestic violence. In the end we decided that police officers could not appear on a stage alongside someone we were investigating, and the conference was called off.

When the media asked me about this, I said that I supported the sheikh's efforts to dissuade young people from embracing terrorism. My remarks, though intended to be conciliatory, provoked a hail of criticism from both sides. Letters poured into the Yard, the Jewish community denouncing the Met for offering to fund the conference, and the Muslim fraternity claiming that we had insulted Sheikh al-Qaradawi. After much negotiation we managed to draw up an agreement with the Muslim Safety Forum that was signed by both parties, and our relations with them were stronger afterwards.

*

One of the last major events that took place towards the end of my commissionership was the publication in December 2004 of the report by Sir William Morris on the practices of the Metropolitan Police Service. When his team had begun work in the previous January, I had welcomed the inquiry, because many of our procedures, especially over complaints, were still based on ancient formulae that dated right back to the Indian Mutiny of 1857. The system was so antiquated that it took ages for any conclusions to emerge: some investigations went on for two or three years, and my view was that justice delayed is justice denied.

I had been the first to give evidence to the inquiry, and I took the opportunity of making some outspoken comments on attitudes to race, gender and so on:

> There is no place in the Metropolitan Police Service for racists. There is no place in the Metropolitan Police Service for anyone who believes it is acceptable to discriminate against people on any grounds of gender, sexual orientation, faith or belief, disability or age. If you do not believe in the fundamental right of people to be treated with respect, dignity and compassion, then I do not want to share my service with you. You should not try to join. If you are a senior police officer or staff member, and cannot claim such a belief as your own, you should get out of the service now. You are not wanted.

I called for a complete overhaul of many of our procedures, but strongly recommended that the office of constable should be retained – and I am glad to say that this plea was upheld. The report called for many changes and improvements, not least in the field of race relations, where (it became clear) some officers were still ill at ease. 'We are concerned,' ran one paragraph, 'that some managers lack the confidence to manage black and ethnic minority officers without being affected by their race.' Bill Morris and his team did an excellent job of analysing the evidence they collected, and I look forward to seeing their recommendations put into practice.

TWENTY-EIGHT
The Trouble with Blunkett

It is essential that police chiefs should have good working relationships with the Home Secretary, since it is to him that they report. For years I had absolutely no problems in this respect. With Michael Howard, who often came to Northumbria while I was Chief Constable there, I got on particularly well. During my time as Deputy Commissioner and my first year as Commissioner, I was on the best of terms with Jack Straw and Charles Clarke, and also with Kate Hoey and Lord Bassam, who were then ministers at the Home Office. I had similar good working relationships with all the Shadow Home Secretaries, and with Simon Hughes in particular, during my period as Commissioner. I always found visits to the Home Office both constructive and entertaining. Because Straw had been in office before I had, I naturally looked up to him as a senior figure. Besides, until the new regime came in, the Home Secretary had been the Police Authority for London, so that he had wide experience and knowledge of the Met.

Then, in the form of David Blunkett, there came along a new Home Secretary who had no previous experience of dealing with the Met, and knew very little about policing. I realised that he might not be as supportive as Straw, since he had not been involved in my selection. However, it was my duty to work constructively with him, but at the same time it was important for me to maintain political independence: as I was continually saying to the Police Authority, the Mayor and others in senior positions, I was determined that the Met should not be used as a political football. Nevertheless, we were public servants, who had to implement the law of the country as dictated by Parliament and ultimately by the duly elected Government.

Soon after Blunkett had succeeded Straw early in 2001, we had our first meeting. I took along (among others) Susannah Becks, my chief of staff at the Yard, and on the other side were the permanent under-secretary, John Gieve, and a couple more officials. The atmosphere felt friendly enough. 'You seem to be giving me all the good news,' Blunkett told me at one point. 'Just like my chief executive in Sheffield, when I was leader of the council!'

I came away feeling quite hopeful. Here, I thought, is a man who knows what he wants and is going to get it. He has no time for people who put obstacles in his way. 'I reckon we can do business with him,' I told Susannah. But she, to my surprise, thought otherwise.

'I'm not sure,' she replied. 'I think he will be very difficult, and can't be trusted.'

'Well – we'll see.'

I respected her opinion, because she is highly intelligent, with excep-tional intuition, and a person of great integrity; and I saw that she found it difficult to deal with someone who did not appear to be straightforward. It took some time for these doubts to be confirmed, but gradually we discerned that he was a real, pugnacious street fighter, immensely determined, who wasn't used to coming up against anyone else as stubborn and aggressive as himself. The civil servants in his department seemed to be frightened of him, and the general feeling emanating from his office was, as one senior member put it, that he had 'thrown away the memory bank of the computer'. Indeed, certain able and experienced officials were soon moved out.

Our real difficulty came in relation to the Reform Programme for the modernisation of the police. Much had been done by Jack Straw and his team to ensure a smooth run-up to most of the changes that were needed; but all that seemed to be ignored in a new, aggressive approach which, I warned Blunkett, seemed confrontational, and would 'end in tears'. My forecast proved all too correct when 14,000 police officers marched in protest on the Houses of Parliament. That demonstration worried me greatly: it should not have been happening, and I got Mike Todd to go along and walk the columns, to make sure proceedings were orderly. It took diplomacy and hard work by many people, led by my old friend Sir Keith Povey, to ensure that Blunkett apologised at the next meeting of the National Federation. After that hiccup, we got back on track, but it had all been so unnecessary. One day I called Susannah into my office and said, 'You're absolutely right. You saw through him straight away.'

At the beginning of October 2001 the *Sun* ran an 'exclusive' by the newspaper's Political Editor Trevor Kavanagh under the headline BLUNKETT GIVES TOP COPPER A ROASTING. The report claimed that the Home Secretary had called me into his office and rebuked me for warning the public that Britain could be the next target for a terrorist attack. This was news to me. I had indeed given a warning, in response to a question put to me by a member of the Police Authority; but the rest of the story was complete rubbish: I had not been called in or carpeted.

Then in February 2002 he suddenly took it upon himself to tell the *Evening Standard* that I had six months in which to get the level of street crime down, or else I would be replaced. 'We will give you the freedom to do the job,' he was reported as saying, 'but if you don't do it, I'll have to intervene.'

That, to say the least, came as a surprise: in recent months street crime had been falling, following my decision to put 1,000 officers, mainly from the traffic division, into the fight against robbery and mugging. Moreover, Blunkett had not thought fit to tell me of his displeasure before spilling it to a newspaper. He had not given me any kind of warning. Not the least curious feature of his outburst was that we had had a social dinner at Scotland Yard the night before, attended by the Met's top team and our wives, at which the atmosphere had been highly cordial. There seemed to be no friction between the Home Secretary and the Met, and he told the company, 'We stand together or go down together.'

When I telephoned him to remonstrate about his remarks, and said he had never given me any warning, he denied having said what had been reported. I subsequently confirmed that the story was true from the *Standard* reporter, who had taped the conversation. Other members of Blunkett's office later denied that he had made a denial. After that I followed some advice I had been given earlier by a number of influential people, who said, 'Be wary of Blunkett, and never go to see him alone, but always take a witness.' At the time this had sounded unduly alarmist, but later I saw how right they were. It was interesting to observe that whenever a denial came out, it was issued not by him but by one of his staff. We could see that they were working under enormous strain, and they sometimes quietly appealed to us for help in sorting out the problems that their chief had created. Fortunately, these difficulties only strengthened our relationships with most Home Office executives.

The only explanation I could give of such *volte-faces* was that they were Blunkett's way of trying to keep people off balance, and so of being able to dominate them. The trouble with me and the Met, I suppose, was that we were *not* fully under his control, and did not submit to his bluster.

Our worst spat came in February 2003, when he reviled me publicly for sending tanks to defend Heathrow Airport, on the grounds that their appearance would terrify the public. In fact the vehicles were light armoured cars, not tanks, and it was David Veness, not I, who had ordered their deployment. Later, Blunkett claimed that I had been devious and less than honest in saying that the 'tanks' were only armoured cars – but this true remark had been made not by me, but by David. The operation had, in any case, been agreed in Cabinet, with the Prime Minister presiding. I told Blunkett I was quite prepared to take responsibility for what Veness had done, but that we must get things right for a change. The wrangle was all the more unfortunate, as these were times of unprecedented danger. I was not surprised to hear, from other sources, that at one point Blunkett had declared chief constables to be the most unpleasant group of people he had ever come across.

For the first two years of my commissionership relations with him remained very difficult. Articles in the press bore no relation to what had been said at the meetings they reported. When he continued to run me down, I eventually rang up two friends close to very senior figures in the Government, and told them that I was not going to stand for any more of it. I did not propose to carry on maintaining a dignified silence, I said. Rather, if it went on, I would come out fighting. The way the police were being treated was just not satisfactory, and if necessary I would go public on that.

Lo and behold, the insults ceased – and indeed there came a complete change of attitude One day Blunkett and I emerged simultaneously from 10 Downing Street after a meeting on street crime chaired by the Prime Minister, and jointly told the media how well we were working together. Thereafter, for his last two years in the Home Office, he actively supported me, and we worked constructively together.

Then, in Stephen Pollard's biography *David Blunkett*, published in December 2004, he appeared to have reverted to his old enmity. The business of the tanks at Heathrow came up again, and the Home Secretary was quoted as saying that I had been a weak commissioner, lacking in judgement. He also alleged that I had failed to discipline officers who had allowed royal security to be breached, and declared that I needed to 'start feeling the pressure' I was under. This corroborated the stories that I'd heard from supportive and friendly press sources during the first two years.

It was reassuring to find that I was in good company: in the book Blunkett had savaged several of his Cabinet colleagues with equal ferocity. Yet what was one to believe? On the day after a bruising serial extract had appeared in the *Daily Mail*, along came a two-page letter from Blunkett himself, delivered to Scotland Yard by hand, apologising for all the rude remarks about me, and alleging that he had never made them. Indeed, he claimed that he had hardly spoken to Stephen Pollard, and believed, on the contrary, that I had been a splendid commissioner, with whom it had been a joy to work. To be fair to him, he had sent a number of letters complimenting me on the success we had achieved over the past few years.

By then, I am afraid, he seemed to be in a thoroughly confused state, demoralised by the problems of his personal life. He appeared to forget that we, the Met, had been guarding him ever since he became Home Secretary, and that I had frequently received queries about his security. It was not our job to make any judgements about his behaviour: our task was simply to protect him, and to say nothing about his private life – which we did.

He seemed to forget, also, that I was there to serve the Home Secretary, not to feud with him. Many officers felt that, when he took office, he came ready-armed with an anti-police agenda. I never believed that. Yet at one point he had the nerve to challenge the honesty and integrity of David Veness, who dealt with him frequently on anti-terrorist matters. David was so upset that he spoke about resigning;

and as he is the most luminously honest man I have ever met – an outstandingly professional officer who was playing an absolutely key role in the fight against terrorism – I talked him out of that and gave the Home Office a very sharp blast.

I believe that in the end Blunkett understood the complexities of policing, and the constitutional position of the Commissioner, who reports to a number of people. He also fought a successful battle in Cabinet to gain extra resources for policing – for which we should all be grateful. But, as Nick Hopkins of the *Guardian* said in relation to myself, Blunkett needed to know not only his enemies, but also his friends.

The most apt comment on our up-and-down relationship was made by David Yelland, the Editor of the *Sun*, just after I had retired. He recalled that, after the first report that I had had a roasting from Blunkett, I said, 'I don't know where this story came from. There were only three of us in that office – myself, the Home Secretary and his dog. And it didn't come from the dog.'

TWENTY-NINE
Looking Back

The title of this book came from a phrase I used during an interview on my first day as Chief Constable of Northumbria. Asked how I intended to tackle the multiple problems I was inheriting – the aftermath of the riots, the car thefts, the ram-raiding, the rivalry between criminal gangs – I replied that policing was not a job for the faint-hearted. My career to date, I said, had shown me how strength of purpose and the support of officers on the street could overcome the most daunting problems.

I officially retired from the Met at the end of January 2005; but as I write, six months later, I am still engaged in running two major inquiries – one into the deaths of Diana Princess of Wales and Dodi Fayed, the other (Stevens Three) into collusion in Northern Ireland.

Obviously I cannot disclose details of either before our reports are published. As for Diana – an announcement by the Coroner that I was to take charge of an investigation came as we were in the middle of an all-day meeting of the Met's top team at Kingston Hill. Dick Fedorcio, my press chief, was called out of the room and told that the news had been on television. As he came back in, he gave me an odd look, and I said, 'What's up?'

'You're now doing the Diana inquiry,' he replied.

I had known for two years that Mohammed al-Fayed wanted me to carry out an inquiry; but all the same the news was a shock. Naturally my mind flew back to that difficult day when I met the Princess in Northumbria, and she gallantly mastered her emotions to carry out her programme.

Now, suffice it to say that our twelve-strong team all devoutly hope that our investigation will put the grim story of her demise to rest once and for all. We recognise that al-Fayed, as a father who lost his son, is no less deserving of sympathy than the Royal Family, and that some of the issues he has raised need thorough examination.

Our relationship with the French police has been excellent – and it was never better than when I went across to look at the scene of the crash for myself, in April 2004. When we drove to the tunnel in a car, the scenario became uncomfortably realistic as paparazzi came curling and swooping round our vehicle on fast motorcycles. Then the tunnel was closed for the duration, and Dick Fedorcio was given twenty riot police to manage the media, who had come out in swarms from all over the world.

I walked the route in the company of senior French detectives and the coroner. Afterwards some people criticised me on the grounds that my interest was macabre, or just a publicity stunt; but I disagreed utterly. I felt I must see where the accident had occurred, to give myself a grasp of all the details, particularly the slight bends and changes of camber in the road – and if I hadn't taken the trouble of going to the scene, I would have been rightly criticised.

The visit brought home to me the tremendously strong interest that people still have in the Princess and her untimely death. By the time this book is published, we will have brought the wrecked Mercedes from Paris to England – for forensic processes have advanced so far in the eight years since the fatal crash that we can now use computers to reconstruct every detail of the vehicle's progress on its last journey, and model exactly what happened to it from the damage it sustained. Our report on the case will go to the Coroner this autumn (2005), and an inquest will be opened next year.

As for Northern Ireland – our inquiries continue into the activities of the undercover agent known as 'Stakeknife', and the next major event – probably in the spring of 2006 – will be the public inquiry into the murder of Pat Finucane, which we will have to serve with the evidence we have collected.

Of all the events that marked my retirement, none was more heart-warming than a dinner given towards the end of 2004 on an evening when I had just returned from a trip to South Africa. After a long flight, I was none too enthusiastic when Cynthia told me that she and our daughter Susannah were taking me out to a restaurant near Tower Bridge for a private celebration – but I thought it best to play along.

When I saw a taxi draw up outside my flat in Bayswater, I thought it was slightly odd that we were not using my official car, but when Cynthia told me that my protection officers would meet us at the restaurant, I did not smell a rat. Then, as I got into the back, I noticed that the driver was exceptionally well dressed, with a smart shirt and tie. No matter: he drove us down to the river and decanted us near City Hall. As I was walking away from the cab, I happened to look round and see him refuse some money that Cynthia was trying to give him.

Rapidly becoming more suspicious, I said to her, 'This is all very strange. What's going on here?' A moment later, round the corner came Ken Livingstone, walking with Len Duval, the Chairman of the Metropolitan Police Authority. Cynthia belatedly let on that we were to have dinner with the Mayor and some colleagues. For a minute or two I assumed it would be a small party of a dozen or so. Not at all: it was a superb, full-scale banquet for 200, planned in absolute secrecy, and included all the ministers I had worked with, members of the Police Authority, and other dignitaries from all shades of the political spectrum. The champagne and other wines, ordered by Ken Livingstone himself, were magnificent, and the speeches were highly flattering. Everything conspired to make it a memorable evening, not least the view across the river to the Pool of London on the other side. I am not ashamed to say that at moments I had a few tears in my eyes. Afterwards, my protection officers took us home in my official car, and I realised belatedly that our taxi had been one the Met's surveillance vehicles, driven by a policeman!

Another wonderful dinner was the one given in my honour by the Prime Minister and Cherie Blair. In a gesture of unprecedented generosity, he allowed me to invite twenty of my own guests to dine at No. 10 Downing Street – so I went to town with a mixture of family and friends. First and foremost was my mother, then aged eighty-four, who had a most wonderful evening. With her came my children and their wives (all of whom also accompanied me to the House of Lords when I took my seat there). Others at the dinner included Jack Straw (who had appointed me Commissioner), Sir David Omand (the anti-terrorist supremo in the Cabinet Office, who had sat on the panel which gave me the job), Sir John Gieve (the present permanent secretary), Sir Keith Povey and my successor, Sir Ian Blair. Tony Blair, as usual, was a magnanimous host, and after the meal made some embarrassingly fulsome remarks about my performance as Commissioner. Another humbling experience came at a ceremony in the Midlands, when Sir Keith Povey and I were given individual presents by the Association of Chief Police Officers, and Chris Fox, the President, praised us for our defence and support of the police in very difficult times.

For my final retirement party at Scotland Yard, attended by 400 people, a video presentation had been put together featuring public figures from the Prime Minister downwards, all passing judgement on my performance as Commissioner.

One thing that I believe has helped sustain me in difficult times is my rudimentary belief in God. I am a very imperfect Christian, but I go to church on Sunday as often as I can – and if I had a stress problem, I would take it not to a psychologist or a psychiatrist, but to the local priest. Attendance at many funerals, and frequent exposure to sudden death, have convinced me that most people no longer realise that we are here on earth for only a short time, and that we will move on. Because of the antiseptic way we now deal with death – hospital staff come along, the police appear, and the body's taken away – we have ceased to appreciate the transient nature of life. But that, I think, is something of which religion does remind us.

Most of the world's religions are based on principles and ideals – and Christian ideals are superb. Even an agnostic cannot argue with them, and I support them wholeheartedly. At the same time, I do not like people who thrust religion at you: I feel it should be a matter of personal choice

My own belief is based on a humanist approach, in that I hold that you should always treat other people as you would wish to be treated yourself. That was one of Christ's basic teachings, and it still seems absolutely right. It doesn't mean that I don't think people should not be told off in a forceful way if they have done something bad, or that it is wrong to put people under pressure to do a proper job. But the bottom line is: never take people's dignity away from them, or do anything to them that they don't deserve.

During my career I have admired a number of people, mostly colleagues, and I have tried to model my behaviour on theirs. I learnt years ago that nobody can get everything right all the time, but that the most important thing is to take responsibility off the shoulders of people working for you. If you're in charge, and subordinates make mistakes, the responsibility is yours as much as theirs. Provided you don't duck that, people will realise that you're there to support them. The role of a commander, at any level, should be to encourage his people, point them in the right direction, and back them up if things go wrong.

Great changes have come over policing during my lifetime, most obviously in the technology available. Instead of a whistle, every PC now has a personal radio; the evidence of fingerprints is massively reinforced by DNA analysis. For chasing criminals, we no longer have to rely on our feet or bicycles, or even on cars, when helicopters fitted with heat-seeking equipment are available.

In the field of anti-terrorism vast improvements have been made. The combined approach, introduced by Dame Eliza Manningham-Buller, the Director-General of MI5, and agreed by us at Scotland Yard, has allowed anti-terrorist police and the security services to work in joint squads, gathering and analysing information and acting together on intelligence in a way that would have been inconceivable a decade ago. The new threat demands no less.

When I was a detective constable, our main aim was to 'no-crime' every incident we went to, and we used to come up with ridiculous prevarications in order to keep apparent crime levels artificially low. As I pointed out earlier, that policy was counter-productive, because if few crimes were being committed, the police did not get the resources they needed. Today, everyone is encouraged to report crime – and even if there is no physical evidence that an offence has been committed, police will accept the word of the person who has made the allegation, and log it as a crime.

Yet the test still is: do the public have confidence in the police service? Do they believe we're doing a good job? From the continual critical sniping in the press – far more frequent now than it used to be, and some of it deserved – you might think the answer was 'No'. But the fact is that the police need the support of the public in their efforts to keep the streets safe, and research shows that at least 80 per cent of people are behind them. One sign of this is the public's willingness to communicate: the number of telephone calls taken by Scotland Yard has gone up by five times in the past ten years. All the same, I do believe that on occasions we have got things very wrong, with an overemphasis on issues like minor traffic offences. A balanced approach is essential, and the public will be rightly incensed if the law is enforced purely to generate revenue or to satisfy what appears to be a senior police officer's personal whim.

I am always irritated when pundits make comparisons between our performance and that of the Americans. Having made many visits to the United States, the longest being my four-month stint teaching at the John Jay College, City University, New York, I have the greatest respect for what the New York Police Department and some of the states have achieved; but they have a different culture, a different way of enforcing the law, and a different legal system. Apart from anything else, every police officer is armed, and I believe it would be a retrograde step if our officers carried weapons as a matter of routine. Lessons can certainly be learnt in specific areas, but it would be a serious mistake to try to lay an American template over police operations in this country.

To me, the most important thing is to manage performance – to maintain a consistent, integrated approach to the containment of crime, so that all strategies and policies combine to produce an overall reduction in crime levels. Reduction must be the key aim. No single strategy is sufficient on its own, because different areas have different needs and different demands. The first essential is to reduce the opportunities for people to commit crimes, by focusing resources on hot-spots so as to win back control of the streets and engage with local communities. There is also a need for 'connect crime' series, in which patterns of offences are identified, and resources are aligned accordingly in big hits (thousand-bomber raids), so that returns are maximised.

It is also important to target active criminals – the prolific offenders – and the networks that support them. If they cannot be arrested for crime, they can be detained for road-traffic offences – anything that will disrupt their activities. Preventative measures – closed-circuit television, overt and covert, the hardening of targets such as cars and houses (estates must be designed so as to frustrate burglars) – all help to make their lives more difficult.

It should never be forgotten that some of the major criticisms of the police have come about as the result of murder investigations. From the Yorkshire Ripper in the 1970s and 1980s to Stephen Lawrence in the 1990s it has been absolutely essential that such crimes be investigated with the utmost vigour and efficiency. For that reason, I was delighted when the Met's murder detection rate went to the highest in the world, at between 95 and 97 per cent. Scarcely less important is the drive against serious and organised crime: if we fail to maintain impetus in that field, we do so at our peril.

If a force places emphasis on crime reduction, detection rates generally rise at the same time. Every force must produce its own overall strategy, and make it clear to everyone, inside the police and outside, what its policy is. The need for strong, unequivocal leadership cannot be overemphasised. One particularly striking set of figures has stayed in my mind ever since my days as an HMI: in a large metropolitan force whose chief repeatedly announced, 'While I am here, crime will continue to fall, and the rate of primary detections will continue to rise,' crime was reduced by 30 per cent in five years, and the proportion of offences detected rose from 24 per cent to 37.

In police work everything must be done with the utmost integrity. Focus on performance undoubtedly brings results, but it can also put excessive pressure on officers and tempt them to manipulate crime figures – always a recipe for disaster. With integrity, there must be trust: leaders must trust their subordinates enough to delegate authority to them, to encourage innovation and to spread confidence. Also vital is accountability: everybody must be held accountable for the actions he or she takes.

I have never wavered in my belief that a householder has a right to protect himself and his home against intruders. After the case of Tony Martin, who received a life sentence for shooting a young burglar at his farm in Norfolk, many people got the impression that you *couldn't* defend yourself. I was, and am, extremely keen that there should be some certainty about what is or is not permissible. In fact the law is quite clear: if you are defending your life or your property, and your loved ones, you may use lethal force if you deem it necessary – and I believe this needs to be more widely understood.

Among my most agreeable memories will always be those of my meetings with Her Majesty the Queen. These began on my own initiative, when I felt there was a need for the Commissioner to have an audience of the monarch to discuss policing issues of national importance, and to talk about the protection of the Royal Family. Everyone knows that we live in very dangerous times, and I thought that perhaps the Queen might want to ask me questions about how we went about our work.

She graciously agreed that I should see her, and so began a series of meetings which took place about every eight months. Our first encounter was rather tentative: I think the Queen was curious to see if she would get anything out of it, and I was not sure what the outcome would be; but I was encouraged to come back. I always met her alone – and I found our discussions extremely enjoyable, not least because she was so extraordinarily well informed about the problems that we were facing. Usually some courtier warned me before I went in that I would have only twenty minutes, but I hardly ever came out in less than ¾ of an hour. Not only did she make me feel very much at ease: her professional grasp of events was exceedingly impressive, and she was scrupulous in not discussing specific operational matters.

Looking back, I realise how exceptionally fortunate I have been. Robust health and an inexhaustible fund of energy are gifts from God worth more than gold. I have never been seriously injured, and – except for the time when I suffered a burst appendix – never seriously ill. All through my career I have had the luck to work with able colleagues, most of them good friends. Whether I have succeeded or failed, I leave it to others to decide. I know that sometimes I could have done a lot better – perhaps that I did not drive an investigation as hard as I might have, or that I did not show enough compassion – and I regret those patches of poor performance. The only thing I can say in my own defence is that I have always tried my utmost to do my best, and I have put every ounce of my energy into leadership. Now, in retirement, I am lucky again, in that I still have a tremendous amount to look forward to, both in work and in recreation, and a wealth of fond memories to look back on.

ACKNOWLEDGEMENTS

Numerous former colleagues contributed to this book, and I am enormously grateful for their help in constructing an accurate record of events. If I have missed out any names, I apologise, but I should particularly like to thank the following: Chris Allison, Dick Andrews, Johnny Batten, Susannah Becks, Joy Bentley, Sir Michael Boyle, Alan Brown (Metropolitan Police), Alan Brown (Northumbria), John Bunn, Hamish Campbell, Peter Clayton, Bob Cook, Tony Coppellotti, Peter Cornish, Dick Fedorcio, Simon Foy, Jim Gallagher, Tim Godwin, Maureen Green, Sue Hall, Mike Hargadon, Bob Holmes, Ashley How, Simon Humphrey, Mavis McCann, Vince McFadden, Tony McStravick, Mike Messenger, Colette Paul, Bob Quick, Steve Richardson, Laurie Sherwood, Alan Slessor, John Stoddart, John Sutherland, Eddie Theobald, Bernard Tighe, Nigel Tilley, Sir David Veness.

I should like to salute not only the officers who worked with me and for me during my forty-three years in the police service, but also all those in other forces who have been prepared to lay their lives on the line in the course of doing their duty. Their loyalty and professionalism have been beyond praise.

Above all, I should like to thank my wife Cynthia for so stoically enduring all the separations and privations that a policeman's wife inevitably suffers when he is away on duty, especially when he is working in dangerous places. Not only has she given me three fine children and managed our various homes with unobtrusive skill; she has also been a rock, a best friend and a perfect life's companion.

INDEX

325